The World's Religions after September 11

The World's Religions after September 11

Volume 1
Religion, War, and Peace

EDITED BY
ARVIND SHARMA

PRAEGER PERSPECTIVES

PRAEGER

Westport, Connecticut
London

Library of Congress Cataloging-in-Publication Data

The world's religions after September 11 / edited by Arvind Sharma.
p. cm.
Includes bibliographical references and index.
ISBN 978-0-275-99621-5 (set : alk. paper) — ISBN 978-0-275-99623-9 (vol. 1 : alk. paper) — ISBN 978-0-275-99625-3 (vol. 2 : alk. paper) — ISBN 978-0-275-99627-7 (vol. 3 : alk. paper) — ISBN 978-0-275-99629-1 (vol. 4 : alk. paper)
1. Religions. 2. War—Religious aspects. 3. Human rights—Religious aspects. 4. Religions—Relations. 5. Spirituality. I. Sharma, Arvind.
BL87.W66 2009
200—dc22 2008018572

British Library Cataloguing in Publication Data is available.

Library of Congress Catalog Card Number: 2008018572
ISBN: 978-0-275-99621-5 (set)
978-0-275-99623-9 (vol. 1)
978-0-275-99625-3 (vol. 2)
978-0-275-99627-7 (vol. 3)
978-0-275-99629-1 (vol. 4)

First published in 2009

Praeger Publishers, 88 Post Road West, Westport, CT 06881
An imprint of Greenwood Publishing Group, Inc.
www.praeger.com

Printed in the United States of America

The paper used in this book complies with the Permanent Paper Standard issued by the National Information Standards Organization (Z39.48-1984).

10 9 8 7 6 5 4 3 2 1

Contents

Introduction

Arvind Sharma

Europe has arguably not known war for the past sixty years, but the world is another matter. Those who were dreaming of a utopian peace after the implosion of the Soviet Union had their dreams shattered on September 11, 2001.

Violence was back with a bang and this time not in secular livery but in sacred garb. And it was back this time not as war between armed parties, but as terror in which an armed minority conducts asymmetric warfare on an unarmed civilian population, disregarding national borders. This new cocktail of violence is not as deadly as the older one yet but its elements are more combustible.

This volume addresses this situation and contains a series of chapters that deal with the themes of war, terror, and peace, in that order.

Part I of the volume is devoted to war, especially to those aspects of war that have become more salient after the events of September 11, 2001. The concept of just war is now being revisited in almost all the religions, and the issue is explored here in the religious context of Christianity and the regional context of South Asia. The famous Hindu text, the Bhagavadgītā, is also reprised once again in this context, and the demonic dimension of war is also explored. Although the prospect of a nuclear Armageddon may have receded somewhat after the end of the Cold War, it is still around to haunt us, and new perspectives on it are also examined. Thus the concept of just war, the complications introduced by the potential for nuclear war, and the demonic element associated with war are some of the themes explored in this part of the book.

The discussion is extended from war to terror in Part II of the book. War is typically engaged in by states, which are legal entities. Thus the violence involved in war is on a different footing from the one involved in terrorism, which often involves non-state sponsors. This difference opens up a whole new dimension of the issue of religion and war that is explored in this part of the book, especially in three theaters: the United States, Turkey, and Lebanon.

Peace is the theme of Part III, as an antidote to both war and terror. But it is not to an innocent, but a hard-won, peace that one returns to, for peace is now more a matter of equilibrium rather than the complete absence of tension. How religion can be both sublimely and sordidly involved in maintaining or disturbing this equilibrium is analyzed in this last part.

Part I

War

CHAPTER 1

The Violent Bear It Away: Christian Reflections on Just War

William R. O'Neill

In a world riven by religious terror and casual slaughter, what shall we say of the *justum bellum?* Is the very notion now a *contradictio in adjecto* in late or post-modernity—war having finally become, in Clausewitz's words, "theoretically limitless"?[1] Or, as Michael Walzer urges, is war still a "rule-governed activity, a world of permissions and prohibitions—a moral world," even "in the midst of hell"?[2] The norms of just war, after all, remain a stubborn inheritance, an "overlapping consensus" of permissions and prohibitions enshrined in international positive law (i.e., the Geneva Conventions and Protocols).[3] But just how are we to make sense of such a consensus?

Several distinct yet overlapping methodological perspectives emerge. We might, following Grotius, assume that the just-war norms derive from the "manifest and clear" dictates of natural reason (e.g., the "secular religion" of human rights and duties).[4] And yet one wonders. Can the Augustinian-Thomistic tradition so readily be trimmed of theological reference? Must an overlapping consensus of differing narrative traditions "bracket" religious belief? Or do scriptural or theological warrants rather support a "reiteratively particularist" consensus in Walzer's words—one logically dependent upon our distinctive religious narratives?[5]

In this chapter, I will propose a *via media* between these rival schools of thought, arguing that distinctive religious attitudes and beliefs play a constitutive role in the (1) justification, (2) modality, and (3) interpretation of the *justum bellum.* Yet the resulting consensus, I argue, rests less on the contingent iteration of particular traditions than on the family resemblance of well-formed narratives.

JUSTIFICATION

Christians, after Constantine, drew on their Greco-Roman and biblical heritage, working multiple variations on the theme of the *justum bellum.* Codified in the *Corpus Juris Canonici,* Ambrose's and Augustine's early speculations were later grounded in Thomistic natural law and refined by the Spanish Scholastics. Still further variations emerged in the seventeenth century, with the doctrine's progressive disenchantment. In the Prolegomena of his magisterial *De Jure Belli ac Pacis* (1625), Grotius writes that the precepts of natural law retain their validity "*etiamsi daremus non esse Deum* [even were God not to exist]."[6] For Grotius, to be sure, the impious gambit "cannot be conceded"; yet for his successors, the speculative hypothesis soon became "a thesis." For Pufendorf, Burlamaqui, and Vattel "the self-evidence of natural law" left God a supernumerary in creation.[7]

Under the spell of modernity's disenchantment, Grotius's heirs regard the validity of the just-war norms as logically independent of the ethical substance of the traditions that "hand them on" (including, a fortiori, "the broad tradition of just war in Western culture").[8] Distinctive religious attitudes and beliefs, as in the "autonomy school" of Christian ethics, serve rather a paraenetic or hortatory function, inspiring us to do what morally (rationally) we are required to do. But such beliefs do not alter the logical force of the *ad bellum* or *in bello* criteria. Consensus, in Walzer's felicitous terms, is "thin," or narrative-independent, as in President Bush Senior's assertion that the Gulf War was "not a Christian war, a Muslim war, or a Jewish war, but a just war."

Yet it seems modernity's final disenchantment is of itself.[9] Not only are the norms of just war dishonored in the breach, but the rationalist foundations of the *justum bellum* have ceased to be perspicuous. Reason is more parsimonious than Grotius believed. Indeed, it is precisely with respect to such foundations that the putative consensus breaks down. James Childress, for instance, proposes a "prima facie duty of nonmaleficence—the duty not to harm or kill others"; the U.S. bishops argue in a similar vein in their "Peace Pastoral."[10] James Turner Johnson demurs: "the concept of a just war" begins not with a "presumption against war," but rather with "a presumption against *injustice* focused on the need for responsible use of force in response to wrongdoing."[11]

Such internal "*différance*" may well support a rival interpretation of the consensus, specifically, that of a merely contingent overlap of "thick" narrative traditions.[12] Intercommunal agreement, that is, rests not on the "manifest and clear" precepts of natural reason, but, in Walzer's words, on the "reiteratively particularist" convergence of normative practices.[13] Thus Christians and Muslims may agree on the *in bello* norm of noncombatant immunity, but their agreement is not foreordained by natural law.

Curiously, Francisco Suárez argued in an analogous manner, distinguishing the merely contingent agreement of states from the *jus gentium* proper, the "rational basis" of which

> consists in the fact that the human race, into howsoever many different peoples and kingdoms it may be divided, always preserves a certain unity, not only as a species, but also a moral and political unity (as it were) enjoined by the natural precept of mutual love and mercy; a precept which applies to all, even to strangers of every nation.[14]

The latter, or "second kind of jus gentium," conversely,

> embodies certain precepts, usages, or modes of living, which do not, in themselves and directly, relate to all mankind; neither do they have for their immediate end (so to speak) the harmonious fellowship and intercourse of all nations with respect to

> one another. On the contrary, these usages are established in each state by a process of government that is suited to the respective courts of each. Nevertheless, they are of such a nature that, in the possession of similar usages or laws, almost all nations agree with one another; or at least they resemble one another, at times in a generic manner, and at times specifically, so to speak.[15]

We cannot, alas, keep "our metaphysics warm" by invoking Suárez's "natural precept of mutual love and mercy." Yet, with a nod to Suárez, we may seek a pragmatic *via media* between a freestanding, "thin" rationalist interpretation and a "thick," narrative-dependent overlap. For we may distinguish two modes of narrative-dependence: although a "reiteratively particularist" interpretation exhibits strong narrative dependence, a weaker narrative dependence permits us to affirm both (1) that the grammar of the just war is "empty" if not embodied or schematized in our particular traditions, and (2) that our traditions are themselves "blind" if not internally disciplined by such narrative grammar. (In Kant's Second Critique, the synthetic role of a schema is played by the type of pure, practical judgments, i.e., a realm or kingdom of ends. By analogy, the ideal of a well-formed narrative schematizes the depth grammar of claim-rights, e.g., in the *ad bellum* and *in bello* norms.[16])

The overlapping consensus of the *justum bellum* rests, then, not in a freestanding (i.e., logically and epistemically autonomous) set of "secular" norms, but rather in the "family resemblance" of rhetorical practices.[17] The *ad bellum* and *in bello* norms exhibit a *concrete* universality such that distinctive religious beliefs may provide for their *ultimate* justification—and, as we shall see, motive force and interpretation—even as our particular religious narratives are "well-formed" precisely inasmuch as they embody (or schematize) the norms.

In short, such a weak narrative dependence allows us to identify, pragmatically, performative contradictions in denying just cause or noncombatant immunity, while grounding such norms in a theological doctrine of the natural law as, in Aquinas's words, our "share in the divine reason itself," our "participation in the Eternal law."[18] Consider the practical import of religious "grounding reasons" in the Augustian-Thomistic tradition of the *justum bellum.*

War, for Augustine, was a tragic necessity, the consequence—and remedy—of fallen nature. The "love of enemies" admits "of no exceptions," yet the "kindly harshness" of charity does not "exclude wars of mercy waged by the good." Inspired by the "severity which compassion itself dictates," such "wars of mercy" presumed that those inflicting punishment had "first overcome hate in their hearts." Neither Ambrose nor Augustine permitted violent *self*-defense; only defense of the innocent neighbor could satisfy the stringent claims of charity.[19] Thomas Aquinas recognized the normative primacy accorded *caritas* in forming justice, posing the *quaestio* in the *Summa Theologiae* II-II, Q. 40, "whether it is *always* sinful to wage war?" Harking back to their Thomistic heritage, the Renaissance Spanish schoolmen Francisco de Vitoria and Francisco Suárez fashioned the just-war tradition as we know it today in the law of nations or international law—law ordained, in Vitoria's words, to "the common good of all," including that of one's enemies.

In the Augustinian-Thomistic tradition, we begin, then, not with simple premises or prima facie presumptions underlying "the concept of a just war," but rather with a grammar embedded in a complex web of belief consisting of nested values, ideals, tales and tropes. Thus, in modern Roman Catholic social teaching, the religiously inspired ideal of the *bonum commune* integrates the "prima facie" rules of nonmaleficence and justice in what we might call, following Sen, a "consequentially sensitive" redemption of basic human rights. *Justice,* extended beyond strategic national interest, recognizes the basic security rights of citizen and noncitizen alike (their claim to *nonmaleficence*). For it is precisely the grave, systemic violation of such claims, for example, in genocide or mass atrocity, that renders a just war "just." But just so, terrestrial peace ("*tranquilitas ordinis*") presumes more than mere nonmaleficence. Duties correlative to basic human rights, including social, economic, and cultural rights, generate structural imperatives of provision and protection—the set of institutional arrangements constituting, for John XXIII, the universal common good.

Other religious traditions, such as Jewish or Moslem, "do likewise," embodying the just-war norms in their distinctive narratives and casuistry, for example, in notions of divine obedience.[20] Such a narrative rapprochement thus permits us to speak of their family resemblance, which as such remains fluid and open-textured. For we interpret and apply the just-war norms of the *jus gentium as* an overlapping consensus, not a grand meta-narrative. Family resemblance is not reified; yet neither is it infinitely malleable. Tacit prejudices distort our use, and, as Gadamer reminds us, notable among such prejudices is the "prejudice against prejudice" itself, the "foundationalist" prejudice that just-war norms function as a freestanding, impartial decision-procedure.[21]

Proceeding *more geometrico,* the use of just-war norms would be independent (logically and epistemically) of their particular narrative embodiment (or schematization). Yet, as we argued previously, the rules of just war are hermeneutically underdetermined. Grammar without narrative *is* empty. But such hermeneutical naïveté may blind us to misuse—distortions arising less from formal incoherence (of the *ad bellum* or *in bello* criteria per se) than interpretative inadequacy. Just as the devil quotes scripture, so we may speak of just war with a Hobbesian inflection.

Hobbes, indeed, does just that. In Hobbes's militant rhetoric, of course, the "state of nature"—no longer naturally pacific—is aptly "called war, as is of every man against every man." And in that inglorious "tract of time" we call history, "wherein the will to contend by battle is sufficiently known," we have but *one* right, that of "self-defense"—the very right Ambrose and Augustine denied.[22] Violent self-preservation, no longer a "stain upon our love for neighbor" in Ambrose's words, is our natural right, writ large upon the "artificial person" of the state.

Neither does Leviathan sacrifice this right, even if it is tempered by the rule of international law. Hobbesian "realism" legislates for general self-preservation in the form of laws of nature, the force of which depends upon general compliance. In a state of partial compliance, governed by weak international law, "reason" will abide by the laws of nature, and of the *justum bellum,* if, and to the degree, they promote self-preservation. There are, in this sense, theoretical limits to Hobbesian realism, underwritten by realism itself. And so, the "violent bear it away"—not merely by abjuring the norms of just war, but by incorporating (schematizing) them within the realist narrative.[23]

President George W. Bush's defense of our war in Iraq, for instance, seems less "a synthesis of idealist and realist elements," in Johnson's words, than a *bricolage* "from many contexts"—a rhetorical *locus* beholden more to Machiavelli's "armed prophets" than to Augustine's "kindly harshness."[24] Now, with the eclipse of Christian narrative's "ontology of peace," proportionality, and, by implication, reasonable hope of success and last resort, are ordered, not to the "common good," including the good of enemy civilians, as a "final end," but rather to the limited aims of strategic self-interest.[25] American exceptionalism, not the universal *bonum commune,* legitimates "preventive war" in U.S. strategic doctrine.[26] So too, we shall see, the *in bello* norm of discrimination is trumped by "political necessity."

MODALITY

In such a *locus,* the *justum bellum* becomes, as the rhetoricians say, a "self-consuming artifact." For it is not only the use of just-war norms that political realism distorts, but their form and force. In accordance with the Geneva Conventions, norms prohibiting torture are general in form, applying to all agents, and nonderogative—claims against torture oblige categorically. Signatory to the relevant Conventions, the United States holds Saddam Hussein's human rights violations as (the remaining) *casus belli.* How, then, to account for George W. Bush's brief for torture, abrogating these very accords? Hobbes, again, is instructive.

Even for Hobbes, the laws of nature "dictate peace." Yet such laws, though "immutable and eternal," obtain only notionally prior to Leviathan. "The laws of nature oblige *in foro interno* only," says Hobbes. "And whatsoever laws bind *in foro interno* may be broken." Indeed, "every man, ought to endeavor peace, as far as he has hope of obtaining it; and when he cannot obtain it, that he may seek, and use, all helps, and advantages of war." Even Hobbes, then, does not banish the rules of war, but so empties them of force that they become nugatory.[27]

Still subtler variations are worked on this theme. Thus we may recognize ordinary "permissions and prohibitions," but only within limits and not "in the midst of hell." Only a "supreme emergency" warrants a teleological suspension of the ethical. *In extremis* only do we permit torture, renditions, and the like. But with (post)modern terror, the extreme becomes quotidian, supreme emergency naturalized. Our Hobbesian logic is thus circumscribed within a "moral world," and to preserve this world, we betray the very tenets that make it moral. Realism is, in effect, moralized, and in such "utopian" realism, the "absorption of politics by the language and imperatives of war," says Jean Bethke Elshtain, becomes "a permanent rhetorical condition."[28]

INTERPRETATION

In the previous sections, I have argued that we must look to the "thick" uses of just war, attending precisely to the family resemblance—or distortions—introduced by the many (narrative) contexts at play in public, political reasoning. Yet distinctive religious beliefs never displace such reasoning in complex, pluralist polities where civility and reciprocity prevail. Our religious teaching, stories, and tropes do not typically dictate specific policies; rather they rein in our *hybris,* permitting us to imagine otherwise, for example, in seeing systematic distortions in our just-war rhetoric.

The Augustinian sense of even legitimate warfare as tragic thus recalls the stringent demands of *caritas,* even to one's enemies, a theme echoed in Pope John Paul II's lament for Iraq that "War is never just another means that one can choose to employ for settling differences between nations. . . . War is not always inevitable. It is always a defeat for humanity."[29] At the heart of Christian narrative, after all, is suffering innocence, crucified love. The polemics of "focused brutality" and "self-confident relentlessness" are never warranted by claims of American exceptionalism, of lost innocence after September 11. *That* innocence, as H. Richard Niebuhr once wrote, was "slain from the foundations of the world."[30] And if the cross speaks of innocent suffering, it does so sans qualification: not only Americans figure in the calculus of innocence betrayed, but all those "crucified on many an obscure hill," including the innocent Afghani civilians killed as collateral damage, the Iraqi children malnourished, the families displaced.[31] Innocence, of course, is never policy, but the metaphor of crucifixion extends our gaze to every cross and every obscure hill, whether in New York, or Afghanistan, or Iraq.

Re-inscribing the *justum bellum* in Christian narrative thus serves to remind us of the original uses (section i) and form and force (section ii) of the *ad bellum* and *in bello* norms. Indeed, religious *différance* casts the Christian churches (and *pari passu,* synagogues, mosques, et al.) in a critical role; theirs must remain a hermeneutics of suspicion in assessing the state's use of just-war rhetoric. And it is against this backdrop, I believe, that we best interpret the "moral reality" of Christian pacifism: first with respect to public reason or deliberation, and then with respect to personal discernment. Were pacifism merely rule-governed behavior, its opposition to just war is patent: in Childress's words, the "duty of nonmaleficence—the duty not to harm or kill others" is not prima facie, but absolute. Yet as Lisa Cahill has shown in an incisive critique, Christian pacifism is rather a "way of discipleship," guided by radical fidelity to the Gospel. To be sure, its maxims preclude violence; yet the leitmotif of discipleship, of "loving your enemy," is decisive.[32]

Where Machiavelli (whose infamy is exceeded only by his emulation) bequeaths us an armed peace in which there is no "place" for *shalom,* the pacifist bears witness to precisely such a place or *locus.* And this witness, precisely as such, plays its role in public reasoning. Christian pacifists may concede, with Augustine, that the "*tranquilitas ordinis*" of earthly peace falls short of the biblical ideal of *shalom.* But Christian narrative is never bracketed (as in modernity's disenchantment), even if it is, at best, only partially translated into public *reasons.* What remains is witness. And though witness is not simply argument, it is, as Rawls himself recognized on reading Martin Luther King Jr., no less relevant to argument, that is, to public *reasoning.* For the regulative ideal of *shalom,* of "love of enemies," remains the *locus* of deliberation—even if disciples, pacifist *or* just-war, differ as to its implications, *hic et nunc.*

Pacifism, then, is no mere exercise of private piety. Neither can we regard the state as simply fallen or "immoral" as in Reinhold Niebuhr's Christian realism.

Public reason, though disciplined by pluralism—and thus the virtues of civility and reciprocity—is not, for that reason, disenchanted. We cannot bracket "mutual love and mercy," as if the City of God and earthly cities were not only distinct (as for Augustine), but entirely separate. Still, there is a surplus of religious meaning. We remain citizens of two kingdoms, and hence of differing, but not opposed, moral rubrics (e.g., Niebuhr's love and justice).

Christian narrative, one might say, sublates natural law; grounding public reasons, yet providing, as well, for existential discernment. In an illuminating essay, Karl Rahner distinguishes "essentialist" ethics—what I have treated here as the generalizable grammar of just-war norms—from "formal, existential ethics," wherein we discern the particular call of God for the disciple as "*individuum ineffabile,* whom God has called by name, a name which is and can only be unique."[33] Obedience to the "grammar" of our narrative traditions frames our existential obedience; yet the "natural precept of mutual love and mercy" does not exhaust it. Whether one should fight, as in the *justum bellum,* or refrain from fighting, as in the Christian pacifist tradition, would here be assimilated to discernment, that is, obedience to the concrete, particular will of God. Yet the state, as I argued previously, is not simply the individual writ large. The state is not an *individuum ineffabile,* and precisely so, falls under different moral rubrics: the state can never claim divine sanction for its war-making; at best, obedience to the divine will would be mediated through generalized *political* norms of the just war.[34]

CONCLUSION

"Christian realism," for Niebuhr, remains a paradox, but Niebuhr's paradox lacks the saving subtlety of Kierkegaard's irony. In times of terror, realism is quickly moralized in the polemics of "focused brutality" and "self-confident relentlessness." Lance Morrow thus urges us to "relearn why human nature has equipped us all with a weapon (abhorred in decent peacetime societies) called hatred."[35] Rage has found a voice, seductive as it is potent. And yet, for the Christian, it is Calvary's silence that enfleshes the great command, "love your enemy." For Christians, this is the very touchstone of discipleship. Christians are summoned to seek those things that "make for peace," to embody, personally and collectively, the "Gospel of peace." The hermeneutics of hatred is not, after all, something we Americans must relearn. It is a weapon we have wielded often and well in the past. Perhaps we must rather relearn, in Augustine's words, that for those called Christian, "love of enemy admits of no exceptions," and that those inflicting punishment must "first overcome hate in their hearts." A hard lesson, to be sure, after September 11, but enmity cannot be a fitting memorial to our grief. Nature, graced even in tragedy, has equipped us with other, better weapons. If September 11's tragedy has taught us anything, perhaps it is to imagine otherwise: in the words of Dorothy Day, whom Machiavelli would deride as an unarmed prophet: "Yes we go on talking about love. St. Paul writes about it, and there are Father Zossima's unforgettable words in the Brothers Karamazov, 'Love in practice is a harsh and dreadful thing compared to love in dreams.' What does the modern world know of love, with its light touching of the surface of love? It has never reached down into the depths, to the misery and pain and glory of love which endures to death and beyond it. We have not yet begun to learn about love. Now is the time to begin, to start afresh, to use this divine weapon."[36]

NOTES

1. Karl von Clausewitz, *On War*, trans. Edward M. Collins, in *War, Politics, and Power* (Chicago: Henry Regnery Company, 1962), p. 65; cited by Michael Walzer, *Just and Unjust Wars: A Moral Argument with Historical Illustrations*, 3rd ed. (New York: Basic Books, 1977), p. 23.

2. Walzer, p. 36. Walzer speaks of the "moral reality" of war as "a rule-governed activity."

3. For the ideal of an "overlapping consensus" see John Rawls, *Political Liberalism*, rev. ed. (New York: Columbia University, 1996), pp. xlvii ff., 133–72; "The Idea of Public Reason Revisited," in *The Law of Peoples* (Cambridge, MA: Harvard University, 1999), pp. 164–80.

4. Hugo Grotius, *De Jure Belli ac Pacis, Prolegomena*, trans. F. W. Kelsey (*The Classics of International Law*, Publication of the Carnegie Endowment for International Peace, no. 3, 1925), par. 11. For the notion of human rights as a "secular religion," see Elie Wiesel, "A Tribute to Human Rights," in *The Universal Declaration of Human Rights: Fifty Years and Beyond*, ed. Y. Danieli et al. (Amityville, NY: Baywood, 1999), p. 3.

5. See Michael Walzer, *Thick and Thin: Moral Argument at Home and Abroad* (South Bend, IN: University of Notre Dame Press, 1994), pp. 7, 10, 16–19.

6. Grotius, *De Jure Belli ac Pacis, Prolegomena*, par. 39.

7. A. P. D'Entrèves, *Natural Law: An Introduction to Legal Philosophy*, 2d ed. (London: Hutchinson, 1970), p. 55.

8. James Turner Johnson, *Morality and Contemporary Warfare* (New Haven, CT: Yale University Press, 1999), p. 219.

9. Cf. Theodor W. Adorno, *Negative Dialectics*, trans. E. B. Ashton (London: Routledge & Kegan Paul, 1973).

10. James F. Childress, "Just-War Criteria," in *War in the Twentieth Century: Sources in Theological Ethics*, ed. Richard B. Miller (Louisville, KY: Westminster/John Knox Press, 1992), pp. 352; see U.S. Bishops, "The Challenge of Peace," par. 80 in David J. O'Brien and Thomas A. Shannon, *Catholic Social Thought: The Documentary Heritage* (Maryknoll, NY: Orbis Books, 1992), pp. 510–11. "The moral theory of the 'just-war' or 'limited-war' doctrine begins with the presumption which binds all Christians: we should do no harm to our neighbors." For commentary, see Todd D. Whitmore, "The Reception of Catholic Approaches to Peace and War in the United States," in *Modern Catholic Social Teaching: Commentaries and Interpretations*, ed. Kenneth Himes (Washington, DC: Georgetown University Press, 2004), pp. 493–521.

11. Johnson, pp. 35ff.

12. See Jacques Derrida, "Difference," in *Speech and Phenomena*, trans. David B. Allison (Evanston, IL: Northwestern University Press, 1973), pp. 126–60.

13. I am indebted to John Kelsay for this term.

14. Francisco Suárez, *De legibus ac Deo legislatore*, in *Selections from Three Works*, vol. 2, trans. Gwladys L. Williams et al. (Oxford: Clarendon Press, 1944), p. 349. Cf. Quentin Skinner, *The Foundations of Modern Political Thought*, 2 vols. (Cambridge: Cambridge University Press, 1978), vol. 2, pp. 174–78.

15. Suárez, pp. 348–49.

16. See Immanuel Kant, *Critique of Practical Reason*, trans. Lewis White Beck (Indianapolis: Bobbs-Merrill Educational Publishing, 1956), pp. 68–71. Kant describes the schema of a concept as "a rule for the synthesis of the imagination," i.e., a rule linking concepts (a posteriori or a priori) to perception (*Critique of Pure Reason*, B 180, trans. Stephan

Körner, in Kant [New Haven: Yale University Press, 1955]), p. 70. The ideal of a well-formed narrative extends the Kantian ideal of a kingdom of ends diachronically (as inscribed in a narrative tradition) and synchronically (as intersubjectively rather than monologically realized). Construed thus, the kingdom of ends is not a type for the abstract, ahistorical subject, but historicized, concretely in social narrative. Cf. Wittgenstein, *Philosophical Investigations*, 3d ed., trans. G. E. M. Anscombe (New York: Macmillan Publishing, 1958), pt. 1, par. 497, 664.

17. See Robert Audi, *Religious Commitment and Secular Reason* (Cambridge: Cambridge University Press, 2000), pp. 86–100.

18. ST. I–II, Q. 91, art. 1 and 2.

19. Cf. Epist. 189, and 209, 2; De Civitate Dei, XIX, 12–13, XXII, 6; Quest. Heat. VI, 10, SEL., XXVIII, 2, p. 428, IV, 44, CSEL, XXVIII, 2, p. 353; De Libero Arbitrio, V, 12, Migne, PL, XXXXII, 1227; Contra Faustum, XXIII, 76 and 79; Epist., 138, ii, 14. Cited in Roland Herbert Bainton, *Christian Attitudes Toward War and Peace: A Historical Survey and Critical Evaluation* (New York: Abingdon Press, 1960), pp. 91ff.

20. Luke 10:37.

21. Hans-Georg Gadamer, *Truth and Method*, 2d revised ed., trans. Joel Weinsheimer and Donald G. Marshall (New York: Crossroad, 1989), p. 270. As Louis Dupré observes, "The Enlightenment's fight against [prejudices] stemmed itself from a prejudice and followed the Cartesian methodical rule that no position ought to be considered intellectually 'justified' before it was proven" (*The Enlightenment and the Intellectual Foundations of Modern Culture* [New Haven: Yale University Press, 2004], p.10).

22. Thomas Hobbes, *Leviathan*, ed. C. B. Macpherson (London: Penguin Books, 1968), pp. 185–86.

23. Matthew 11:12.

24. Johnson, p. 23; following classical rhetorical usage, *loci* comprise the "storehouse of arguments" whereby general warrants are "topically" applied to specific cases. Such "commonplaces," deriving from consensual ("common sense") presumptions, schematize warrants (and backing), in part, by fixing motives. Cf. Cicero, *Topics*, II, 7; *Partitiones Oratoriae*, 5; Chaim Perelman and L. Olbrechts-Tyteca, *The New Rhetoric: A Treatise on Argumentation*, trans. John Wilkinson and Purcell Weaver (South Bend, IN: University of Notre Dame Press, 1969), pp. 83–85.

25. Jean Bethke Elshtain, "Reflections on War and Political Discourse: Realism, Just War, and Feminism in a Nuclear Age," in Miller, p. 400.

26. As Michael Walzer observes, "Hobbes argues that only an absolute sovereign can free [citizens] from . . . fearfulness and break the cycle of threats and 'anticipations' (that is, pre-emptive violence)" (Walzer, p. 77).

27. Locke argues that, "the not taking God into this hypothesis has been the great reason of Mr Hobbeses [*sic*] mistake that the laws of nature are not properly laws nor do oblige mankind to their observation when out of a civil state of commonwealth" (John Locke, *Two Treatises of Government*, ed. P. Laslett [Cambridge: Cambridge University Press, 1963], pp. 93–94).

28. Elshtain, p. 407.

29. John Paul II, "Address of His Holiness Pope John Paul II to the Diplomatic Corps" (January 13, 2003) (http://www.vatican.va/holy_father/john_paul_ii/speeches/2003/january/documents/hf_jp-ii_spe_20).

30. H. Richard Niebuhr, "War as Crucifixion," in Miler, p. 70.

31. Niebuhr, p. 70.

32. Lisa Sowle Cahill, *Love Your Enemies: Discipleship, Pacifism, and Just War Theory* (Minneapolis: Fortress Press, 1989), pp. 1–14.

33. Karl Rahner, "On the Question of a Formal Existential Ethics," in *Theological Investigations* 2, trans. Karl H. Kruger (Baltimore: Helicon, 1963), pp. 217–34. "Essential ethics"

refers to the set of universal, action-guiding moral norms ascertained by natural reason (e.g., respect for persons' basic rights); we need not assume that such norms rest upon a foundationalist or essentialist metaphysics.

34. Such a mediating approach permits a limited rapprochement with Islamic emphasis upon divine obedience as the primary sanction for just war. See John Kelsay, *Islam and War: A Study in Comparative Ethics* (Louisville, KY: Westminster/John Knox, 1993); John Kelsay, "Islam, Politics, and War," *Sewanee Theological Review* 47, no. 1 (Christmas 2003): 11–19; John Kelsay, "Islamic Tradition and the Justice of War," in *The Ethics of War in Asian Civilizations*, ed. Torkel Brekke (London: Routledge, 2006), pp. 81–110.

35. Lance Morrow, "The Case for Rage and Retribution," *Time Magazine*, Sept. 11, 2001.

36. Dorothy Day, "Love Is the Measure," *The Catholic Worker*, June 1946, p. 2.

CHAPTER 2

Turning War Inside Out: New Perspectives for the Nuclear Age

Marcia Sichol

To understand or change the war system, we need to understand the constituent elements at lower levels of analysis in a sophisticated way. The cook knows salt, the composer strings, and the gardener soil; the war scholar should know gender.[1]

During these post-9/11 days, we are witnessing something greater and of longer duration than armed conflicts. As a member of a congregation of women religious who believe that God lives and acts in our world, and as an ethicist who also believes in the power of human reason, I have felt the need to address not only the regional armed conflicts that have ensued, but also what I believe is the growing global conflict between religion and reason. Both religion and reason have a role to play during the current violence. Certainly religion should help people of all faiths to purify intention, and to rid the mind and heart of hatred and prejudice. Whereas people's religious beliefs emerge from a variety of religious sects and cultures, reason appeals to universal ethical principles. Religion can help one to live by such principles; it ought not to be abused by appealing to sectarian beliefs that contradict them. No side in a conflict can use revelation to prove it is on God's side; rather, I maintain that God works through human beings who do their best to reason rightly.

In this chapter I assume that the role of theology and religion is and ought to be different from the role of philosophy and reason in making the case for war or for pacifism. Theology and philosophy have long been close partners in the Christian just-war tradition, with each appealing to human reason in making its arguments for and against war. In our century, the presence of nuclear weapons has given rise to new theories about war. These theories are but the latest within a tradition in the West dating back to the Greeks 4,000 years ago. In my book, *The Making of a Nuclear Peace*, I analyzed three contemporary just-war theorists, each of a different academic discipline and religious faith, but each male, and found that none of them succeeds in giving an ethical justification for the use of nuclear weapons. The fact that both religion and reason—theology and philosophy—have been dominated by men for centuries prompted me to ask, "What if I change one piece of the matrix and examine female thinkers? Does gender make a significant difference in making judgments about war? Will taking a 'feminine turn' in moral reasoning offer clues to the uncovering of the underlying principle governing centuries of the just-war tradition?" Will I find a new paradigm for a more adequate just-war theory for the twenty-first century? What I discovered was not what I expected and yet turned out to be more than I expected.

DOES GENDER MAKE A DIFFERENCE? YES . . . AND NO!

The first step toward answering my questions followed from the realization that nuclear war is a bioethical issue on a global scale, affecting the lives of the human race as well as the planet's entire ecosystem. Bioethics has brought casuistry back to respectability in moral philosophy, and its widespread practice signals a change in perspective, what I have called a "feminine turn." Women customarily pull out moral principles from cases at hand, much as lawyers, physicians, and business people function. Today many men, too, are finding that this "feminine turn" in moral thought holds great promise of providing a more adequate approach to resolving today's moral dilemmas than the deductive approaches of the past.

Not Gender, but Perspective

In my research, I discovered that Hannah Arendt, a woman who did not actually write much about just war per se, nevertheless has developed concepts that illumine the moral ground on which the just-war tradition stands. A Jewish American philosopher who escaped from Nazi Germany, Hannah Arendt is a woman many feminists have abandoned as not "feminist" enough. Nevertheless, her work has invigorated feminist thought.

What captured my attention was Arendt's explication of Immanuel Kant in relation to aesthetics and the perspectives of "actors" and "spectators"—whom I call "insiders" and "outsiders." The "best people," Kant says, come to a situation not as actors, but as spectators, for only the spectator gets to see the whole while the actor focuses on the part he or she plays. More important, it is the spectator who serves as judge—he or she determines what is and is not acceptable. When it comes to war, this analysis aptly pertains to the role of the majority of women in the world.

THREE TWENTIETH-CENTURY WOMEN

The claim that most women are outsiders, as along with many men who are excluded from war-fighting or policymaking for whatever reason, is supported by the fascinating stories and statistics in the writings of three twentieth-century women: Vera Brittain (1893–1970), Jean Bethke Elshtain (1940–), and Joanna Bourke (1963–).[2] Of the three, Vera Brittain's published letters reveal a woman who is closest to being an insider in that she served as a nurse on the front in World War I. After losing the four most significant men in her life and then seeing her own British soldiers treating injured Germans with dignity and respect, she moved from being an avid war supporter to becoming an active pacifist. In her book, *Women and War,* the American historian Jean Bethke Elshtain analyzes women's behaviors in wartime and finds that there are no simplistic divisions between "violent men and pacific women."[3] She cites statistics to show that only 15 percent of the men engaged in combat in World War II, for example, actually fired their weapons in battle. Wartime analyses show that men are strongly opposed to killing even when society gives them permission to do so. Joanna Bourke, now professor of history at Birkbeck College, University of London, in what has been called "a masterpiece of revisionist history," *An Intimate History of Killing: Face-to-Face Killing in Twentieth Century Warfare,* shows how women are an integral part of the slaughter of war and the myths surrounding it.[4] Her position, which the writings of the two other women support, is that society is the chief determinant in deciding what aspects of gender should dominate in men and women. As women become insiders, such as, war-fighters and policy-makers, society encourages them to shed their more "feminine" qualities. In the nuclear age, it is easy to see that the barriers against women in the military are fast disappearing. Little physical strength is needed to push a button. As a former Marine Vietnam veteran has said:

> [A]ll you do is move that finger so imperceptibly, just a wish flashing across your mind like a shadow, not even a full brain synapse, and poof! in a blast of sound and energy and light a truck or a house or even people disappear, everything flying and settling back into dust.[5]

THE *DIS*-COVERING OF THE DEEP VALUE IN THE JUST-WAR TRADITION

Relating Arendt's analysis to war, the three authors show that *most* men and women are not actors, not insiders, but spectators. As outsiders they are the majority affected by war. As judges who determine what is acceptable, they also have tremendous power—the power that, I believe, gave rise to the just-war tradition. The outsiders were the ones who needed a safe space to make homes, to care for families, to attain human flourishing. In prehistoric days, defense of one's borders fell to the physically strong male. In our time defense of one's borders has expanded beyond individual nations to regions and alliances. But what underlies this concern for defense of borders is the desire to preserve that kinship or bondedness that now reveals itself as global in scope. In the eighteenth century, Kant spoke of the bondedness of peoples in his *Perpetual Peace* (1795) when he referred to the kinship "steadily increasing between the nations of the earth [that] has now extended so enormously that a violation of right in one part of the world is felt all over it."[6] In the twenty-first century we have actually reached the point where war threatens the entire global family. This situation demands human action to save ourselves from ourselves.

A NEW PARADIGM

One can find instances of individuals' acts to resolve conflicts without resort to war-fighting in the twentieth century in Gandhi, King, Mandela, and others. Thinkers from the East are among those "previously excluded" to whom I have referred. If the twenty-first century does turn out to be, as some have suggested, the century of India or China, the West would do well to enter into conversation with these thinkers in what Arendt calls the "public space." Respect for such a public space offers the best chance to resolve conflict because discussion can focus on the boundaries beyond which policymakers may not go. Such public dialogue is called for by the bondedness of peoples, which provides justification for self-defense or defense of one's neighbors against unjust aggression.[7] The presence of nuclear weapons makes it impossible to conduct a just war because these weapons threaten the very value just wars are meant to preserve.

In her analysis of the human condition, Arendt finds that the greatest surprises in history come about through one human being's act. And it is through the human act that religion can assist reason. Ironically, Arendt turns to a religious figure—to Jesus of Nazareth, who, she says, links the power to forgive with the power of performing miracles. In fact, she, a scholar from a Jewish background, calls the Incarnation the "most succinct expression of hope for the world."[8] The Incarnation is God's way of seeing humanity from the perspective of the lowly, a child born into a people among the most despised by the powerful elite in Rome. This is the very perspective we have been considering as the perspective of the outsider—the perspective of the most vulnerable of the world. Paradoxically, it is at the same time the perspective of power, for if the marginalized act in concert against policies and actions that are harmful to them, their combined power can force changes made by global insiders. In the United States, women's movements led by such women as Sojourner Truth, a former slave; Elizabeth Cady Stanton; and others show the changes such combined power can effect. The civil rights movements in the United States and South Africa and Gandhi's independence movement in India are but three examples of this use of power from the twentieth century. This perspective of power is available to each woman and each man, regardless of where they stand in society. Peace will only be possible if both genders make this "feminine turn"—perhaps it should be called a "more fully human turn"—and stand with the most marginalized to examine social and political realities from the perspective of those underneath. Such is the human act that is "the miracle in the making"—a peace that is more than a truce, but a peace that is forged through sustained work: not the work of war, but the struggle to enter into conversation with those from many perspectives, especially the perspective of the most vulnerable, still overwhelmingly a woman's perspective.

NOTES

1. Joshua S. Goldstein, *War and Gender* (Cambridge: Cambridge University Press, 2001), p. 408.

2. Brittain was an English woman studying at Oxford who left her studies to serve as a nurse in World War I. Her wartime experience would mark her for life. Elshtain, an American, now the Laura Spelman Rockefeller Professor of Ethics at the University of

Chicago, co-chairs the recently established Pew Forum on Religion and American Public Life. She was born just as America was entering World War II; the wartime culture seems to have marked her as a woman and an academic. Bourke, born in New Zealand to Christian missionary parents, traveled widely. Bourke is a revisionist historian, who is presently professor of history at Birkbeck College, University of London. Her work ranges from social and economic history to the history of the emotions. She says of her work, "Gender has always been a major site of investigation."

3. Jean Bethke Elshtain, *Women and War* (Brighton: The Harvester Press, 1987).

4. Joanna Bourke, *An Intimate History of Killing: Face-to-Face Killing in Twentieth Century Warfare* (London: Granta Books, 2000).

5. Bourke, p. 14, citing William Broyles, a former Marine and editor of the *Texas Monthly* and *Newsweek.*

6. Immanuel Kant, *Perpetual Peace: A Philosophical Essay,* trans. with introduction and notes by M. Campbell Smith (New York: Garland Publishing, 1972), p. 142.

7. Marcia Sichol, *The Making of a Nuclear Peace* (Washington, DC: Georgetown University Press, 1990). This is the topic of the final chapter, in which I trace this core value throughout the just-war theories of Walzer, Ramsey, and O'Brien, as well as in the work of the classical just-war theorists.

8. Hannah Arendt, *The Human Condition* (London: The University of Chicago Press Ltd., 1998), p. 247.

CHAPTER 3

Demonic Religion and Violence

Lloyd Steffen

The religious extremism that played so prominent a role in the events of September 11, 2001, and in their aftermath, was bewildering to many. Questions arose then, and are with us to this day, about how and why religion seemed to inspire violence when it would seem to many religious people that "true" or "authentic" religion seeks to advance peace in the world and restrain aggression and violence.

The question that has been placed at the forefront of this congress—literally on the masthead of communications from the organizers—is this: "Can religion be a force for good?" The answer to the question is suggested in the asking. Of course religion can be a force for good. But the fact is that it need not be. Religion can motivate people to act destructively, even self-destructively, and human history provides ample examples of situations where religion has been involved in motivating people to violence and destruction, which can take form as war and crusade, killing (including terrorist killing), and even suicide.

I do not accept the claim some would make that true or authentic religion resists destructiveness and serves only the good. I think that view is naïve about the nature of religion—for religion as a social and cultural power can legitimate by its appeal to transcendent authority both life-affirming and destructive acts. The moral issue that faces religious people is, I believe, this: "How will people choose to be religious?" There is no single way to be religious—the options are in fact many. So when we ask whether religion can be a force for good, we can say with assurance and ample evidence that of course it can be. Religion, however, does not always align with goodness; it does not always promote the goods of life, including the preeminent good of life itself. Religion can serve ends subversive of goodness, attack the goods of life, and even advance a spiritual vision that affirms a necessary and sought-after destructiveness. Religion can be a part of what is good and beautiful in life, but the simple reality is that religion can repudiate goodness. When it does so, religious people will justify that repudiation by appeal to a transcendent context above or outside of ordinary human moral sensibilities.

I want in this chapter to look into a way of being religious that is essentially involved with destructiveness. Contrary to those who affirm the religious possibility in light of a normative moral vision of goodness that then shuns destructive religion as perversion, I want to claim that the religious consciousness has long understood that it contains within it a destructive negativity of enormous power, because religious destructiveness appeals to transcendent sources to justify and legitimate such destructiveness. This negativity in the moral context is termed fanaticism or absolutist contradiction; in the religious context it is recognized as "the demonic." Returning to the September 11 experience, I will cite examples of this demonic spiritual reality. I shall then expose some characteristics of the demonic, arguing that the demonic option is always before religious people. Then, given that there is no such thing as "true religion," but only options for ways to be religious, I shall conclude by arguing that how one is religious is ultimately a moral rather than a religious matter. My constructive argument is that the decisions people make to be religious one way rather than another are essentially moral decisions even if implicitly made, and that those decisions and the actions that flow from them in the interpersonal sphere of human relations are always open to moral critique, and should be. Religion that can be shown to draw on or participate in the demonic option ought, in my view, to be rejected on moral grounds, despite the claim that could easily be made that such religion is true religion grounded in a transcendent authority superior to human moral reflection and exempt from the categories of moral assessment and evaluation.

THE DEMONIC

> You must remember to make supplications wherever you go, and anytime you do anything, God is with his faithful servants. He will protect them and make their tasks easier, and give them success and control, and victory. . . . Pray for yourself and all your brothers that they may be victorious and hit their targets and ask God to grant you martyrdom facing the enemy and not running away from it, and for Him to grant you patience and the feeling that anything that happens to you is for Him. . . . Before you enter [the airplane] you make a prayer and supplications. Remember this is a battle for the sake of God. . . . If God decrees that any of you are to slaughter, dedicate the slaughter to you fathers and [unclear], because you have obligations toward them. If you slaughter, do not cause the discomfort of those you are killing, because this is one of the practices of the prophet, peace be upon him. When the confrontation begins, strike like champions who do not want to go back to this world. Shout, "Allahu Akbar," because this strikes fear in the hearts of the nonbelievers. Know that the gardens of paradise are waiting for you in all their beauty. . . . When the hour of reality approaches, the zero hour, whole-heartedly welcome death for the sake of God. Always be remembering God. Either end your life while praying, seconds before the target, or make your last words, "There is no God but God, Muhammed is His Messenger."[1]

These words are just some selections from the "Final Instructions to the Hijackers" found in Mohamed Atta's luggage in an abandoned car at Boston's Logan Airport. The appeal to religious authority—to God, in fact—for sanction and justification of a murder-suicide mission directed at noncombatant civilians is unmistakable. I acknowledge that the motivations for these actions are complex and involve much more than religion—political, economic, historical, social, and cultural motives background the September 11 attacks. But, that said, clearly religion is involved. If religion always involves some appeal to transcendence, some idea of an ultimate value (it need not be absolute, only an Anselmian idea of "that than which nothing greater can be conceived"), these instructions make such an appeal. The instructions assured the hijackers on religious grounds that their impending deaths not only had meaning but divine blessing. The writers of the "Instructions" understood that religious sources of sanction, being attached as they are to an ultimate and transcendent power, are sufficiently powerful to overrule ordinary prudential reasoning and the self-regarding duty of self-protection it entails.

It takes an enormous power to inspire a person to engage in an act of self-killing and also to understand such an act as something other than what a moral point of view would term it—suicide. The instructions provided a way for the hijackers to frame what they were doing religiously so that their impending actions were not interpretable as suicide, which their religion, Islam, explicitly prohibits, and a powerful interpretive framework is required to overrule ordinary moral sensibilities and make something mean religiously what it does not and cannot mean morally. From a moral point of view, this document is inspiring murder and suicide; the religious construction around the acts renders them protected acts of faithful servants carrying out God's will, acts that are blessed and will be rewarded. The religious interpretive scheme overrules the moral point of view and provides a divine sanction for murder and suicide.

Let me offer one more, short example of a September 11–related religious reflection that I believe falls under the purview of demonic religion. Two days after the attacks, Pat Robertson, a prominent American televangelist, interviewed another prominent Christian evangelical televangelist, Rev. Jerry Falwell, on the *700 Club* television program. Robertson offered the view that "We have insulted God at the highest levels of our government. And, then we say, 'Why does this happen?' Well, why it's happening is that God Almighty is lifting his protection from us."[2]

Falwell said in the interview that the September 11 attacks were clearly divine retribution for American's sins: "what we saw on Tuesday, as terrible as it is, could be miniscule if, in fact, if in fact God continues to lift the curtain and allow the enemies of America to give us probably what we deserve." With Pat Robertson concurring, Falwell reflected that the responsibility for the attacks rests with "the pagans, the abortionists, and the feminists, and the gays and lesbians . . . the ACLU, People for the American Way, all of them who have tried to secularize America. I point the finger in their face and say: 'You helped this happen.'"[3] There is more in the actual interview, but this statement gives us enough to work with.

These statements suffice to show how Robertson and Falwell interpreted the September 11 attacks as divinely sanctioned just retribution for America's egregious moral sins, which Falwell identifies as feminism, abortion rights, gay rights, and the like. This attack was in Robertson's words "deserved." I think it worth pointing out that the hijackers would have concurred with this opinion in the main, as they were willing to die for their belief that God sanctioned what they were doing and would reward them later. The hijackers shared with Robertson and Falwell the idea that this attack was ultimately authorized and sanctioned by God. In sum, the hijackers and the American televangelists agreed that God was angry at America, and that this attack was a justified act, a just desert approved by God—a deserved punishment for America's sins. The hijackers do not specify the sins and their list would have certainly differed from that offered by Jerry Falwell, but those details are not important for my purposes. The use of religion and how religion is framing interpretation of this event is my issue.

I want to say that the religious appeal here invokes a vision of a wrathful God hell-bent on destruction and punishment. The God appealed to in the "Instructions" and by the televangelists is authorizing murder, and suicide as a permissible means for committing the murder, and religion is effecting an interpretive transformation of the moral meaning of these acts. From a religious point of view, the meaning of the attack must be first referred to and conformed to divine will. For the hijackers, those to be murdered are legitimate targets of the divine wrath—those to be "slaughtered" are characterized as "allies of Satan" and "brothers of the devil"; for the televangelists, the attacks are a divine retribution against a nation turning Godless and secular and opposing the divine will. We can assume that the hijackers and the televangelists continue to think of God as good and just, and that even if the acts authorized are destructive of some, that destruction has positive meaning, because it is falling on enemies of God. For the hijackers, the killing and self-killing are justified and will yield the result of life with God in paradise; for Falwell, the attacks are a wake-up call so that America repents of its evil secularizing ways and forges a new bond with God as a nation not only under God but of God and with God in all things.

From a moral point of view, the destruction of September 11 can be described and evaluated as murder and suicide, with murder being by definition unjustifiable and suicide at least presumptively so. Yet religion is providing an interpretive frame that trumps and then suppresses this moral evaluation with a sanction so powerful that individuals actually proceed motivated by religion to murder and to kill themselves in the process, or, in the case of the televangelists, to interpret the horrors of the day as "deserved." My claim is that this is not only an example of the power of religious reframing of moral matters but, in authorizing immoral action, it exposes a particular way of being religious that can be associated with "the demonic." What do we mean by "demonic religion"?

THE DEMONIC CHARACTERIZED

The demonic is difficult to describe without falling into negatives, but saying what the demonic is by saying what it isn't in one sense accurately conveys the most important thing about the demonic, which is its negativity. The negativity is located in the fact that demonic religion is not what many people seek and find in religion, that is, something positive, creative, constructive, and ultimately life-affirming. The demonic is none of these things. Paul Tillich, one of the few modern Christian theologians to give concerted attention to the demonic, once described the demonic as "the Holy (or the sacred) with a minus sign before it, the sacred anti-divine."[4] In that brief characterization is the heart of the matter. Demonic religion is not false religion or untrue religion, and it is not a negation of religion from outside religion. The demonic, rather, is religion of a certain sort, a way of being religious that negates what we might call life-affirming religion, which is religion conformed in its central vision to goodness and to the promotion of goodness.

The demonic presents its possibility wherever ultimacy and ultimate power are at issue and likely to be divinized or made absolute, and this could include politics, economics, and art, as well as religion. But the demonic is a term religion has claimed as a way of describing a negativity internal to religion, a possibility that is alluring in its offer to satisfy the basic spiritual needs all human beings have for such things as community, identity, meaning, and a self-understanding formed around a sense of doing good and existing in relation to ultimate values and realities. The demonic allures with its involvement with ultimacy and transcendent power, and it can empower those who grasp it, that empowerment being a negativity in the realm of spiritual meaning.

The demonic offers something life-affirming religion often cannot: certainty. That certainty is of a certain sort, for it arises from a belief that the transcendent is absolute and is to be known as such, that that absolute and transcendent spiritual reality communicates itself to human beings with absolute clarity, that human beings have the capacity to understand that communication in the purity of its absolute expression. The demonic offers certainty—absolute certainty—with no hesitancy or humility, questioning or interpretive freedom permitted to surround it. It offers absolutist ideas—and commands actions out of that absolutism—thus giving a permission slip to move past reasonableness into contradiction with goodness itself. If absolutism encompasses everything, it encompasses its own contradiction, and that contradiction will eventually will out—every example of absolutism will eventually express contradiction, as did the hijackers in their absolute belief that that a sure way to gain life—and thus promote the good of life—is to kill others and even oneself. There may be a way to understand that religiously and in light of transcendence, but the moral point of view, based as it is on reason and universalizable notions of goodness and other-regarding benevolence, sees only contradiction and negativity. An extraordinary clarity about moral and religious meaning attends the demonic: when viewed from the moral point of view this feature is deemed the "fanatical" as self-regarding duties like that of self-preservation or self-defense are willingly surrendered to the absolute.

What are the major characteristics of the demonic? I suggest three.

Destructiveness

First, the demonic expresses itself in destructiveness. Destruction in religion, as in life itself, is not always bad, or wrong, or evil. Destruction is in dialectical relation with creativity, so that while we would attribute wrongdoing to an arsonist whose actions threaten lives, we also would not want thoughtlessly to equate the fact of a forest fire with evil when the natural logic is that fire clears old growth so that new growth might begin, thus creating new life and preserving the forest. (In the Hindu trinity a god of destruction, Shiva [and his wife, the destroyer goddess, Kali], is set alongside a creator god [Brahma] and a preserver god [Vishnu].)

So if we accept that destruction is not in itself evil and may be integral to the life-affirming values of creation and creativity, what does it mean that the demonic is destructive? The demonic emphasizes a persistent destructiveness aimed ultimately—spiritually—at absolute destruction. Demonic destruction is drawn out of dialectical relationship with creativity and purposefully seeks ultimate realization as absolute negativity. The demonic, in other words, identifies a religious negativity wherein destruction is unrelenting and unrelieved—except by a turn away from the demonic itself. When the demonic is fully engaged the destructiveness seeks to go absolutely negative with no hope for reclaiming life and goodness out of its movement.

We can glimpse a picture of such absolute negativity in the demonic picture of God presented in 1 Samuel 15, in which God commands King Saul to undertake a total annihilation of the enemy, to inflict on the defeated Amalekites a slaughter of "man and woman, child and infant, ox and sheep, camel and donkey." The picture of God in this part of the story reflects an absolute, unrelieved negativity that shocks King Saul, who disobeys parts of the order, leading to God bemoaning the day God made Saul King—the demonic picture is unrelenting in its vision of destruction. Saul's refusal to follow the divine order in all of its details incurs God's wrath, and ultimately the omnicide is carried out—by priests! Thus is the demonic vision kept "in-house," with religious authorities and institutions able to sustain and even carry out the demonic vision.

The demonic is pictured dramatically in stories of divinity as well as in the lives of the faithful—such as the priests who undertook to carry out what they took to be God's instruction that all the enemies should be killed. Any form of religious life—and any religious tradition—that engages in a destructiveness aimed at a totalized vision of annihilation of life and the goods of life—even if offered in the name of goodness or God or values such as freedom or even life itself—participate in the demonic form of spiritual striving, seeking to bring about a realization of this possibility in its absolute negativity. (That realization is, I think, always beyond human grasp, for to realize the absolute possibility, whether of goodness or destruction, would be to render the individual something other than human, but totalized as spirit—the possibility that is a god. The demonic points to a spiritual direction of negativity, even as life-affirming religion points toward a vision of goodness, that, in light of human fallibility, is never—and cannot be—totally realized.)

Subversion of Freedom

Life-affirming religion endorses a spirituality marked by an expansive inclusivity, where the dangerous power that human beings can claim over one another is diffused and shared, and all people are invited into the creation of forms of life that preserve and promote the goods of life. In the life-affirming spiritual option, the goods of life, including the good of life itself, are received as gifts, shared and cared for, valued, and extended to others in a vision of benevolent other-regardingness and impartial justice. And freedom is a critical condition for the enjoyment of religion or spirituality connected to such a vision of goodness. The demonic is not aimed in this direction but away from it. It neither seeks to promote and preserve the goods of life for all—it actually subverts the condition of freedom itself. The demonic aims not at freedom but seeks to grasp a spiritual power that is characterized by exclusivity, by authoritarianism and regimens of restrictive obedience, which is why political forms that adopt this spiritual context are often referred to as "demonic." As detachment and ego-diffusiveness is a sign of freedom, the demonic concentrates and seeks increasing ego extension and dominion. It is a lesser characteristic of this loss of freedom, but noticeable nonetheless, that the demonic is humorless, whereas freedom shows itself in play and humor, detaching the ego from itself and opening itself in freedom to possibilities outside its control. Humor is one common way this is accomplished.

As freedom is the defining condition of spirit and spirituality, those who use their freedom to renounce freedom exemplify this characteristic of the demonic turn. Tillich is of some help at this point, because he looked broadly—even past religion—to consider the affairs of spirit and freedom in human life. And in many arenas where freedom was the issue, Tillich invoked the category of the demonic to explore this spiritual negation of freedom, seeing it in art; in politics and economic systems, including fascism and capitalism; and even in science itself. In all of these arenas of life, human persons were turning away from freedom and surrendering to some notion of negative and absolute ultimacy that subverted freedom, and with that subversion, the idea of moral agency and human autonomy. Tillich looked into his own Christian tradition and identified the demonic renunciation of freedom in everything, including formulas of condemnation, inquisitions, the tyrannies of Protestant orthodoxy and the fanaticism of sects, and church doctrines. Tillich was specifically critical of the doctrine of papal infallibility.

Self-Deception

The third characteristic of the demonic is that it prepares fertile ground for the cultivation of self-deception. People are motivated to action by goodness, and the demonic furnishes ideas of goodness to cover up the best, most reasonable (moral) interpretation of their acts. Self-deception is a psychological maneuver whereby individuals keep certain interpretations away from direct confrontation, the idea being that when self-deceived, individuals can act in one way yet operate out of a self-understanding that indicates that what is being done is really good, even if others cannot see it. (In this self-deceivers are not delusional and unhinged from reality, but see that what they are doing looks like something wrong or evil; in the self-deception they hold the secret information and the big picture interpretation that reveals it is not really wrong or evil but actually good—like the televangelists saying that a particular instance of mass murder, the 9/11 attacks, were deserved, an interpretation that goes against the best most reasonable moral interpretation, but which is tied to God employing a powerful and ultimately good reminder that God wants America awakened so that it will become what it ought to be in God's own eyes, namely, a nonsecular, God-fearing country.) The self-deception hides the meaning of the destructiveness so that the destructiveness can continue its spiral toward absolute destructiveness.

Demonic religion succeeds because destructiveness is not confronted as spiritually negative action: self-deception is a willed interpretive act aimed at reconstructing negative and destructive acts so that they conform to goodness. Once deemed good, those destructive acts can be undertaken as projects that have sanction thought to be goodness itself, as in the idea that God is good and would never issue a command to do evil. The disparity between what an action would most reasonably mean and how religion is able to cover up that meaning so that even murder and suicide might be deemed positive, life-affirming expressions of the goodness of God exemplifies how self-deception enters demonic spirituality to blunt confrontation with the best, most reasonable interpretation of these destructive acts.

INTERPRETING THE "INSTRUCTIONS" AND THE ROBERTSON-FALWELL INTERPRETATIONS AS "DEMONIC"

These three characteristics of the demonic now allow us to interpret the demonic features in the examples of 9/11 justifications presented earlier. First, the "Instructions." The "Instructions" appeal to God and the goodness of God. This good God, who as good would not (could not?) commit an evil act, authorizes and sanctions the hijackers to commit murder and suicide, bequeathing to them a divine blessing and promise of a reward in paradise. An ordinary moral point of view evaluating this justification would determine that the acts being contemplated are wrong and evil, as is any transcendent authority that would sanction them. But the moral point of view is being abrogated for a religious interpretation in which these evil acts are referred to God for transcendent justification beyond the reach of the moral point of view, so that these acts are being conformed with the divine purposes that are good although obscure to human beings who lack the ability to see their true purpose as consonant with goodness itself. The hijackers deceive themselves into thinking that something evil is really good; they kill themselves but in such a way that it is not to be thought of as suicide; they engage in a destructiveness that goes so far as to overrule a basic self-regarding duty to preserve one's own life; and so gripped are they by the vision of destruction that they are not free to question the moral meaning of what they are doing. Rather than being concerned that they are murdering passengers and airliner crews, they turn attention to the moral requirement, a good end as stated in the "Instructions," of dispatching their direct-kill victims in such a way that they do not cause undue suffering. They thus show compassion to the enemies of God in how they kill them, and completely avoid the idea that they are committing murder. Destruction, the subversion of freedom, and self-deception are apparent throughout the "Instructions."

The Robertson-Falwell perspective also demonstrates the presence of demonic religion. The murder and mayhem is present to them as a deserved punishment from God, who acts to destroy life to make a point about God's nonsecular vision of American life. All those who oppose this vision oppose God—and the condemnation of abortion rights advocates, gays, and lesbians is issued without qualification, and the causal links to the destruction itself and to God as the real cause of it is absolute and clear. God has an absolute power to transform murder into a "wake-up call" having to do with America's culture wars, and on 9/11, God exercised that power. God revealed through these acts a divine displeasure, and destruction is an acceptable means of delivering the divine message—if God wills it, it is by definition permissible and appropriate, even good. It is the way God has chosen in God's freedom to get America's attention.

We see in the Falwell remarks an appeal to an absolute power, for an absolute power is punishing and delivering justice—which is ordinarily a good thing, is it not?—through these terrorist acts. These look like terrible acts, but if seen from God's point of view—and this is what Falwell and Robertson are in a sense claiming to see—this destructiveness is in fact a good thing, a needed reminder from God that America has made bad choices, and change is needed. This destruction might lead to religious revival and an America free of gay people and abortion activists and the like—however that might be accomplished in the dark spiral of destruction. But the point is that if God is sanctioning these acts as a punishment, which is the claim, this death and destruction is really a moment of chastening, and that cannot be, coming from God, anything other than ultimately a good thing—really good, terrible as it may seem on the surface. So again, murder and suicide are transformed into meaning something other than what a moral point of view would see—murder, suicide, and mayhem. The demonic interpretation of the 9/11 attacks is reinterpreted to mean something other than an act of murder and suicide: in this we see a self-deceptive interpretation that negates the freedom to avow the evil before one, that uses the event to reaffirm an absolutist idea that all that happens is from God and because of God, and that embraces a defiance of the moral point of view. The demonic has transformed the meaning of violence so that it comes to bear an interpretive valence of real and deep goodness rather than of an apparent evil—this is what demonic religion accomplishes. People gripped by demonic religion suspend moral interpretation and transform acts of destruction and violence in such a way that they come to mean something religiously that they cannot mean morally.

Demonic religion ultimately subverts, and then defies, the moral point of view.

CONCLUSION: THE PRIMACY OF THE MORAL POINT OF VIEW

The moral point of view shuns association with spiritually negative absolutism and all that springs from it, including the violence of destruction and the appeals for sanction grounded in absolute certainty. The moral point of view, rather, envisions goodness and seeks to connect a universal sense of goodness through various goods of life important in the common life, goods such as life itself, practical reasonableness, speculative knowledge, friendship, relation with ultimacy, and many others. These goods are essential to human flourishing, and they express a benevolent attitude of other-regardingness. Demonic religion sets itself in opposition to such goods and seeks to subvert their value, even destroy them, accomplishing this end either by postulating an ultimacy that is destructive and evil, which is rare, or by the ruse that the destruction and violence unleashed under the sanction and at the will of the absolute is not really a negative but only apparently seems so.

An absolute power can claim power sufficient to translate murder and suicide into meaningful, life-affirming acts. The moral point of view, being grounded in reason and appealing to a universal sense of good will, refuses to accept this absolutist translation and judges the demonic as a way of being religious that is destructive of the moral life. Demonic religion ultimately opposes the moral point of view itself, and a moral critique of violent acts committed in the name of a demonic vision of transcendence will finally, at some point, direct its focus on the religious possibility of the demonic itself, not just the acts that express it behaviorally. And a moral critique will call into question, and ultimately judge, that religious possibility—that possibility of the demonic—as unworthy of people of good will. It will be evaluated as a destructive religious possibility, one to be feared because of the power it holds to affect human action, one that not only does not lead to human flourishing but actually contributes to human destructiveness.

Demonic religion can be discerned as a way of being religious in human actions and attitudes. It will be a form of religion that focuses on ultimacy and transcendence as all religious forms do, but in the demonic mode it will exclude and separate, it will confer value on insiders at the expense of outsiders, and it will render opponents enemies and sanction hatred, even violence, against those who do not conform to its directives. It will identify outsiders or even internal opponents as "enemies of God" or as heretics and require their exclusion, their punishment, and their dehumanization in the name of purity, which is a value that absolutists come to value above all others. The demonic is present when in the name of religion people are demeaned and dehumanized, are subjected to harm and terror, or, when afflicted with harm, be it from disease, natural disaster, or acts of human violence, are told they deserve such harm because of their defiance of true religion. Demonic religion becomes a way of wishing ill on others in the name of the sacred or the holy.

Demonic religion is a religious possibility that is a real option for any religious person—it is seductive and meets needs, as I said, and some vigilance is in order to keep it at bay. Some of the spiritual techniques that are continually calling persons into postures of spiritual humility and fostering benevolent attitudes toward both individuals and a universal humanity of which the individual is a part, connected each to all and all to each one—such things as prayer, meditation, fasting, developing compassion and undertaking works of charity, practicing forgiveness, and so on—become life-affirming actions that help individuals resist the demonic option and keep self-deception at bay. But the demonic is always an option in the religious realm. The other option—the other direction on that continuum of ways to be religious—points toward a life-affirming religious possibility in which religion acknowledges goodness and affirms the essential goodness of the moral point of view itself: other-regardingness becomes an expression of a transcendent concern for others that arises from the heart of religion itself; attitudes expressing compassion, benevolence, and justice become hallmarks of the religious life itself; and the religious option comes to be a way to express goodness not simply in the realm of action but in the spiritual realm as well. In life-affirming religion all persons are spiritual persons and are to be regarded as such, respected as such, and honored as such.

Religion that is unloosed from its moral hinges is not only prone to become destructive, but is, I think, doomed to do so. The power religion is dealing with, the power of ultimacy, is simply too unwieldy, and too easily distorted when attempts are made to manipulate it. Because religious life is so prone to involvement in demonic fixtures—these things happen on a continuum, they do not plunge into absolute evil all at once—the moral point of view is essential for testing and providing critique of actions undertaken in the religious realm. The moral point of view will provide an external resource to evaluate how actions and attitudes connect with ultimate values. It will in freedom question the meaning of actions and, in light of rational understanding, determine whether a religiously inspired action conforms to goodness; and the moral point of view will inquire whether religion itself, in any of its many particular and diverse expressions, is advancing life-affirming values or offending against them.

We are not keen on subjecting religion to moral scrutiny this way, yet this moral scrutiny of religion is important if religion is to be included among the goods of life, an aspect of human existence that promotes life and contributes to human well-being and not its destruction. It can do either, and the decision to go one way or the other is not a religious decision but a moral decision about how one is going to be religious—a decision that can be made explicitly or implicitly, one that needs to be made more consciously than we are used to making it.

Can religion be a force for good? Yes, of course it can. But the moral point of view would want to say something more, namely, "It should be, it must be—and it must itself oppose those who would attack goodness by their religions of violence and destruction."

NOTES

1. These statements are taken from "Final Instructions to the Hijackers of September 11, Found in the Luggage of Mohamed Atta and Two Other Copies," reprinted in Bruce Lincoln, *Holy Terrors: Thinking about Religion after September 11* (Chicago: University of Chicago Press, 2003): pp. 93–98.

2. "Transcript of Pat Robertson's Interview with Jerry Falwell Broadcast on the 700 Club, September 13, 2001," reprinted in Lincoln, *Holy Terrors,* p. 104.

3. "Transcript of Pat Robertson's Interview," p. 106.

4. Paul Tillich, *What Is Religion?*, trans. and ed. James Luther Adams (New York: Harper Torchbook, 1963), p. 85.

CHAPTER 4

The Bhagavadgītā and War: Some Early Anticipations of the Gandhian Interpretation of the Bhagavadgītā

Arvind Sharma

GANDHI IN DIALOGUE

I propose to tackle this topic in three parts. First, I shall narrate an actual piece of dialogue between Mahatma Gandhi and one Dr. Kagawa, who has been identified as "a student of religion." Having presented that piece of dialogue, we shall next analyze it to identify the basic features of the Gandhian interpretation of the Gītā. Having done that, we shall finally see if the Gandhian frame of reference toward the Gītā has any precedents within the Hindu tradition.

We turn now to the first part of the chapter and recount the dialogue between Mahatma Gandhi and Dr. Kagawa that was reported on January 21, 1939, in the *Harijan*. It runs as follows:

> **Dr. Kagawa:** I am told you recite the Bhagavadgītā daily?
>
> **Gandhiji:** Yes, we finish the entire Gītā reading once every week.
>
> **Dr. Kagawa:** But at the end of the Gītā Krisha recommends violence.
>
> **Gandhiji:** I do not think so. I am also fighting. I should not be fighting effectively if I were fighting violently. The message of the Gītā is to be found in the second chapter of the Gītā where Krishna speaks of the balanced state of mind, of mental equipoise. In 19 verses at the close of the 2nd chapter of the Gītā, Krishna explains how this state can be achieved. It can be achieved, he tells us, after killing all your passions. It is not possible to kill your brother after having killed all your passions. I should like to see that man dealing death—who has no passions, who is indifferent to pleasure and pain, who is undisturbed by the storms that trouble mortal man. The whole thing is described in language of beauty that is unsurpassed. These verses show that the fight Krishna speaks of is a spiritual fight.

Dr. Kagawa: To the common mind it sounds as though it was actual fighting.

Gandhiji: You must read the whole thing dispassionately in its true context. After the first mention of fighting, there is no mention of fighting at all.[1] The rest is a spiritual discourse.

Dr. Kagawa: Has anybody interpreted it like you?

Gandhiji: Yes. The fight is there, but the fight as it is going on within. The Pandavas and Kauravas are the forces of good and evil within. The war is the war between Jekyll and Hyde, God and Satan, going on in the human breast. The internal evidence in support of this interpretation is there in the work itself and in the Mahābhārata of which the Gītā is a minute part. It is not a history of war between two families, but the history of man—the history of the spiritual struggle of man. I have sound reasons for my interpretation.

Dr. Kagawa: That is why I say it is your interpretation.

Gandhiji: But that is nothing. The question is whether it is a reasonable interpretation, whether it carries conviction. If it does, it does not matter whether it is mine or X.Y.Z.'s. If it does not, it has no value even if it is mine.[2]

BHAGAVADGĪTĀ: THE GANDHIAN INTERPRETATION IN OUTLINE

A close review of this dialogue reveals that Mahatma Gandhi changed his response during the conversation from a historical to a rational one. The key question asked by Dr. Kagawa was: has anybody interpreted the Gītā like you? Mahatma Gandhi began by saying yes, but then instead of citing any name of such a predecessor he started to explain how and why the Gītā should be understood allegorically. Dr. Kagawa, recognizing Mahatma Gandhi's failure to cite a precedent to his interpretation then remarked: "That is why I say it is your interpretation." Again failing to cite a precedent, Mahatma Gandhi appealed to the merit of the interpretation itself, rather than its author, as a worthy criterion of its value. So the question raised by Dr. Kagawa remained unanswered in a sense. Let us now try to answer it by asking the original question: has anybody interpreted the Gītā like Mahatma Gandhi before Mahatma Gandhi? Before an answer to the question is attempted it is helpful to realize that on the basis of Mahatma Gandhi's dialogue with Dr. Kagawa, Mahatma Gandhi's interpretation seems to have two major components:

1. The Gītā teaches nonviolence.
2. The Gītā is to be taken allegorically and not historically.

No one denies that the Gītā refers to fighting—the question is whether this fight refers to a spiritual struggle in the heart of man or to actual warfare on a battlefield. Thus Dr. Kagawa's question—has anyone interpreted the Gītā like "you"—breaks down into two distinct though allied questions:

1. Has anyone interpreted the Gītā as preaching nonviolence before Mahatma Gandhi?
2. Has anyone interpreted the Gītā allegorically before Mahatma Gandhi?

ANSWERS TO THE QUESTIONS

The answer to the first question seems to be that no one appears to have claimed, as Mahatma Gandhi did, that the Gītā preached nonviolence explicitly. It may be argued that the message is implicit in the Gītā itself, and this is what Mahatma Gandhi did, but no one seems to have claimed this prior to Mahatma Gandhi. Having said this, however, it may now be pointed out that there are some hints in ancient Hindu literature that, although not reaching the point of articulation achieved in Mahatma Gandhi, seem to be headed in that direction. To see this it is important to realize that one of the reasons why Mahatma Gandhi thought that the message of the Gītā was nonviolence was that, according to him, that was the message of the Mahābhārata itself, of which, as he said, "the Gītā is a minute part."[3] Thus he wrote while remarking on the message of the Gītā:

> The author of the Mahābhārata has not established the necessity of physical warfare; on the contrary he has proved its futility. He has made the victors shed tears of sorrow and repentance and has left them nothing but a legacy of miseries.[4]

In this context certain passages of the Bhāgavata Purāṇa make interesting reading. Indeed, "it is usually said that the Bhāgavata Purāṇa begins where the Mahābhārata ends, seeking to correct a story which tells of gambling, dishonouring of women and a devastating war which ends in a pyrrhic victory."[5] In the fifth chapter of the first canto we actually find Vyāsa, the putative author of the Mahābhārata, being criticized by Nārada:

> It was a great error on your part to have enjoined terrible acts (acts involving destruction of life) in the name of religion on men who are naturally addicted to such acts. Misguided by these precepts of yours (in the Mahābhārata) the ordinary man of the world would believe such acts to be pious and would refuse to honour the teachings that prohibit such action.[6]

In other words, Nārada complained that the justification of violence involved in the Mahābhārata and especially in the Gītā could have disastrous consequences in general, and urged sage Vyāsa to compose a devotional work to offset this effect, namely the Bhāgavata Purāṇa. Thus we find that even as far back as tenth century CE, the date usually assigned to the Bhāgavata Purāṇa, there was a certain uneasiness in certain Hindu minds with the violent nature of the Mahābhārata episode. The ancient thinker writing in the name of Nārada, to be sure, took a different tack than Mahatma Gandhi—he wanted a new work to turn people's minds toward the worship of Lord Krsna and away from the terrible war and its justification. Mahatma Gandhi thought that the work itself implied condemnation of violence. But both the pseudonymous Nārada and the famous Mahatma were grappling with the same issue: the violent nature of the Mahābhāratan narrative and its reconciliation with higher spiritual ends. The Gandhian solution, though, must be regarded as unique, for Nārada explicitly recognized the violence involved in the Mahābhārata and condemned it, but Mahatma Gandhi commended it as a warning to others. This difference in attitude between using it as a warning rather than as an example allowed him to claim, as none had done, that the real message of the Mahābhārata and the Gītā was nonviolence.

How then do we answer the first question: did anyone interpret the Gītā as preaching nonviolence before Mahatma Gandhi did so? The answer seems to be that no one interpreted the Gītā the way it was interpreted by Mahatma Gandhi before him, even though it may be argued that the message of nonviolence is implied in the Mahābhārata itself, and even though we detect previous undercurrents of dissatisfaction with the violence involved therein. No one before Mahatma Gandhi seems to have clearly and unambiguously stated the message of the Bhagavadgītā—and indeed of the Mahābhārata—to have been nonviolence. Now the second question: did anyone interpret the Gītā allegorically before Mahatma Gandhi? The answer to this second question can be given in the affirmative in view of certain facts that have come to light in the course of an examination of Abhinavagupta's commentary on the Bhagavadgītā known as the Gītārthasaṁgraha. Before this evidence is presented, however, it seems useful to emphasize that Mahatma Gandhi's claim that the Gītā preached nonviolence rests heavily on the antecedent claim that the Gītā must be interpreted allegorically. Mahatma Gandhi was himself fully conscious of this fact, as is clear from the prefatory note with which he commences his Gujarati commentary called *Anasakti Yoga* on the *Bhagavadgītā*.[7] The remarks translate thus:

> No knowledge is to be found without seeking, no tranquility without travail, no happiness except through tribulation. Every seeker has, at one time or another, to pass through a conflict of duties, a heart-churning.[8]

Having thus provided a spiritual rather than a historical orientation, Mahatma Gandhi translates the first verse of the Gītā and then follows it up with the following annotation:

> The human body is the battlefield where the eternal duel between Right and Wrong goes on. Therefore it is capable of being turned into the gateway to Freedom. It is born in sin and becomes the seed-bed of sin. Hence it is also called the field of Kuru. The Kauravas represent the forces of Evil, the Pandavas the forces of Good. Who is there that has not experienced the daily conflict within himself between the forces of Evil and the forces of Good?[9]

Thus Mahatma Gandhi equates the Kurukṣetra, the battlefield where the Mahābhārata war was fought, with the human body, the Kauravas with the forces of Evil in the person, and the Pāṇḍavas with the forces of Good. Fresh evidence, as pointed out earlier, suggests that the tradition of such an allegorical interpretation of the Gītā seems to go back at least as far as the tenth century CE.

The reasons for making this claim are as follows. Abhinavagupta is a name with which many if not most students of Indian culture are familiar; he is well-known for his commentaries on such well-known works of Hindu prosody and dramatics as Ānandavardhana's *Dhvanyāloka* and Bharata's Nāṭyaṣātra.[10] He is also a well-known exponent of the system of Kāśmīra Śaivism known as Trika.[11] His dates are not known with complete certainty but he is believed to have been born between 950 and 960 CE. and is thus assigned to the tenth century CE.[12] He also wrote a commentary on the Bhagavadgītā, hitherto untranslated.[13] In this commentary, in his gloss on the first verse of the Bhagavadgītā, after making his own remarks, Abhinavagupta refers to a tradition of interpreting the Gītā in which the Kurukṣetra is equated with the human body, very much in the way Mahatma Gandhi did.[14] The relevant passage runs as follows:

> Herein some speak of an alternative interpretation. [They explain the word *kurukṣetra* as] the field of the Kurus: Kurūṇām = karaṇānām—organs of sense; kṣetra (field) = that which favours, that is, the field of the senses is the favourer of all the properties of transmigration as being that which helps to bring them about (i.e. the human body). Whereas *dharmakṣetra* (the field of *dharma*) is to be understood from the sentence, "This is the highest *dharma*; to see the soul by means of Yoga," namely, as being the body of the [aspirant for whom the Gītā is] intended, a body which offers salvation by its attainment of *apavarga* through the abandonment of everything opposed to *dharma*. [So that the question asked by king Dhṛtarāṣṭra may be paraphrased thus:] Standing in that [battle] where passion and detachment, anger and forbearance, etc., have come together in mutual conflict, for the senses, etc., always aim at the injury of the body—what have my ignorant volitions, comparable to ignorant men, accomplished, and what have (my) wise (volitions), the Pāṇḍavas, comparable to men of knowledge, accomplished? That is to say, who has defeated whom?[15]

CONCLUSION

The parallels between these remarks on the first verse of the Bhagavadgītā recorded in the tenth century CE. and the remarks made by Mahatma Gandhi in the twentieth century CE. are quite obvious. This enables us to offer the conclusion that whereas Mahatma Gandhi was certainly original in regarding the message of the Bhagavadgītā to be that of *ahiṁsā*, he was certainly not the first to think up the allegorical interpretation on which he based his opinion.[16] To conclude: although the claim by Mahatma Gandhi that the Gītā preaches nonviolence seems to be unprecedented, the allegorical interpretation of the Gītā on which it is based is not unprecedented in ancient Hindu exegetical tradition that grew up around the Bhagavadgītā.[17]

NOTES

1. This statement, though substantially true, is not entirely accurate, as later chapters do contain references to fighting (e.g., IX.34). However "in thirteen out of eighteen chapters of the Gītā (viz. Chap. IV–X and Chap. XII–XVIII) we do not meet with a single reference to the scene of the battlefield of Kurukṣetra, nor to the Epic story or incidents of any kind, which might remind us of the fact that Kṛṣṇa and Arjuna had anything to do with the Bhārata war or that the object of the teaching of the Gītā was to induce Arjuna to fight, so preoccupied and deeply absorbed are both the speakers of the dialogue in topics relating to modes of spiritual culture, the ethical ideal and subtle metaphysical concepts" (S. C. Roy, *The Bhagavad-gītā and Modern Scholarship* [London: Luzac & Co., 1941], pp. 146–47).
2. M. K. Gandhi, *Hindu Dharma* (Ahmedabad: Navajivan Press, 1958), pp. 178–79.
3. Gandhi, p.159.

4. Gandhi, p.140.

5. T. S. Rukmani, *A Critical Study of the Bhāgavata Purāṇa* (Varanasi: Chowkhamba Sanskrit Series, 1970), p. 6.

6. Rukmani, p. 6; *Bhāgavata Purāṇa* 1.5.15.

7. Mahatma Gandhi, *Anasakti Yoga* (Ahmedabad: Navajivan Prakasana, 1970).

8. Mahadev Desai, *The Gītā According to Gandhi* (Ahmedabad: Navajivan, 1946), p. 135.

9. Desai, *The Gītā According to Gandhi*, p. 135.

10. See Benjamin Walker, *Hindu World*, vol. II (London: George Allen & Unwin Ltd., 1968), p. 221; Kanti Chandra Pandey, *Abhinavagupta: An Historical and Philosophical Study* (Varanasi: Chowkhamba Sanskrit Series Office, 1935), p. 9.

11. See A. L. Basham, *The Wonder That Was India* (London: Sidgwick and Jackson, 1956), p. 335.

12. Pandey, p. 8; Basham, p. 335.

13. See Pandey, pp. 52–55.

14. K. S. Ramaswamy Sastrigal seems to attribute this view to Abhinavagupta himself when he remarks: "Abhinava Guptacarya says that kṣetra means the body and that the war referred to is between the righteous and the unrighteous tendencies in man" (*The Bhagavadgītā*, vol. I, with translation and notes [Srirangam: Sri Vani Vilas Press, 1927], p. 47). But Abhinavagupta introduces this discussion with the remark: "In this respect some offer the following alternative explanation," and hence seems to be citing an alternative interpretation rather than developing his own (see Wasudev Laksman Shastri Pansikar, ed., *Śrīmadbhagavadgītā* [Bombay: Niranayasagar Press, 1912], p. 8).

15. Translation by the author.

16. The allegorical interpretation of the Gītā became quite current around the turn of the century (see W. Douglas Hill, *The Bhagavadgītā* [London: Oxford University Press, 1928], p.99) and continues to be popular (see A. L. Herman, *The Bhagavad Gītā: A Translation and Critical Commentary* [Springfield, IL: Charles C. Thomas, 1973], pp. 107–8). It is important to realize, however, that Mahatma Gandhi seems to come by the allegorical interpretation on his own, for he says quite clearly that "Even in 1888–89, when I first became acquainted with the Gītā, I felt that it was not a historical work, but that, under the guise of physical warfare, it described the duel that perpetually went on in the hearts of mankind and that physical warfare was brought in merely to make the description of the internal duel more alluring" (Mahadev Desai, p. 127). It should be further noted that according to Mahatma Gandhi his "first acquaintance with the Gītā began in 1888–89 with the verse translation by Sir Edwin Arnold known as the Song Celestial" (Mahadev Desai, p. 126). This translation does not project the Gītā as an allegory (see Edwin Arnold, *The Song Celestial or Bhagavad-Gītā* [Boston: Roberts Brothers, 1888], p. 9), unlike the translations or studies by Annie Besant (*The Bhagavad Gītā or The Lord's Song* [London: Theosophical Publishing Society, 1904], preface; *Hints on the Study of the Bhagavad-Gītā* [London: Theosophical Publishing Society, 1906], pp. 6ff). Hence it is potentially misleading to state, as some have done, that Mahatma Gandhi was first introduced to the Gītā through Annie Besant's translation (see Agehananda Bharati, "The Hindu Renaissance and Its Apologetic Patterns," *The Journal of Asian Studies*, 29, no. 2 [1970]: 274–75). Similarly, Mahatma Gandhi refers to his attempts to read Bal Gangadhar Tilak's commentary on the Gītā (Mahadev Desai, p. 125.), which again does not espouse an allegorical interpretation of the Gītā. It seems that the similarity in the exposition of the Gītā referred to by Abhinavagupta and its exposition by Mahatma Gandhi provides a case of exegetical convergence that spans several centuries.

17. This paper was delivered at the first conference of the Australian Association for the Study of Religions held at Adelaide in 1976.

CHAPTER 5

Just-War Theory in South Asia: Indic Success, Sri Lankan Failure?

Katherine K. Young

In this chapter, I will compare the views of Indian Buddhism, Jainism, and Hinduism on just war and ask the following question regarding each: did these religious traditions have any effect on wars in South Asia? I find that Buddhism did not move successfully beyond monastic withdrawal as its initial reaction to warfare, even though it struggled to develop the two-wheel doctrine (which acknowledges the distinct roles of both the Buddha and the King). In its early period, Jainism, too, did not find a way to reconcile its central doctrine of nonviolence with the duty of kings to regulate and protect society. By contrast, Hinduism engaged the problem directly and eventually emerged with a just-war theory.[1] Along with the nature of the state and strategies to prevent religious conflict, this made a big difference in practical terms. In fact, even Buddhist and Jain kings came to rely on it, making it an Indic approach.[2] A few exceptions notwithstanding, this approach eliminated religious wars. In that case, what went wrong in Sri Lanka, where the Indic theory had taken root? To answer that question, I will examine other variables in what follows.

THE VEDIC AGE AND ITS WARFARE (1500–900 BCE)

In the Vedic age, warfare was constant.[3] According to the texts (there is little archaeological evidence), tribes adopted heroic views of fierce manhood. They celebrated raw power and experienced it as sacred, because of its dramatic relation to life and death. They harnessed and directed this power, their goals being to protect lands and herds.

Conflict, violence, and perpetual crisis were central to this worldview. Consider the many characteristic struggles: gods (*devas*) versus anti-gods (*asuras*); sages versus deities; sages versus ordinary people; sage versus sage; group versus group.[4] Mock ritual attacks and ritualized verbal contests reflected the reality of constant warfare between nomadic tribes.[5] Indra was the warrior god par excellence and chief god of the Vedic pantheon. Brahmin priests composed "power songs" to make their king victorious. Warfare itself was sacralized as a religious ritual (*yajña*). The reward for death in battle was heaven. This constant violence appears in maxims: "big fish eat little fish," for instance, and "relative or no relative, crush the foes: conquer those who attack, conquer others by attacking."[6]

Within this ethos, however, warriors gradually developed a code of morality.[7] "Family honor or disgrace, protection of life or murder, possession of wives or adultery, possession of goods or stealing, truth swearing or false witnessing—all are the ken of the warrior class."[8] Violence continued during the transition from tribal societies (described in the *Ṛg-Veda*) to early chiefdoms and kingdoms.[9] This transition accompanied a second phase of urbanization, which began in the Gangetic plain between 1000 and 800 BCE. Late Vedic texts acknowledge both defensive and offensive wars. The ideal ruler is a *cakravartin.* From the words *cakra* (wheel) and *vartin* (one who turns), this compound word means "one whose wheels are moving" and by extension "one whose chariot rolls everywhere without obstruction, an emperor or sovereign of the world."[10] Because early chiefdoms and kingdoms competed for resources and territories, these early states were usually unstable. On the margins, moreover, warfare continued.

By the end of the Vedic age, warrior ethics had brought some order to tribal and then royal rivalries. That order made it possible to establish norms. And those, in turn, made it possible to establish ethical principles for the everyday (*pravṛtti*) world. But for many people, warrior codes were not enough.

POLARIZATION IN THE AXIAL AGE (900–200 BCE)

Because of constant warfare, some people withdrew from society as ascetics (Pāli *samaṇas*; Sanskrit *śramaṇas*) and established nonviolence (*ahiṃsā*) as a central religious virtue.[11] Stress produces a "fight or flight" response, so we could classify asceticism and nonviolence with "flight." This gave rise to Buddhist, Jain, and Upaniṣadic worldviews.

The idea of a legitimate war is comparatively undeveloped in Indian Buddhism. This is because Buddhism began partly as a reaction to constant warfare during the Vedic Age. Although the Pāli Canon was redacted only in the third century BCE, some parts went back to the period of the Buddha himself (who is now increasingly placed in the fourth century BCE).

The eightfold path to enlightenment for monastics includes not killing under "right action." (Conviction for murder, one of early Buddhism's four monastic prohibitions, leads to expulsion.[12]) This path also includes refusing to trade in lethal weapons under "right livelihood." The Buddha forbade his followers to witness military parades, discuss war, or go "to see an army fighting, to stay with an army, or watch sham fights or army reviews" even though he used militaristic language such as "all-conquerer" (*sabbābhibhū*) as a metaphorical description of himself.[13] In fact, men who fought in wars would be reborn in hell or as an animal.[14] Nonviolence is first among the five precepts, moreover, for lay people.[15]

But the Buddha was from the warrior (*khattiya*) caste, as were many of his followers. This made him take a more pragmatic attitude toward rulers (such as Pasendi, a fellow Kosalan, and Bimbisāra and Ajātasattu, who ruled Magadha, where the Buddha spent much of his time teaching), than his teachings against violence suggest.[16] The political realities of his age—expansionist oligarchies and kingdoms, though not yet empires—meant that warfare still prevailed.[17] An early Buddhist myth about the origin of the state involves a contract between an outstanding person (*mahāsammata*), who ends anarchy in exchange for a share of the produce.[18] The Buddha admitted that it was hard to rule without force in some circumstances.[19] He avoided conflicts with rulers, moreover, by not allowing soldiers to become monks.

According to Steven Collins, the "king's use of force and violence in putting down lawlessness is seldom questioned, much less criticized, the only advice given is that he should act with justice in giving punishments."[20] The five powers of a warrior (*khattiyabāla*) include strength of arms.[21] The Buddha praised warriors as the highest caste (theoretically displacing Brahmins). Praising them became politically useful, once monks began to live in monasteries, endowed by kings, instead of wandering around the countryside. Moreover, kings built *thūpa*s (S. *stūpas*), which became pilgrimage centers after the Buddha's "final enlightenment."[22]

Several prominent scholars think that Pāli texts advocate a two-wheel doctrine.[23] Both the Buddha and the king turn the wheel (*cakka*) of Dhamma, a word often used for Buddhist teachings.[24] Collins argues that this doctrine is not about a simple parallel. It is about two modes of the Dhamma, which involve two views of kingship and war. The first mode involves the good king in the real world, which requires him to be flexible and therefore willing to negotiate so that "the punishment fits the crime." This is an "ethics of reciprocity," a *lex talionis* ("an eye for an eye"). It requires care, not haste, and avoids anger. According to Collins, the texts present this point of view as "a law of human nature if not a policy."[25] The second mode, he says, involves bad kings in a bad world.[26] All kings must participate in violence, after all, which is always wrong according to the "context-independent and non-negotiable" first precept: "do not kill." In other words, this is an ethics of the absolute. To eliminate violence means renouncing the world to become a monk and therefore abandoning the world to its karma. This does not mean the triumph of *ahiṃsā* in daily life. Most people will not choose monasticism, even though that is the ideal way of life. Monasticism is a transcendental vision, really, that is theoretically accessible to everyone in one rebirth or another. What people do not do now, they might do in the future.[27]

To reconcile the opposition between accepting kings who are good and rejecting all kings as bad, Buddhism has proposed the nonviolent king. This utopian paradox had roots in a work from the early Pāli canon (probably from before 250 BCE).[28] The *Cakkavatti-sīhanāda-sutta* is the twenty-sixth sutta of the Dīgha-nikāya. In this sutta, the Buddha tells his monks about "a king called Daḷhanemi (Strong-tire), a Wheel-turner, righteous, a king of righteousness (*dhammiko dhammarāja*), a conqueror of the whole world, who had achieved stability in his country and possessed the Seven Jewels . . . he had more than a thousand sons, who were valiant, of heroic (physical) form, crushing enemy armies. He conquered this earth, surrounded by the ocean, and lived from it, without violence, without a sword, according to what is right [*dhammena*]."[29] When it was time to pass power on to his son, so the story goes, the king became a renunciate. The celestial wheel-jewel, which symbolized his nonviolent and just rule, slipped from its place in the sky. When the new king asked about this event, his father taught him how to rule justly

> for the army, for your noble warrior client(-kings)s, for Brahmin householders, . . . for ascetics and Brahmin (-renouncers). . . . The ascetics and Brahmins in your territory, my dear, who abstain from drunkenness and negligence, who practice forbearance and gentleness, each one conquering himself, calming himself, quenching himself . . . you should go to them from time to time and ask: "What, sir, is good ('wholesome,' *kusala*)? What is not good? What is blameworthy, what blameless? What is to be practiced, what not? Doing what would lead to suffering and harm for me in the long run? Doing what would lead to happiness and benefit for me in the long run?" You should listen to them, and avoid what is bad (unwholesome, *akusala*); you should take up what is good and do that. That is the noble turning of a Wheel-turning king.[30]

The new king leads his army, following the wheel-jewel, in all directions. But he does not need to fight rival kings, because they immediately say, "Come, great king, welcome, great king, it's yours [i.e., take possession of this territory], great king, give us your orders [or: instruction, *anusāsa*]."[31] The wheel-turning king says, "'No living being is to be killed. What is not given is not to be taken. Misconduct in sexual matters is not to be indulged in. Lies are not to be told. No intoxicant is to be drunk. (Now) kings in the east became clients of the wheel-turning king."[32] The rival kings voluntarily become his vassals, in other words, and the king establishes righteous rule by instituting the five precepts for lay people. In this way, his kingdom prospers.

This advice and expansion, with the miraculous help of the Cakka, continues with power passing from one king to another. Eventually, though, a king chooses to ignore the Dhamma. His kingdom does not prosper. Along with lies and violence, not giving to the poor causes trouble for his kingdom. And that, in turn, causes even more violence. Over the generations, things go from bad to worse. Included in the myth's list of woes is lack of respect for ascetics and Brahmins. Finally, people realize that they should start doing good deeds instead of bad ones and abstain from killing.

A list of predictions of what will happen follows. By doing good deeds, the good society will slowly make a comeback. Moreover, the future Buddha (Metteyya) will emerge.[33] Then King Sankha will reign. After living in the palace, he will give it away "as alms (for the use of) ascetics, Brahmins, indigents, tramps, and beggars. In the presence of the Blessed One Metteyya he will cut off his hair and beard, put on yellow robes, and go forth from home to homelessness. He will be a renouncer" as are other "sons from good families."[34] The story ends with a general statement about the Dhamma as a refuge and about overcoming evil (Māra) by acquiring merit through wholesome states of mind.

I do not see how we can know whether the *cakkavatti* originally got his empire by nonviolence (although the second sequence of restoring righteous rule definitely says so) or by violence in view of the passage that refers to his thousand sons "who crush enemy armies." The sutta as a whole is equivocal, in short, even though its support for defensive violence is unequivocal. In any case, Collins points out that the imperial myth of the *cakkavatti,* with its "cosmo-geography" appears in early Buddhist texts as a thought experiment—that is, before the advent of empires in ancient India.[35] Still, he thinks that it inspired later kings who wanted empires and legitimated those who managed to win them. If so, they would have ignored the *Cakkavatti-sīhanāda-sutta* or recognized its ambiguity. By contrast, Balkrishna Gokhale thinks that the nonviolent king is an ideal. "In spite of these seeming compromises in practice," he says, "early Buddhists hoped to minimize the violence inherent in the power of the State by ordaining that this power be, at all times, restrained by morality."[36] But he provides no clues on how the ideal offers any practical advice on restraint, aside from the extreme view that violence is categorically wrong.

* * *

Jainism, a religion that developed in the Axial age alongside Buddhism, if not a bit before, too holds *ahiṃsā* as the supreme value, categorically for monastics (who scrupulously avoid taking the lives of sentient creatures) and provisionally for lay people who avoid doing so by minimizing the violence of some occupations (such as hunting, agriculture, or the military), avoiding some foods (such as meat, fish, and even some vegetables), and making intention more important than act. Like the early Buddhist view, the Jain one focuses on the personal quest for salvation, not the welfare of humanity in general.[37]

Jains attribute the following story about war from the *Bhagavatīsūtra*, belonging to the Jain canon (which was redacted in the fifth century CE from fragments and oral traditions) to Mahāvīra, the last *tīrthaṅkara.* He describes a war between Koṇika (the emperor of Magadha, where Mahāvīra lived) and a federation of eighteen kings, which resulted in 840,000 dead warriors. Unlike the Brahmanical texts, which promise heaven to warriors who die in battle, this one says that only two gained heaven in this war.[38] One of these, Varuṇa, had taken lay vows—including the vow never to strike anyone first—before being drafted into the army. On the battlefield, he asks his adversary to shoot first. Although Varuṇa manages to kill this adversary, even so, his own wound is mortal. Sitting on the ground and vowing to renounce all forms of violence, he pulls out the arrow, dies peacefully, and attains heaven. The other warrior supports Varuṇa in his final moments. But his wound, too, is mortal. He dies and is reborn again as a human.

This Jain story acknowledges the reality of war and being drafted by the king. If drafted, a Jain who has taken his lay vows may act only defensively—even on the battlefield. He attains heaven because of his final vow, renouncing all violence, and his peaceful death. But what if he nonetheless kills an enemy warrior? He might satisfy the religious principle at stake, I would argue, but hardly the military one. Waiting for an offensive move by the enemy, after all, would generally result in defeat.

* * *

This period witnessed two extreme positions in Brahmanical circles: flight and fight. Regarding flight, not only Buddhists and Jains withdrew from society, but some Brahmins as well. The Upaniṣads share ideas with the *samaṇas* (S. *śramaṇas*) such as individualism, asceticism, withdrawal to the forest, detachment from the material and social world, and theories of karma, rebirth, meditation, knowledge over action, and liberation. Scholars still debate whether these Upaniṣadic ideas are borrowings (especially striking is the fact that teachers are often Kṣatriyas and the Upaniṣadic language is a vernacular as in Buddhism and Jainism) or internal developments. The latter would be via the Ṛg-vedic long-haired ascetics (*keśins*) and silent ones (*munis*), ideas of ritual heat or power (*tapas*), the internalization of Vedic rituals, and so forth. These details aside, the Upaniṣads offer a distinctive view on the nature of liberation: that the absolute (*brahman*) is the true self (*ātman*). The word *ahiṃsā* occurs first in the *Chāndogya-upaniṣad.*[39] Withdrawal for spiritual development became known in brahmanical circles as *nivṛtti* (escape, abandon, cessation) in contrast to *pravṛtti* (action within the world).

But doctrines of war were hardening as well. This was the fight response to stress. So important was warfare that passages on it (scattered through genres such as the Dharma-śāstras) became the Dhanur-Veda, the Veda of Warfare (Veda being the category of scripture par excellence). In his *Artha-śāstra* (ca. 300 BCE), Kauṭilya elaborates on the imperial ideal of the *cakravartin,* saying that the king should rule from the Himālayas to the ocean. Kauṭilya had some personal experience with imperialism, after all, as chief minister for King Chandragupta (ruled 321–297 BCE), whose Mauryan empire stretched throughout northern and central India. Scholars have characterized Kauṭilya as a rugged political realist at best and paternal despot at worse.[40] He gave the first comprehensive view of the state in terms of a king, minister, country, fort, treasury, army, ally, and enemy. His premise was that the purpose of a king is to establish order, thereby preventing chaos, which also exists because every ruler acts to maximize his own self-interest and power for expansion of the kingdom.[41] According to R. P. Kangle, Kauṭilya did acknowledge some rules for just warfare; for example, the following should not be attacked: those who have fallen, turned their backs, surrendered, whose hair is loose as a sign of submission, who have abandoned their weapons, who are visibly afraid, and who are not taking part in the fight.[42]

The king is ultimately accountable, however, not to justice but to his own power to ensure the existence and order of the state, which might necessitate force and stratagems such as spying, arresting people on mere suspicion, torture, and even assassination. When he conquers another king, he treats him according to his strength; if he is more powerful, he may offer terms of peace and win him over; if he is equal in power, he may enter into alliance with him, But if he is weaker, he may "be completely destroyed, unless he becomes desperate and fights for his life, when peace may be made with him."[43] Because of his political realism, Kauṭilya wanted the king to have total control over religion and to build shrines and control their wealth to achieve that. Religion is helpful only to the degree that the king can harness it to achieve his own goal.[44] If promise of heaven helps warriors to fight more valiantly, so be it.[45]

* * *

To conclude, Buddhism, Jainism, and Upaniṣadic religion in the axial age never got beyond attempts to reconcile their initial response to war (withdrawal from society) and their observation that every society had to maintain not only order but also security (which might involve war). This is especially striking given the fact that Buddhism and Jainism developed in warrior circles and targeted local rulers for proselytism. Despite some pragmatism, the best that Buddhists could do was to recognize the paradox of a nonviolent king. Buddhism remained equivocal over the idea of the *cakkavatti* (world-conquerer) praising nonviolence on the one hand, but occasionally admitting the need for defensive war on the other. Because hell was the Jain penalty for participating in even a defensive war, not many Jains wanted to discuss ethical conduct on the battlefield. Jainism initially rejected the idea of the *cakravartin.* As theirs was a flight response, the Upaniṣadic ascetics too failed to address the realities of war. This created a moral vacuum that allowed a soft despotism to develop in the form of *Kauṭilīya Artha-śāstra.*

OVERCOMING THE EXTREMES OF FLIGHT OR FIGHT: JUST WAR IN THE CLASSICAL AGE (300 BCE TO 400 CE)

Perhaps in reaction to *Kauṭilīya Artha-śāstra,* Brahmins began to shift power from warriors to themselves. Especially as priests or advisors (*purohitas*) to kings, Brahmins tried to tame tyrannical royal power with discussions of the *just* king, one who brings peace and harmony to his realm and upholds dharma through righteousness and concern for the welfare of the people (*lokasaṃgraha*). Now, ethics (*dharma*) would constrain power and politics (*artha*). In the process, Brahmins transformed royal imagery. This implied a stable and peaceful kingdom. Nonetheless, it acknowledged the inevitability of offensive wars and therefore the need for defensive ones. In addition, it acknowledged that warriors would have to fight in these wars according to a new code of ethics and that civilians deserved protection. As both intellectuals and priests, Brahmins did not participate in warfare, which was the prerogative by birth of warriors. Even so, they had to make sure not only that their own kingdom's warriors refrained from attacking them but also that these warriors protected them from the attacks of enemy rulers.

This new concern with ethics can be seen in the integration of the concept of *nivṛtti* into *pravṛtti.* Brahmins expanded *nivṛtti* during the classical period. The ethical corollary of *nivṛtti* is a list of virtues, which appeared first in the Upaniṣads and then in the *Yoga-sūtra,* such as "non-violence, truthfulness, non-stealing, celibacy, renunciation of possessions, and self-control."[46] Although these lists originally defined the ethical behavior only of renunciates and ascetics (*sannyāsins* and *tapasvins*), classical authorities reclassified them as common (*sāmānya*) and therefore for everyone. *Mānava-dharma-śāstra,* for instance, refers to nonviolence, truthfulness, non-stealing, purity, and restraining the sense organs.[47]

Making *ahiṃsā* applicable to all people helped Brahmins to compete with Buddhists and Jains. The latter had attacked the Brahmanical tradition for its legitimation of violence in both animal sacrifice and warfare. But making *ahiṃsā* a virtue for everyone created, in turn, a conflict between common (*sāmānya*) dharma and particular (*viśeṣa*) dharma. Particular dharma, which includes the duties that pertain to both caste and stage of life, makes killing (*hiṃsā*) a duty for Kṣatriyas under specific conditions.[48] So how could they fulfill the obligation of *ahiṃsā?* The supreme evaluation of *ahiṃsā* created problems for Brahmins, too.

Whether they became ascetics proper (and some did) or merely non-warriors who lived nonviolently, they now faced a dilemma: should they continue to uphold the warrior culture or encourage a shift to a nonviolent one for both society in general and Brahmins in particular? The general consensus favored nonviolence.

How to attain that ideal, however, was another matter. Conflict over that led to the exploration, through stories, of possible solutions. Some stories displace the command for violence from mortals to the gods or God.[49] Some argue that war can be legitimate but add that everyone should develop a spiritual state of detachment in action. Others argue for silence in the face of conflict. And still others argue that war is never legitimate.[50]

The epic *Rāmāyaṇa* (composed sometime from the fourth century to the second century BCE) introduces the king's social responsibility in connection with Rāma. Kingship and warrior dharma are now about selflessness and compassion, not selfishness and power.[51] Although the epic still refers primarily to extended families or tribes, it replaces the tribal code of warrior ethics with a righteousness one that has transcendental authority and relies on personal conscience.[52] It encourages kings to develop the *yogin*'s equanimity in the midst of conflict. One passage implies that Rāma cannot be righteous without giving up violence, which originates in greed and tyranny.[53] From this, you would think that warrior circles have embraced nonviolence. From the *Rāmāyaṇa* as a whole, though, you realize that Rāma has renounced only the old warrior ethic. According to the new one, he remains ready to defend justice through violence.[54] Obviously, this epic reflects conflict over violence and nonviolence.

The old views about warfare prevail, however, in the Mahābhārata (the oldest strata of which dates from the beginning of the classical period). This epic is about a great war between the Kauravas and the Pāṇḍavas, two sides of a family. It contains the famous text, the Bhagavadgītā.[55] The latter was probably composed in the first century BCE. The Mahābhārata often compares the bloody battle of Kurukṣetra with a sacrifice. For one thing, it killed a whole generation of warrior chieftains.[56] Moreover, the "idea that by sacrificing one can compete over chieftainship is of course the essence of the agonistic legacy."[57] Even Brahmins developed a taste for big-time power. In their redactions of the epics, they try to convince others that their magical power is superior to conventional military power. Stories show them competing with warriors by using a power with fiery qualities (*tejas*) and divine weapons (*brahma-astra*) that they create from it.[58] Rivalry between the two elites, Brahmins and Kṣatriyas, had been common before caste rigidified and Brahmins, who composed the scriptural texts, made themselves superior to Kṣatriyas (just as Buddhists and Jains were making themselves superior to Brahmins).

The Bhagavadgītā explores violence and nonviolence ostensibly from the perspective of Kṣatriyas (Brahmins were the authors of the texts). On the eve of a great battle, Arjuna does not want to fight. This battle would cause the destruction of his whole family, after all, even though it is about justice (the Pāṇḍavas' rightful succession to the throne) according to the prevailing rules of just warfare. He must choose between protecting his family and protecting the state: loyalty to kin versus loyalty to polity (both of which are closely connected in a royal family, which must preserve its own lineage but also its kingdom).

Like a modern conscientious objector, Arjuna argues that war originates in greed and is therefore inherently wrong. The suffering that war creates is absurd, he adds, and leads to hell. Far better to renounce this world altogether by becoming an ascetic. But Lord Kṛṣṇa, his charioteer, disapproves. He calls Arjuna's action ignoble (*anārya*), womanly (*klība*), useless (*ajuṣṭam*), and generally dishonorable (*akīrtikara*). Arjuna denies that he wants anything—victory, kingship, pleasure, enjoyment, or sovereignty over the three worlds—if it requires him to kill members of his extended family, violate ancient family laws (*kula-dharmaḥ sanātanaḥ*), or foster unrighteousness (*adharma*). Better to die than do any of those things.[59] Once again, Kṛṣṇa disagrees. He argues, now at a more philosophical level, that life involves both death and birth; there will always be another birth.[60] But this cycle belongs to the ordinary level of existence. The ultimate level transcends this opposition altogether, involving neither killing nor being killed.[61]

The Gītā's solution for this conflict between *ahiṃsā* and *hiṃsā* is to insist that warriors do their military duty but adopt a new yogic perspective: renunciation in action (*niṣkāma-karma-yoga*). This allowed them to act in the world (the requirement of *pravṛtti*) but also to move beyond the oppositions that characterize everyday life with a spiritual centeredness that negated the effects of karma (the requirement of *nivṛtti*). This point of view also allowed them to gain the benefits of both *nivṛtti and pravṛtti,* thereby overcoming the deep polarization between violence and nonviolence. With this new way of understanding dharma, Kṣatriyas could not withdraw and become sages. Doing so would erode their distinctive function: protecting society. But they had access to the spiritual domain by cultivating not only dharma but also yogic equanimity. God himself (that is, Kṛṣṇa) manifests both violence (*hiṃsā*) and nonviolence (*ahiṃsā*) in the cosmic cycles but also transcends both.[62] He tells Arjuna to seek equilibrium in the midst of action and to act without wanting any of its results. Only by developing spiritually beyond illusion and greed can he work for the ideal society (*Rāmarājya*).[63] A just war (*dharma-yuddha*), in other words, requires both just reasons and just means.

More specifically, it requires (1) legitimate reasons for war (expanding a kingdom or defending it after failing to secure peace in any other way); (2) clarity (announcing both the war and every battle); (3) discrimination (restricting warfare to particular places, times, and people—the Kṣatriyas—so that Brahmins, the aged, women, children, peaceful citizens, the mentally ill, and the military support staff would be protected); (4) fairness and equality (including only combatants of the same size, who have adequate weapons, and who fight according to a military code that allows the surrender of those who are afraid, tired, disabled, or without adequate weapons); (5) containment (restricting war to duels between two Kṣatriyas of equal status and ability); and (6) reconciliation after victory (welcoming defeated kings and allowing them to keep their kingdoms and customs in exchange for tribute).[64]

Although the Mahābhārata refuses to absolutize nonviolence by calling nonviolence a general principle and violence an exception, it does encourage warriors to avoid cruelty and promotes the principles of a just war (some of which are like those developed in the West).[65] But it recognizes one important exception. If an enemy does not play by the rules of righteous warfare, no regulations apply; the war is obviously unrighteous (*kūṭayuddha*).[66] In other words, anything goes (a point that Kauṭilya makes). Ethics is promoted but not at the expense of foolishness.[67]

In short, Brahmins thought a great deal about violence and nonviolence. I see the following pattern: thesis (constant warfare without much regulation in the Vedic period); antithesis (polarization between flight and fight in the Axial Age); and, after a millennium of trying to move beyond these problematic extremes, synthesis (nonviolence as the Hindu norm; violence as just war the exception). The opposition between flight and fight had been theoretically overcome.

Gradually, this view spread to new regions through contact with local rulers, their ritual legitimation, and syncretism.[68] Because of fluctuating tribute systems and gradual integration of local chiefdoms, the state had porous boundaries. This prevented demarcation of strict in-groups and out-groups based on language, territory, and ethnicity. Although borders enlarged beyond the northern river valleys because of southward migrations, the "land" remained somewhat unified despite various names.[69] This was not an empire as such but a civilizational ethos.

Consider the case of Tamilnadu. The earliest Tamil literature (from the first century to the third), called *caṅkam,* is about love and war. Some poems describe conflicts ranging from minor cattle raids to major wars. So important is war, poets discuss it in connection with five characteristic types of landscapes (*tiṇai*) that are found in Tamilnadu. The *Tolkāppiyam* associates cattle raiding with mountains; preparing for war and invading with pastoral lands; besieging towns with plains; attacking and displaying royal power with seashore; and achieving victory with desert. Other poems celebrate the tyranny of chiefs who plunder and then burn towns and agricultural fields.

But still other poems, no doubt under northern influence, celebrate kings for their justice and impartiality.[70] With that in mind, one *caṅkam* poem chides a king for his ruthless looting of other kingdoms: "[Y]our bards are wearing lotuses of gold and the poets are getting ready to ride fancy chariots drawn by elephants with florid bow-shields: is this right, O Lord rich in victories, this ruthless taking of other men's lands while being very sweet to protégés?" But usually, poems demand justice *within* kingdoms.

> [O]ne might measure the depth of the dark sea, the width of the earth, the regions of the winds, the empty, eternal sky, but he could never measure you, your wisdom, kindness, compassion. Those who live in your shade know no other flames than the blazing of the red sun and the fire that cooks their rice. They know no warrior's bow, only the rainbow. They know no weapon, only the bow. O Lord who devours the lands of others, destroying your foes with warriors who are skilled in the art of war, no enemies eat the soil of your land, only women compelled by the longings of pregnancy. Arrows are stored in your guarded fortress, justice lives in your scepter. Even if new birds come or old birds go, nothing threatens the benevolence of your rule. That is why all breathing creatures in your kingdom live in fear that you might come to harm.[71]

In Tamilnadu, too, we find the idea of just warfare. "Your valour in battle adheres to the principle of declaring the procedures of just warfare as you say: 'Oh cows and cow-like gentle Brahman folk, women, sick persons . . . we will shoot our arrows fast! Go to your places of safety.'"[72]

* * *

All this had an influence on Buddhism and Jainism, but they remained conflicted. In the classical period, the description of the good king appears in the Buddhist Jātaka tales. He has ten virtues: almsgiving, morality, keeping the precepts, liberality, honesty, mildness, religious practice, non-anger, *nonviolence*, patience, and non-offensiveness.[73] Mahāyāna Buddhism takes the idea of the good king one step further by identifying him as a *bodhisattva* in disguise.[74] The *bodhisattva*'s aim is to transform all sentient beings into enlightened ones, which would mean eliminating violence from the cosmos. This is another example of "the utopian paradox of the nonviolent king," who "transcends violence by conquering nonviolently."[75] The approach culminates in the "king as the future Buddha," Metteyya.[76] As such, it is very similar to the *Cakkavatti-sīhanāda-sutta*. According to the *Vimalakīrti Nirdeśa Sūtra*, "When enemies line up for battle, he [the *bodhisattva*] gives equal strength to both. With his authority and power, he forces them to be reconciled and live in harmony."[77] This alludes to the just-war theory developed in the Mahābhārata. The *Ārya-satyaka-parivarta-sūtra* "teaches that the righteous ruler should seek to avoid war by negotiation, placation or having strong alliances. If he has to fight to defend his country, he should seek to attain victory over the enemy only with the aim of protecting his people, also bearing in mind the need to protect all life, and having no concern for himself and his property. In this way, he may avoid the usual bad karmic results of killing."[78]

During this period, Mahāyāna Buddhism also developed the idea of skillful means (*upāya-kauśalya*), which legitimated actions that were ostensibly against the precepts if they were for the welfare of the world. If the motive is virtuous or the lesser of two evils, taking life is not reprehensible.[79] This opened the hermeneutical door to warfare for offence or defense as occasionally occurred in East Asia.[80] But other Mahāyāna works such as the *Brahmajāla Sūtra* argue that *bodhisattva*s should not participate in war, watch battles, kill, praise killing, and so forth.[81]

Jain works promise a harsh destiny for anyone involved in warfare. In the Jain version of the Hindu epic *Rāmāyaṇa*, Rāma's brother Lakṣmaṇa, who fights the demon Rāvaṇa in a just war, ends up in hell with Rāvaṇa. If going to hell was the result of kingship or being a warrior, no matter how just the reasons and means, would not Jains avoid even defensive wars or alternatively ignore Jain teachings about nonviolence? And if the latter, would this not create a vacuum of ethics on the topic of war?

* * *

To conclude, in the classical period, Mahāyāna Buddhism had developed the concepts of the *bodhisattva* and of skill-in-means (*upāya-kauśalya*). These led to consideration of the Mahābhārata's just-war thinking, although Mahāyāna Buddhism seemed conflicted on this topic. Jainism, too, made some half-hearted concessions to the need for defensive wars. But Brahmins—who were on the defensive because of the demand for nonviolence yet still recognized the importance of alliances with kings—began to experiment with ways of overcoming polarization between violence and nonviolence, eventually finding a conceptual solution and embedding it in the great Mahābhārata epic, especially in its Bhagavadgītā section.

THE MEDIEVAL PERIOD (400–1300 CE)

In this period, Buddhist and Jain rulers began to subscribe to the Brahmanical view of just war, making it into a general civilizational or Indic view. Between the fifth and ninth centuries, the Indic view of kingship spread to Southeast Asia. Just as in India, tributary polities and lack of administrative integration created a patchwork of political units, the lesser ones maintaining much internal autonomy after acknowledging the spiritual authority of the region's main ruler, a *cakravartin.* [82] This patchwork focused on "human loyalties rather than territorial acquisitions, which admittedly was often more ideal than real."[83] "Moreover, spheres of influence could shift from one centre to another, so that any sense of statehood was fluid and contingent."[84] The cosmological orientation of the major center was replicated by lesser ones, creating multiple centers.[85] But the Indic view of just war was not always present. "In war, Buddhist temples might be destroyed and famous Buddha images or relics taken booty. . . . This was because they were seen as the source of auspicious magical power that would benefit whoever possessed them. . . . When one reads of this devastation, one might wonder whether it is the case that, having overridden the prime Buddhist precept against killing, Buddhist soldiers may sometimes lose all inhibitions in war and become very violent."[86]

By medieval times, Jain thinkers, too, were integrating the Brahmanical theory of just war. In Tamilnadu, the post-*caṅkam* text *Tirukkuṟaḷ* (fourth or fifth century) has sections on righteousness (Tamil *aṟam;* Sanskrit *dharma*), statecraft (T. *poruḷ;* S. *artha*), and pleasure (T. *kāmam;* S. *kāma*) following the classical Brahmanical view of the three mundane goals of life. Tiruvaḷḷuvar, its Jain author, says that a king should be virtuous, wise, energetic, generous, gracious, and protecting but also impartial and just.[87] Justice requires him to punish injustice, of course, in order to prevent tyranny and cruelty.[88] Agricultural fertility and social harmony are the results of justice.[89] This became a major theme of the Tamil epics, the Buddhist *Maṇimēkalai* and the Jain *Cilappatikāram.*[90] In the latter, a bent royal scepter represents injustice, a straight one justice. The *Tirukkuṟaḷ* makes similar points but adds that a good kingdom is one that "accommodates immigrants."[91] This text also alludes to the *cakravartin.* One passage says that the "whole world is his who chooses the right time and place" and that a "world-conqueror bides his time unperturbed."[92] Note the Indic pattern here: the *cakravartin* who may legitimately expand his kingdom but also must be just.

John Cort analyzes four narratives of Jain kingship in medieval Western India.[93] The fourth one is about King Kumārapāla. "[T]he life of Kumārapāla provided the narrators with the opportunity to describe a king who is fully involved both personally and politically in a Jain moral universe, and therefore in a Jain theory of kingship."[94] This latter image drew from the *cakravartin* model:

> The Jain king was a leader of the congregation of Jain devotees (*sanghapati*) rather than a divine emanation. The Jains saw a king such as Kumārapāla as a special householder, and therefore as lesser than an *ācārya* in terms of the spiritual hierarchy of the fourteen stages towards liberation (*guṇasthānas*). . . . When the Jain *cakravartin* was on his tour of world conquest, the individual victories were possible only by the *cakravartin* taking off his royal regalia and assuming the state of a temporary mendicant. . . . Kumārapāla is depicted as a quasi-mendicant. In the narratives of the twelve

> *cakravartins* in the Jain universal history, ten of them renounce their kingship at the end of their lives to become mendicants and eventually either attain liberation or rebirth in a heavenly realm, just as the Jinas themselves renounced the possibility of universal kingship for the greater victory over ignorance and karmic bondage.[95]

Jain borrowings of Brahmanical just-war theory are especially clear in Jinasena's *Ādipurāṇa* (from approximately the ninth century CE). This tells the story—with hints of the Mahābhārata and the Gītā—about a conflict at the heart of a royal family.[96] In this case, though, the conflict is between two brothers. And its view of justice relies on the Jain doctrine of acknowledging many perspectives (*anekāntavāda*), because it takes into account justice not only for one aggrieved party but for all of them (king Bharata, his brother Bāhubali, and the king's ministers). The story takes place at the beginning of the current temporal cycle (the advent of civilization).

The first holy man (*tīrthaṅkara*), King Ṛṣabha, introduces "both the secular laws legislating the conduct of society as well as the monastic laws governing the pursuit of salvation."[97] (This part of the story is very similar to the Buddhist two-wheel doctrine.) When he renounces the world, his eldest son, Bharata, takes over. But his younger son, Bāhubali, refuses to acknowledge Bharata as king and threatens war. Like the Mahābhārata, this story shows how Bharata's advisors contain a war that would devastate the land. They do so by requiring a wrestling match between the two brothers alone. The story concludes in a characteristically Jain way by having Bāhubali win, not Bharata (who would have been the rightful king). This version allows Bāhubali to feel remorse for humiliating Bharata and for wanting possessions rather than salvation. As a result, he renounces the world and becomes a monk.[98] Despite some pragmatic discussions on the role of kings to protect Jainism but also on the fact that kings will want to expand their kingdom and extend the religion, there are no specific rules regarding just war, only the advice of monks. Kings behave much like monks and, like the Buddhist *cakkavatti,* rule and even punish without violence. Even so, a ruler is still inferior to the monk.[99]

In the century after the *Ādipurāṇa,* which contains that Bharata-Bāhubali tale, Somadeva (a Jain lawgiver who drew from the Mahābhārata's just-war theory), promoted its principle of discrimination. He argued that kings could fight other kings and their warriors but not the weak or downtrodden.[100] By this time, we see that Jainism subscribed to the general Indic view but also developed a more specific Jaina one—the legitimacy of defensive war to protect the Jain community and its teachings, although it keeps nonviolence as its ideal by suggesting that kings should punish wrongdoers without violence.[101] By the twelfth century, in Amritchandra's *Puruṣārthasiddhi-upāya,* killing in self-defense is called a kind of *virodhi-hiṃsā* ([legitimate] injury generated by standing in opposition), which legitimated defense of person and property.[102] All this comes very close to the idea of a state religion in which the king protects the Jaina community.

WHY ALMOST NO RELIGIOUS WARS IN INDIC INDIA?

Ancient India certainly had plenty of opportunity to become a land of religious wars. According to one Buddhist passage, "truth is one without a second" (*ekam hi saccam na dutiyam atthi*).[103] According to another, Buddhism is different from the four religions that are false and the four that are unsatisfactory (this implies a dichotomy between truth and falsehood). Any religion is true only to the extent that it contains aspects of the noble eightfold path.[104] These passages suggest that Buddhists consider themselves superior to the followers of other religions. In fact, several Buddhist *Nikāyas*—the *Brahmajāla-sutta, Tevijja-sutta,* and *Sandaka-sutta*—often criticize Brahmins, especially their animal sacrifices and their theology. In the *Tevijja-sutta,* for instance, the Buddha attacks Brahmins for believing that there are many paths to fellowship with Lord Brahmā, because no one has actually seen Brahmā.[105] Early Jainism was also hostile toward Brahmins. But Vedic religion, too, set the stage for the superiority of its worldview with the statement that "truth is one" (*ekaṁ sat*).[106] By classical times, this rivalry could have led to religious wars because Buddhists, Jains, and Brahmins alike cultivated royal support and wanted to advise kings.

Religious wars did not happen because the just king supported, or at least did not harm, the religions within his realm. Indic rulers realized that it was advantageous for a prosperous kingdom that had multiple religious and ethnic identities to keep peace among them by a rhetoric of honor, by substantial material support, and by never allowing hierarchy based on royal preference to disintegrate into religious wars. This created a fragile religio-political balance albeit within a nominal hierarchy.

But there are other reasons, too, why South Asia had almost no religious wars before the Muslims arrived. This region's culture relied on both pluralism (beginning with the Vedic pantheon) and henotheism (each deity superior in turn to the others). Later on, this spawned new deities, cults, philosophical schools, and guru lineages. Although Buddhism and Jainism ostensibly rejected the Vedic pantheon, this cultural penchant for pluralism entered through the backdoor, as it were, with the recognition of seven previous Buddhas, twenty-four previous (Jain) *tīrthaṅkaras*, popular tree spirits (*yakṣīs*), and so forth. Even when Hindus referred to supreme deities (Śiva, say, or Viṣṇu) or the absolute (Brahman), they acknowledged their many names and forms that had integrated lesser gods such as local ones or those of the old Vedic pantheon. Each of these three religions gradually acknowledged pluralism, moreover, by avoiding exclusive definitions of truth. Jainism produced a doctrine called *anekāntavāda,* which accepts many perspectives. Mahāyāna Buddhism developed its concept of skill-in-means (*upāya-kauśalya*), which acknowledges that seekers find truth to the extent of their intellectual capacities. Hinduism produced its own version, called *adhikāra-bheda.* In addition, it produced the notion of six *darśaṇas* (or schools of thought). All of these religions, moreover, borrowed from each other. The result was porous boundaries. People could have their own religious affiliations. So could families. Because there was no concept of conversion but only religious preferences, hierarchy inherent in views of supreme truth was muted by pluralism and the rhetoric of respect. People ranked ideas, arguments, customs, and even groups but rarely castigated or condemned any of them as evil. Akin to the concept of henotheism in the pantheon—each supreme in turn—this had a calming effect on interreligious relations in the best of times.

As I have argued elsewhere, these religions also used specific strategies to prevent just wars from becoming religious wars.

> One technique is to remain silent regarding other religions. A second is to state philosophically or mythically what may be offensive to other religions. An argument based on logic, for instance, creates distance from the immediate context: through logic something can be said to be true yet not be interpreted personally. Similarly, stories of the gods and demons can allude to truth and illusion without directly incriminating particular religious groups. Thus, silence, logic, and mythos are distancing mechanisms that operate as a form of etiquette to avoid overt clashes. Unlike etiquette, though, there is an attempt to redirect the orientation of one of the participants, albeit as graciously as possible. Then, too, the clarity of logic or the opaqueness of myth or even the wall of silence can still be interpreted by a religious group as strategy, aggression or proselytism. There are, in fact, two official arenas that allow for overt interfaith competition in classical India: the philosophical debate and the religious poetry contest. Each has its decorum, its umpire (*madhyastha*), and its judge. Such court or public competitions operate much like the duel in other societies. Potential conflict is siphoned out of society by a prearranged battle of wits fought according to formal procedure; by extension, this becomes a struggle for ascendancy between two contending persons, groups, or ideas. It is noteworthy, however, that this Indian "duel" is intellectual and nonviolent.[107]

These strategies were usually effective in preventing religious wars, despite political expansion from the Gangetic plain and intense proselytizing. Each religion offered support for the state in ways that looked more and more like those of its counterparts.[108]

Historically, the Indic (Jain, Buddhist, and Hindu) pattern was that religious leaders as represented by monastics/ascetics (*śramaṇas*) or Brahmins (*brāhmaṇas*) wanted special status with the ruler. They could tolerate, at least for short periods, secondary status as long as there was no abrogation of customary rights and no interference in the internal affairs of the religion such as to reform them. Should either of these two conditions not be fulfilled, however, they would react to regain preferential treatment by the ruler. The creation of a state religion was the most problematic of all.

* * *

There were several contexts in which this religious peace was disturbed: during the rule of the Śuṅgas (second century BCE); during the rule of the Bengali Hindu king Saśanka (seventh century CE); and during the rule of some Tamil kings (fifth to ninth century CE).[109]

To understand why the Śuṅga (Brahmin) dynasty's battle to end Buddhist rule over the Mauryan empire was a marker event in the history of interfaith relations in India, we need to know why Aśoka upset the balance of religious power and interfaith relations despite his many generous policies.[110] Aśoka led a massive war against the Kalingas. After the slaughter, he was moved by deep remorse to study and inculcate Buddhist teachings. He said that conquest by the Dhamma "is the only true conquest."[111] He did not give up his army, however, and even warned rebellious tribes to reform or be killed.[112]

Aśoka placed fifty-foot stone pillars, inscribed with edicts, at thirty places along trade and pilgrimage routes. One edict calls for expansion by teaching the Dhamma in places such as Syria, Egypt, Macedonia, and Sri Lanka. But Aśokan edicts also want members of all religions to live everywhere in the kingdom. They argue that religious concord (*samavaya*) "alone is commendable" and that people should "both hear and honor each other's Dharma."[113] (The edicts sound very much like the *Cakkavatti-sīhanāda-sutta.*) In this way, Aśoka succeeded in making Buddhism a state religion, albeit one that would support other religions once he established Buddhist power.

Despite his ostensible respect for other religions, though, Aśoka banned the Vedic rituals of Brahmins in the capital (because they involved animal sacrifice) and ridiculed their rites of passage.[114] Brahmins obviously did not appreciate this Buddhist attack in the name of religious propaganda and reform and by what amounted to a Buddhist state religion, especially because foreign invaders, the Kuśaṇas, were converting to Buddhism.[115] A Brahmin general killed a Mauryan king in 185 BCE and thus established the brahmanically oriented Śuṅga dynasty to reverse the power of Buddhism.[116]

Although evidence for a Śuṅga massacre of Buddhists and banishment of other Buddhists comes only from a Buddhist story about the supernatural, I think that these events probably occurred. As I mentioned, strategies for maintaining peaceful relations among religious communities included the following: diffusing tension by using only coded language for critiques and projecting critiques onto the gods. In any case, the Śuṅga dynasty (185–173 BCE) reasserted the preeminent role of Brahmins as royal ritualists and advisors. Of interest here, though, is that the Śuṅgas, once they gained power, tried to diffuse religious tension by enlarging the famous Buddhist sites of Sanchi and Bharut. Avoiding state religions—with the power to intervene in religious affairs and use government offices for proselytizing—would become a cornerstone of the Indic just-war policy.

Besides the Śuṅgas, another religious conflict occurred during the rule of the seventh century CE ruler in Bengal, Śaśāṅka. We know little about him except that he was a Śaiva, vehemently anti-Buddhist, and supposedly destroyed the *bodhi* tree. Perhaps a provincial governor under the Guptas, his animosity was likely sparked because the area of Samataṭa to the east had become a major Buddhist power, which threatened his rule. He killed the Buddhist ruler Rājyavardhana, possibly fought with Harṣavardhana, and ruled until about 637.

In Tamilnadu, *caṅkam* poems have little to say about religion in general, although they sometimes do refer to the Tamil god Murukaṉ. Buddhism had played a major role just north of Tamilnadu in Andhra, especially under the Sātavāhana kings (from 230 BCE to 199 CE), and in Sri Lanka. But it did not in Tamilnadu, no doubt because the Mauryans had tried to invade Tamilnadu. Because this might have occurred under the reign of Aśoka, Tamils might have associated invasion with Buddhism and might have henceforth tried to keep Buddhists out of Tamilnadu. It is also possible that continual fighting between Tamils and Sri Lankans created a discouraging environment for monks. Be that as it may, after the third century CE, Buddhists began to arrive in Tamilnadu. Two famous Buddhist authors hailed from Kāñcī (but also had stayed in Buddhist establishments in Sri Lanka): Buddhadatta and Buddhaghoṣa. In his *Manorathapūraṇī,* Buddhaghoṣa says that Pāli Buddhism flourished in Kāñcī.[117] When Xuanzang (Yuan Chwang/Hsuan-tsang) visited South India in about 637, he said that there "were more than 100 Buddhist monasteries with about 10,000 monks all of the *Sthavira* School."[118]

Jains, too, began migrating into Tamilnadu in the third century (although some monks were established in the area of Maturai early in the *caṅkam* period) and established themselves there by the fifth. They lived mainly around Kāñcī and Tiruchirāppaḷḷi but also in the deep south, mainly Kaḻukumalai in Tirunelvēli district and some places in Maturai district. These places included rocky hills, which were appropriate for Jain caves (*paḷḷi*), where monks lived.

But all was not well in Tamilnadu from the fourth century to the fifth. Clues to this appear in the story of the Kalabhra Interregnum.[119] Some scholars, based on clues in the Vēḷvikti grant of the Pāṇṭiya kingdom, hypothesize devastation in the Pāṇṭiya and Cōḻa regions and the abrogation of Brahmin rights. For further substantiation, they refer to the Buddhist author Buddhadatta (who describes the Kalabhras as "the hub of the Cōḻa country's chariot"), to legends about a ruler named Accutavikkanta who locked up the Pāṇṭya, Cēra, and Cōḻa kings, and to later Śaiva legends.[120] The so-called Kalabhras remain unidentified, although some scholars think that they were either Buddhists from Sri Lanka or Jains.[121] Others dismiss the Kalabhra Interregnum as but a myth. But even in that case, it likely symbolizes rising tension among the three Indic religions.

In the seventh century, Vaiṣṇava and Śaiva Tamil poet-saints called the Āḻvārs and Nāyaṉmārs criticized Buddhists and Jains. They helped extend a popular temple-based religion, moreover, from the Deccan into Tamilnadu. Of great interest to them was the need to overcome a time of darkness, the *kaliyuga*, a myth that likely went back to Śuṅga times and was popularized by the Purāṇas. In the *Tēvāram*, for example, the Nāyaṉmār Campantar refers to "kings who had been seduced by the false doctrines of the heretic Jain and Buddhist monks."[122]

Mahendravarman I, a Pallava king, was probably a Jain. So was Kūṉ-Pāṇḍya (Neṭumāraṉ), a Pāṇḍya king. According to Śaiva hagiographies, the Nāyaṉmārs converted them to Śaivism.[123] The Nāyaṉmār Appar describes how he had followed the "base, ignorant Jains" before converting to Śaivism. These Tamil poet-saints reacted negatively to Jain or Buddhist newcomers, probably because of the longstanding fact that they were rivals in the religious marketplace or because they were recent newcomers (Digambaras from Karnataka or Buddhists from Andhra) who spoke only northern languages and had little interest in Tamil literature.[124] A caricature of Jains in the *Mattavilāsa-prahasana* and antagonistic rhetoric in the *bhakti* hymns were responses, no doubt, to the growing strength of Jainism in Tamilnadu.

Interreligious conflicts, especially between the fifth century and the seventh, were probably more common by this time than ever before despite the Indic just-war theory found in Tamil Buddhist, Jain, and Hindu texts. These might have been due to stress. Migration had always been a way to decrease tension between groups. But migrants were already reaching the subcontinent's geographical limits. This might have increased interreligious tension.[125] It might also have increased the desire for a state religion. Jainism had come close to that idea with the legitimation of war to protect the religion and the Jain community (*kula*). The idea of protection of the religion became a more explicit rationale for war in the Sri Lankan Buddhist chronicle, the *Mahāvaṁsa*, as we will see in the next section.

I leave the story of the Indic history of just-war theory here except to point out that while it had been relatively successful on the subcontinent and in Southeast Asia, it proved disastrous to counter the military advance in the late medieval period first of the Muslims and then of the Western colonial powers. Was this because members of the Indic religions had forgotten the idea that some wars were really unjust (*kūṭa-yuddha*) and necessitated different tactics? And was it because they had not experienced the alignment of religion *and* military power, thanks to the Indic model?

* * *

To conclude, by the medieval period, the merits of the Indic just-war theory were recognized by Buddhists and Jains and became common practice both in the subcontinent and beyond. Although part of the success of the just-war theory was related to the prevailing view of the tributary state with porous boundaries and the monitoring of interreligious and religion-state relations, the latter created only a fragile balance of powers and on occasion broke down—the cases of Śaśāṅka and some Tamil rulers (but also Aśoka in the classical period). In all of these, the problem was alignment or fear of alignment of one religion and the state in times of great stress, which then provoked a political reaction by another religion to gain the same advantage. As tensions increased, the use of state power to defend the religion was entertained by Buddhists, Jains, and possibly Hindus in Tamilnadu too, although that was not always made explicit and patronage of all religions once power had been established was used to smooth over differences.

THE SRI LANKAN FAILURE?

Given this background, what is the connection, if any, between the Indic just-war theory and what is happening today in Sri Lanka? First, we need to understand how this confrontation occurred. By the fifth century BCE, some Prakrit-speaking people had migrated from northern India to Sri Lanka (then called Tambapaṇṇi), which was inhabited by an indigenous people. Tamils too were settling on the island. Buddhism was probably introduced during the reign of Aśoka. After that, Anuradhapuram became a prominent Buddhist-dominated city-state.

The island sustained invasions from Tamilnadu during the *caṅkam* period (first century BCE to third century CE). In the fifth century, six Tamil conquerors ruled in the island for three decades. Peter Schalk thinks that they were from Tamilnadu or at least had strong connections with "the other shore," but the conflict was only a territorial one between regional powers.[126]

Nevertheless, these invasions inspired the *vaṃsa* literature, which refer to them as threats to Buddhism. The *Mahāvaṃsa* (the Great Chronicle), written in Pāli in the fifth century CE, provides some clues by which to reconstruct the early history of Sri Lanka, although much of it is myth, beginning with three visits of the Buddha himself. Of interest here is its description of the coronation of kings with parasol and holy water following the Brahmanical model (in this Buddhist context, however, the ritual was performed by the ruler and family members[127]). We are told how kings opened up the land for settlements, established town-planning, and brought the whole island under their rule. Paṇḍikabhāya, for instance, unified the entire island and in good Indic style was a patron not only of Buddhists but also Jains,

Ājivikas, and Brahmins, even though he especially supported Buddhist missionaries.[128] The chronicle mentions many wars, some of them between branches of ruling families or petty chiefs. Some chapters mention wars with Tamils (P. Damiḷa) in Sri Lanka. Duṭṭhagāmaṇi, for instance, "conquered in one day seven mighty Damiḷa kings. He of mighty power established peace and gave over the booty to his army. Duṭṭhagāmani said 'This effort of mine is not for the joy of sovereignty; it is for the establishment of the Faith of the Buddha forever.'"[129] On another occasion, he fought thirty-two Damiḷas and finally killed their leader Eḷārā and "brought the kingdom of Lanka under one parasol."[130] But then he felt great remorse. Eight enlightened saints (*arahants*) comforted him saying

> By this act of yours, there is no hindrance in the way to heaven. Ruler of men, only one and a half men were killed here. One was established in the refuges [the Buddha, the Dhamma, and the Sangha] and the other only in the five precepts. The heretical and evil others who died were like animals. You will make the Buddha's Faith shine in many ways. Therefore, Lord of men, cast away your mental confusion.[131]

This text reminds me of Aśoka, except that no one (aside from Duṭṭhagāmaṇi) has compassion for the slaughtered. It legitimates genocide, in fact, because it affirms the slaughter of non-Buddhists—that is, non-humans! Sri Lankan kings used religion to rally their people, thereby contravening the Indic pattern of avoiding state religions. Even in Tamilnadu, an effort was made to have a king of one's own religion, although that did not result in a state religion as was being attempted in Sri Lanka. But it is possible that Duṭṭhagāmaṇi felt enormous stress because the Tamils were mobilizing against him.

One Tamil ruler of the fifth century was a Buddhist—either a local Tamil Buddhist or a Tamil from the mainland who became a Buddhist to facilitate his rule of Sri Lanka. Both Buddhist and non-Buddhist Tamil invaders followed the Indic model of supporting all religions. Inscriptions mention royal gifts to the Buddhist *sangha,* for instance.[132]

From the eighth century to the tenth, more Tamils invaded Sri Lanka. This state of affairs fostered the consolidation of two rival linguistic identities: Sinhala versus Tamil. Schalk thinks that about this time the distinction between Sinhalas and Tamils as ethnics also occurred: "these aggressive Tamils were generalized to represent anti-Buddhist Tamils in general. Anti-Buddhists were always aliens. *Sīhala/siṁhala* did no longer refer to any islander, but to the defenders of Buddhism."[133]

Some tenth-century inscriptions say that Sinhala royal decrees segregated and marginalized Tamils even in villages. A Tamil could no longer hold the office of district headman. Sinhalas could no longer marry Tamils. Whether because of political mobilization to make Buddhism a state religion or real persecution or both, Sinhalas came to believe that the Tamil invaders were anti-Buddhist and therefore threats to Buddhist society. They demonized even local Tamils as anti-Buddhists. This was a major turning point, although invasions from Tamilnadu continued into the twelfth century.

The colonial period exacerbated this Sinhala sense of persecution. This led to pro-Buddhist, anti-Tamil mobilization. Sinhalas perceived Western invaders as the equivalent of Tamil invaders. They worried that Christians were converting Buddhists, taking over Buddhist schools, and making administrative jobs dependent on the use of English. Exacerbating their resentment were Tamils who learned English, gaining upward mobility through the colonial administration. The Sinhalas reacted to this epistemic rupture by linking territory, ethnicity, and language even more closely. After independence in 1948, they tried to consolidate their control over the island by colonizing Tamil-dominated districts. They made Sinhala the language of education and administration. They used quotas for Tamil speakers to counter what they considered the over-representation of Tamils in the civil service. These changes led to anti-Tamil riots in 1956, 1958, and 1977. The constitution of 1978 gave "Buddhism the foremost place." More riots followed in 1981 and 1983. The result, as we know, was a civil war.

I will not discuss the details of this escalating conflict. But I do want to point out that today both Sinhalas and Tamils lack a just-war theory. In the past, realizing that Hindu kings could threaten them, Sri Lankan Buddhists gradually rejected the Indic view of just war that Buddhists had periodically used on the mainland and in Southeast Asia. Rather, they have looked only to their own Buddhist sources for guidance on war. They have found little except the paradox of the nonviolent king and the *Mahāvaṃsa*'s call to defend the faith and dehumanize Tamils. As for Sri Lankan Tamils, they have lacked the political experience of ruling a state. They have either not known about or could not take advantage of the Indic model, which had existed in Tamilnadu, because that had been displaced with the advent of colonial rule in India. As a result, Sri Lankan Tamils have no political experience in advising leaders about justice and interreligious relations. Neither side, in short, plays by any rules for just warfare.

Distinctive variables in Sri Lanka have made its history different from that of the mainland and led to a different approach to war. First is the longstanding fact of Buddhist dominance, which began even before state formation encompassed the whole island but increased after that. Second is the fact that Sri Lanka is an island. This means that since political unification, its boundaries have been both visible and firm. Third is the fact that Sinhalas perceive the Tamil invasions as catastrophic ruptures, not merely ad hoc rotations of rule by kings of each religion. Fourth is the mythic legitimation of Buddhist exclusivity in the island's major sacred chronicle, the *Mahāvaṃsa,* and its indirect legitimation of genocide. This tradition departed, at least rhetorically, from the Indic one of tolerance and avoidance of religious wars. Fifth is the rupture caused by Western colonialism in Sri Lanka, which challenged Buddhist dominance in unprecedented ways and upset majority/minority power relations. Because Sri Lankan Tamils had not exercised political power over Buddhists for many centuries, they had no practical experience with the Indic principles of just war and resorted to their own devices. The result has been recent civil war on ethnic, linguistic, territorial, and religious grounds.[134] All these factors undermined the Indic just-war theory, which Buddhists have used in Southeast Asia and elsewhere.

Tessa Bartholomeusz tests modern Sri Lankan writings on war against just-war theory.[135] She finds that those who support war against the Tamils today argue that it is a just war (*dharma yuddhaya*). They often look to the *Cakkavatti-sīhanāda-sutta* (because it says that a king should have a strong, fourfold army!) and to the *Mahāvaṁsa* as precedent. The current war has a just cause, authorized by the ruler, and a right intention. "King Duṭṭhagāmaṇi was righteous in his killing because his pure intention was to honor the dead and save the dharma. He temporarily suspended his vow of *ahiṁsā* to accomplish this."[136] Despite the fact that the Sri Lankan Constitution today gives Buddhism the foremost place while protecting all other religions on the island and guarantees freedom of religion, many Buddhists argue that the Tamils need to be defeated in order to protect Buddhism, just as King Duṭṭhagāmaṇi did.

As S. J. Tambiah says, "The Buddhist scheme by contrast in stating that the universal cosmic law (*dhamma*) is the root and fountainhead of kingship, raised up the magnificent *cakkavatti* world ruler as the sovereign regulator and the ground of society. By virtue of this grand imperial conception the way was made hitherto unknown in India or, in face of an inability to found them for logistical reasons, at least to stake imperial claims. The rhetoric of kingship reached a high point in the Buddhist kingdoms. But the paradox is that it is within the brahmanical regime of thought that a school of *artha* emerged and attempted to investigate and systematize the foundations of political economy and statecraft and to prescribe for the achievement of their objectives. The Buddhist writers did not produce this kind of differentiated 'science' of administration. Thus the curious asymmetry forces upon us the reflection whether the grandly conceived virtue-endowed rulers may not, for lack of pragmatic rules and constraints relating to the conduct of *artha,* either turn themselves into 'absolute' monarchs practicing a degree of both liberality and tyranny unknown in India or suffer from the shifting sands of instability and disorder in their domestic and external relations."[137]

CONCLUSION

Are there lessons to be learned from the Indic view of just war and its history? I think so. First, every just-war theory is a moral argument. The Indic one offers an opportunity to analyze theory both in the making and in practice, thanks to its long history. Its development can be traced from constant tribal warfare at the dawn of history to state formation throughout the subcontinent and reflects fight/flight responses to stress, experiments with political theory, and religion-state relations. It took a lengthy struggle to develop this just-war theory, make it a civilizing virtue, and contain violence.

The fact that this theory relies on religious pluralism and cultural heterogeneity might provide insights for pluralistic societies in the West. Especially relevant is its state with porous boundaries, allowing freedom of movement and cross-cutting loyalties, which has its contemporary analogue in the European Union. This is a time of transition in the West because of migration, worldview affiliations (both religious and secular), and demographic change. Consequently, we should expect high stress and monitor developments carefully.

Learning from the Indic experience, we could prevent polarization not only between religions but also between religions and states by recognizing religious pluralism (avoiding state religions and giving equal treatment to all, or at least to the major ones) and acknowledging the ways in which religions have fostered prosperity and harmony. The Indic experience—I am thinking here of Aśoka—provides a warning that state interference in religious affairs for the sake of reform, even on justifiable grounds, can have long-term repercussions. (As a reaction, Brahmins became especially tough competitors in the religious marketplace, for instance, which contributed gradually to the disappearance of Buddhism in the land of its birth, and to the diminishment of Jainism.) If we must reform religion, we can do so more effectively by promoting public education and debate than by wielding state power.

The Indic experience shows that religions can be extremely powerful cultural forces, especially when politicized. We need to respect them but also to monitor them, because religious people sometimes try to implement totalizing worldviews. The state should work with them, in other words, not against them—but maintain a system of checks and balances. Religions can inform both the state and its citizens. In this sense, they belong to civil society. But the delicate balance that governs relations not only among religions but also between them and the state can easily collapse if the state becomes too closely aligned with one religion, one ruler, or one territory. Additional factors—ethnicity, language, and political aggression—can complicate all this and lead to major conflicts.

The Indic theory is pragmatic. As I say, it relies on the premise that everyone must understand and agree to the rules of just warfare; otherwise, this or that war is unjust and requires other measures. It is striking, therefore, that Muslim invaders during the medieval period did not meet a more effective resistance. The lesson here, then, is that the Indic policy worked effectively when both sides held similar values but not when one side held different ones. The Islamic/Indic encounter was indeed a clash of civilizations; the Islamic theory of just war favored a state religion (and only then tolerated other religions as under Akbar); the Indic one did not. More importantly, the Indic theory of just war and its general religious tolerance had made Indians forget about the possibility of *kūṭa-yuddha:* all-out war with the aim of political *and* religious dominance.

Another lesson could be the most important of all. An idealized and romanticized approach to nonviolence can actually create extreme violence. Either absolutizing nonviolence or failing to see the occasional need for violence undermines political realism. This creates an ethical vacuum that unscrupulous political and religious leaders can easily exploit. Just-war theory might be a step in the direction of pacifism, because it requires good reasons for war (thereby preventing some wars) and constrains the violence of wars that do break out. And it can do more than that. Rulers who treat all beings as members of their families and believe that their duty is to foster the welfare of everyone (*lokasaṃgraha*) might well avoid war whenever possible. There is more hope, I think, in gradually institutionalizing more and more ways of containing violence than there is in any categorical withdrawal from violence. Containing violence, in short, leads to the dharma of nonviolence. It allows progressively fewer episodes of violence, even just violence, and so is an exercise in prudential wisdom.

NOTES

1. My discussion of just war in Hinduism is taken from Katherine K. Young, "Hinduism and the Ethics of Weapons of Mass Destruction," in *Ethics and Weapons of Mass Destruction: Religious and Secular Perspectives*, ed. Sohail H. Hashmi and Steven P. Less (Cambridge: Cambridge University Press, 2004), pp. 287–88.

2. I use the word Indic here to refer to the religions that originated in the subcontinent and shared a civilizational ethos. After the coming of Islam and then colonial powers, that ethos substantially changed.

3. We know nothing about the existence or nonexistence of violence in the preceding Indus Valley civilization, because the Indus language has not been deciphered and because there is little indication of violence in the archaeological remains.

4. David Gitomer, "King Duryodhana: The Mahābhārata Discourse of Sinning and Virtue in Epic and Drama," *Journal of the American Oriental Society* 112, no. 2 (1992): 222.

5. Tamar C. Reich, "Sacrificial Violence and Textual Battles: Inner Textual Interpretation in the Sanskrit Mahābhārata," *History of Religions* 41, no. 2 (2001): 145.

6. Kauśītaki-brāhmaṇa XX.8.6.

7. Note that this is not a theory from primitive immorality to civilized morality. Rather, it seems that in the transition from small-scale societies to large-scale ones, the moral code of the former broke down, and it took some time for a new one to develop.

8. Mary Carroll Smith, "Warriors: The Originators of the Moral code in Ancient India," in *Reprinted Papers for the Section on Asia Religions—History of Religions, American Academy of Religion Annual Meeting* (Tallahassee: Florida State University, 1974), p. 60.

9. For general discussions of state formation, see Ronald Cohen, "State Origins: A Reappraisal" and "Evolution, Fission, and the Early State," in *The Early State*, ed. Henri J. M. Claessen and Peter Skalnik (The Hague: Mouton Publishers, 1978), pp. 31–75, 87–115. For discussion of kingship and state formation in India, see Carl Gustav Diehl, "Political Authority and Structural Change in Early South Indian History," *Indian Economic and Social History Review* 13, no. 2 (1976): 125–57; "The Structure and Meaning of Political Relations in a South Indian Little Kingdom," *CIS*, n.s. 13 (1979): 169–206; Nicholas B. Dirks, "Political Authority and Structural Change in Early South Indian History," *Indian Economic and Social History Review* 13, no. 2 (1976): 125–57; *The Hollow Crown: Ethnohistory of an Indian Kingdom* (Cambridge: Cambridge University Press, 1987); *Ancient Indian Kingship from the Religious Point of View* (Leiden: E.J. Brill, 1969); Kenneth R. Hall, "Peasant State and Society in Chola Times: A View from the Tiruvidaimarudur Urban Complex," *Indian Economic and Social History Review* 18 (1981): 393–410; *Trade and Statecraft in the Age of the Colas* (New Delhi: Abhinav, 1980). See also J. C. Heesterman, "The Conundrum of the King's Authority," in *Kingship and Authority in South Asia*, South Asian Publications Series, no. 3, ed. J. F. Richards (Madison: University of Wisconsin-Madison, 1978), pp. 1–27; *The Inner Conflict of Tradition: Essays in Indian Ritual, Kingship, and Society* (Chicago and London: University of Chicago, 1985). See also Hermann Kulke, "Early State Formation and Royal Legitimation in Late Ancient Orissa," in *Sidelights on the History of Orissa*, ed. Manmath Nath Das (Vidyapuri, Cuttack: Pitamber Misra, 1977), pp. 104–14; "Fragmentation and Segmentation Versus Integration? Reflections on the Concepts of Indian Feudalism and the Segmentary State in Indian History," *Studies in History* 4, no. 2 (1982): 237–63. See also Burton Stein, "The Segmentary State in South India History," in *Realm and Region in Traditional India*, ed. Richard G. Fox (New Delhi: Vikas, 1977), pp. 415–32; *Peasant State and Society in Medieval South India* (Delhi: Oxford University Press, 1980). See also Y. Subbarayalu, *Political Geography of the Chola Country* (Madras: State Department of Archaeology, Government of Tamilnadu, 1973). See also Romila Thapar, *Ancient Indian Social History: Some Interpretations* (New Delhi: Orient Longman, 1978); "State Formation in Early India," *International Social Science Journal* 32 (1980): 655–69; "The State as Empire," in *The Study of the State*, ed. Henri J. M. Claessen and Peter Skalnik (The Hague: Mouton Publishers, 1981), pp. 409–26; Kamil V. Zvelebil, "The Nature of Sacred Power in Old Tamil Texts," *Acta Orientalia* 40 (1979): 157–92; "Power and Authority in Indian Tradition" in *Tradition and Politics in South Asia*, ed. R. J. Moore (New Delhi: Vikas, 1979), pp. 60–85.

10. The word *cakravartin* first appears in *Maitrī-Upaniṣad* 1.4 in the context of kings who had renounced kingship to become ascetics, which suggests that the concept was already in existence.

11. References to terms for Theravāda Buddhism are in the Pāli language (P.). Sanskrit language (S.) terms begin in the section on King Aśoka. Later in the article, references to Tamil language appear denoted with a T.

12. *Pārājika* is "one who merits expulsion" for committing one of four actions: (1) sexual intercourse, (2) theft, (3) murder, or (4) falsely claiming spiritual attainments (T. W. Rhys Davids and William Stede, eds., *The Pali Text Society's Pali-English Dictionary* [Chipstead, Surrey: Pāli Text Society, 1921–25], p. 454; hereafter referred to as *PTS Dictionary*).

13. D.I.7, cited by Peter Harvey, *An Introduction to Buddhist Ethics* (Cambridge: Cambridge University Press, 2000), p. 254; Harvey, p. 254, citing Vin. IV.104–7.

14. Harvey, p. 254, citing S.IV.308–9.

15. These include (1) *pāṇātipātā veramaṇī*, abstinence from taking life; (2) *adinnādānā*, (from) taking what is not given to one; (3) *abrahmacariyā*, (from) adultery (otherwise *kāmesu micchācārā*); (4) *musāvādā*, (from) telling lies; and (5) *surāmerayamajjapamādaṭṭhānā veramaṇī*, abstaining from any state of indolence arising from (the use of) intoxicants (*PTS Dictionary*, p. 712–13).

16. "The early Buddhists regard the institution of war as strictly within the jurisdiction of *attha* and *āṇā* and take a somewhat neutral attitude toward it. The Buddhist works are full of injunctions against violence but these are, more often than not, related to the level of individual and inter-group relations. The horrors of war are duly recognized but no decisive or overt effort seems to be made to insist on outlawing war itself. Perhaps in this the Buddhists reconciled themselves to their inability to influence the conduct of the state beyond giving it ethical advice. They did envision an ideal state which would eschew the use of force or violence. . . . But for all practical purposes the Samgha largely withdrew itself from considerations of war" (Balkrishna Govind Gohkale, "The Early Buddhist View of the State," *Journal of the American Oriental Society*, 89, no. 4 [1969]: 734).

17. This is similar to the context of *Kauṭilīya Arthaśāstra* captured in the maxim "big fish eat little fish" (*mātsyanyāya*). See the discussion of Kauṭilya later in this article.

18. For the myth of the origin of kingship, see Steven Collins, *Nirvana and Other Buddhist Felicities: Utopias of the Pali Imaginaire*, Cambridge Studies in Religious Traditions (New York: Cambridge University Press, 1998), p. 448; Agañña-sutta of the Dīgha-nikāya summarized by Balakrishna Govind Gokhale, "The Early Buddhist View of the State," *Journal of the American Oriental Society* 89, no. 4 (1969): 733.

19. Gokhale cites Samyutta-nikāya I.116: "Nor is it known that the Buddha advised total disarmament by a state. One measure that the Buddha took in expressing his disapproval of the institution of war was to forbid the monks from witnessing army parades and reviews. In spite of these seeming compromises in practice, early Buddhist political thought insists on the principle of nonviolence and non-injury as the *ideal* basis of statecraft and hopes to minimize the violence inherent in the power of the state by ordaining that this power be, at all times, restrained by morality" (Balakrishna G. Gokhale, "Early Buddhist Kingship" *The Journal of Asian Studies*, 26, no.1 [1966]: 21).

20. Collins, p. 735.

21. Gokhale, "Early Buddhist Kingship," p. 17, citing the *Tesakuna Jataka*.

22. According to the early Buddhist texts, the king should be *khattiya*, the highest caste (SN I.69; AN, V, p. 327, cited by Gokhale, p. 17 note 21).

23. The two realms were the temporal (*diṭṭ(h)adhamma*) and the spiritual (*samparāya*), also called *attha* and *dhamma* or *āṇācakka* (wheel of command) and *dhammacakka* (wheel of the law) (Gokhale, citing SN a I.81). Gokhale argues that Buddhists contributed "the theory of two 'wheels,'" two distinct realms of action by positing two separate but equally important ideals of a *cakkavatti*, the leader of the temporal realm, and the

bodhisattva, preeminent in the spiritual domain. The theory of the two domains is well expressed by a putative statement of Ajātasattu (circa 493–462 BCE) at the commencement of the First Buddhist Council held in Rājagaha when he said to the assembled monks, "Yours is the authority of the spirit as mine is of power (*dhammacakka* and *āṇācakka*)" (Gokhale, "Early Buddhist Kingship," p. 22, citing N. K. Jayawicrama, *Vinaya Nidāna* [London: Luzac & Co., 1962], p. 8). The two wheels were to be complementary, the *saṅgha* being the conscience of the state (Gokhale says that in brahmanical political thought we have practically no such theory of separation of powers, and for obvious reasons). See also Frank Reynolds, "The Two Wheels of Dhamma: A Study of Early Buddhism," in Gananath Obeyesekere, Frank Reynolds and Bardwell L. Smith, *The Two Wheels of Dhamma* (Chambersburg, PA: American Academy of Religion, 1972), pp. 6–30; Trevor Ling, *The Buddha, Buddhist Civilization in India and Ceylon* (London: Temple Smith, 1973); S. J. Tambiah, *World Conqueror and World Renouncer: A Study of Buddhism and Polity in Thailand against a Historical Background* (Cambridge: Cambridge University Press, 1976).

24. The *cakkavatti* (universal monarch) is the *dhammiko dhammarāja* or great person (*mahāpurisa*) endowed with the thirty-two marks (*mahāpurisalakkanani*), and has special powers (*iddhis*) (Gokhale, "The Early Buddhist View of the State," p. 737, citing MN, III, pp. 65ff). Similarly, in the Mahāvāgga, Buddha says "I am a king, an incomparable, religious king (*dharmarāja*); with justice (*dhammena*) I turn the wheel, a wheel that is irresistible." (Pandurang Vaman Kane, *History of Dharmaśāstra: Ancient and Mediaeval Religious and Civil Law* [Poona: Bhandarkar Oriental Research Institute, 1973], vol. 3, p. 66). Tambiah (p. 43) traces the early Buddhist sources for the *cakkavatti* to the *Mahapadāna Suttanta* and the *Maha-Parinibbana Sutta*.

25. Collins, p. 420.

26. See the Mūgapakkha (Temīya) Jātaka, Jataka Pali No. 538; cf. Temiyachariya, Cariyapitaka iii.6; Buddhavamsa Atthakatha 51. Some popular Jātaka stories are illustrated in sculptures and inscriptions by the third century BCE. The collection of Jātaka tales is usually dated before the first century BCE; commentary on them occurs before the fifth CE (Uma Chakravartim, "Women, Men, and Beasts: The Jataka as Popular Tradition," *Studies in History* 9, no. 1 [1993]: 44).

27. Collins, p. 35.

28. Oskar von Hinüber. *A Handbook of Pāli Literature* (Berlin and New York: Walter de Gruyter [Indian Philology and South Asian Studies], 1996), pp. 19–20.

29. Collins, pp. 602–3. Some of these jewels or insignia of Buddhist kingship belong to the larger Indic tradition—wheel, conch, white umbrella, white elephant, and white horse.

30. Collins, p. 604.

31. Collins, p. 605.

32. Collins, p. 605.

33. Joseph M. Kitagawa, "The Career of Maitreya, with Special Reference to Japan," *History of Religions*, 21, no.2 (1981): 107–25.

34. Collins, p. 613.

35. Collins, pp. 66–67.

36. Gokhale, "Early Buddhist Kingship," p. 21.

37. Padmanabh S. Jaini, "Ahiṃsā and 'Just War' in Jainism" in *Ahiṃsā, Anekānta and Jainism*, ed. Tara Sethia (Delhi: Motilal Banarsidass, 2004), pp. 47–61.

38. Jaini, pp. 58–59 citing the *Bhagavatī-sūtra* (Viyāhapaṇṇatti), VII, 9 (#302ff).

39. *Chāndogya-upaniṣad* III.17.

40. Roger Boesche, *The First Great Political Realist: Kautilya and his Arthshastra* (Boulder, CO: Lexington Books, 2002), pp. 14–17.

41. Boesche, p. 82.

42. R. P. Kangle, ed., *The Kauṭilīya Arthaśāstra* (Delhi: Motilal Banarsidass, 1988), Part 3, p. 260.

43. Kangle, part 3, p. 260, citing 10.3.54–57.

44. Boesche, pp. 56–57.

45. See *Arthaśāstra* 10.3.43; Kangle, part 2, p. 441.

46. *Yoga-sūtra* 2.20–31.

47. *Mānava-dharma-śāstra* 10:63; these values must have been in existence for some time. Already, *Kauṭilīya Arthaśāstra*, that masterpiece of pragmatic military strategy, had listed nonviolence, truthfulness, purity, absence of envy, and forbearance as virtues that apply to all people (*Kauṭilīya Arthaśāstra* 1:3:13), although these did not apply to the military, which was to have absolute power over the populace. Otherwise, Kauṭilya upholds *sāmānya dharmas* such as *ahiṁsā.* He "regards them as obligatory on individuals with as much sincerity as does Aśoka [the Buddhist emperor (273–232 BCE) who renounced all violence]. The only thing is that he does not agree that the conduct of public life should be guided by rules of individual morality . . . the preservation of the state at all costs is the foremost duty of the ruler and in the interests of the state have to take precedence over all other considerations" (Kangle, part 3, pp. 281–282).

48. One of the four Hindu castes is the *ksatriya.* It formed the military core, although the *Arthaśāstra* says that *vaiśyas* and *śūdras* may form fighting units (*Kauṭilīya Arthaśāstra* 9.2.21–24).

49. Mary Carroll Smith, p. 60; Gitomer, p. 224.

50. Reich, p. 168.

51. *Rāmāyaṇa* II.101.30.

52. *Rāmāyaṇa* II.101.19; II.16.53.

53. *Rāmāyaṇa* II.18.36 and II.101.20.

54. "[T]his epic pits good (the god-king Rāma) versus evil (the demon Rāvaṇa) in a kind of *dharma-yuddha* [just war]. In this head-on struggle, there is little moral ambiguity involved, no need for discussions of subtle rules. The battle is over the fact that Rāvaṇa has abducted Sītā, Rāma's wife, which is an obvious moral wrong. It is assumed that Rāma, the embodiment of dharma, must answer such an obvious affront. . . . [But], the scale of violence in this epic is limited. The battle is mainly between Rāma and Rāvaṇa, and it is fought in the terrestrial realm, although extraordinarily powerful weapons are at times used, as in the *Mahābhārata*" (Young, "Hinduism and the Ethics of Weapons of Mass Destruction," pp. 277–307).

55. The *Gītā* is found in *Mahābhārata, Bhīṣmaparvan* 23–40.

56. Reich, p. 146.

57. Reich, p. 160.

58. Jarrod L. Whitaker, "Divine Weapons and *Tejas* in the Two Indian Epics," *Indo-Iranian Journal* 43 (2000): 89–90.

59. *Gītā* 1.46.

60. *Gītā* 2.27.

61. *Gītā* 2:19.

62. Hindu art, for instance, reveals a deep (yogic) passivity (the contemplative visage) yet expresses action, even violent action, within the world (represented in some forms by many arms with hands holding weapons).

63. M. M. Agarawal, "Arjuna's Moral Predicament," in *Moral Dilemmas in the Mahābhārata*, ed. Bimal Krishna Matilal (New Delhi: Motilal Banarsidass, 1989), pp. 136–37.

64. Megasthenes, the Greek ambassador in the fourth century BCE, testifies to the fact that war was contained so that citizens—peaceful citizens, the mentally ill, and military support staff—were not harmed (Young, "Hinduism and the Ethics of Weapons of Mass Destruction"). See also *Mahābhārata* 8.49.22; 8.66.62–63 and 7.118.7–8; 7.131.3; and the discussion in V. R. Ramachandra Dikshitar, *War in Ancient India,* 2d ed. (Delhi: Motilal Banarsidass, 1948). A problem for the Hindu theory of just war is whether the epics

themselves were models of behavior. One study of the *Mahābhārata* has analyzed it from the perspective of a war-crimes tribunal. Were there legitimate reasons for the war? Was it fought according to the rules? (M. A. Mehendale, *Reflections on the Mahābhārata War* [Shimla: Indian Institute of Advanced Study, 1995]). After careful scrutiny of all the battles, M. A. Mehendale concludes that it was not a just war, because it did not always maintain the principle of equality, especially in large battles (Mehendale, p. 23). In this context, it is important to remember that everything in the epic is more extreme than it would be in real life, because there is another level of the *Mahābhārata* narrative. This war initiates the change from the *dvāpara-yuga* to the *kali-yuga*, that is, one cosmic period of time to another (curiously, the epic presents this like the change of the *kalpas* at an even more cosmic scale when the universe is destroyed), and this occurs at the level of *daiva* or fate, not *puruṣakāra* or human effort. By contrast, there are fewer rules mentioned in the epic *Rāmāyaṇa* and no instances of unjust stratagems or a change of the *yugas* (Mehendale, p. 65). This epic is often lauded as the embodiment of *dharma*.

65. Alf Hiltebeitel, *Rethinking the Mahābhārata: A Reader's Guide to the Education of the Dharma King* (Chicago: University of Chicago Press, 2001), pp. 177–214.

66. Dikshitar, p. 61.

67. Torkel Brekke, "Between Prudence and Heroism," in *The Ethics of War in Asian Civilizations: A Comparative Perspective*, ed. Torkel Brekke (London: Routledge, 2006), pp. 113–44. Brekke sees two basic approaches in the Hindu tradition to the ethics of war, although sometimes they were mingled. One, exemplified by Kauṭilya, emphasizes the means and as such is consequentialist and pragmatic. It recognizes that the end (protection of order) justifies the means and that "acts are good or bad only in respect of their result" (p. 122, 126). The other, exemplified by the *Gītā*, embodies the heroic idea of chivalry and the duel, a common form of fighting, as a sacrifice or religious game. Out of that developed a deontological ethic that made duty (*dharma*) more important than outcome and right acts as goals in themselves apart from their results, as long as they are carried out with right intention. This led to an extensive code of ethics for fights, a *jus in bello*, which emphasized proportionality so that the means corresponded to that of the opponent. Brekke thinks, however, that this view did not get abstracted to create a more generalized ethic of war as occurred in Europe (p. 137). (I disagree, as will be apparent in my argument for an Indic view.) Finally, Brekke claims that the consequentialist tradition ignores *jus in bello*, but the deontological tradition ignores *jus ad bellum* (pp. 137–38). Whereas Brekke's ideal types furnish some insight to two major paradigms, like all ideal types they distort complexity even in the examples given. Brekke claims that divine kingship, for example, lines up with the deontological position. The example, however, is the *Mahābhārata*, which is characterized as deontological but has a contractual form of kingship. Or the deontological position ignores the causes for war but its key example, the *Mahābhārata*, is all about the breaking of a contract (Duroyodhana's refusal to return the kingdom to Yudhiṣṭira as agreed) as the very reason for war.

68. Already in the Pāli Canon, most of the insignia of Buddhist kingship belong to the larger Indic tradition (conch, white umbrella, white elephant, white horse), but in the Buddhist context, kingship is not obtained through Vedic sacrifices (particularly those involving animal sacrifice). Rather, devotion to Buddhist teachings (*dhamma*), justice, morality, purity, and piety, make the king a *dhammiko dhammarājā* (Gokhale, "Early Buddhist Kingship," pp. 19–20). Ritual coronation by monks was important in Pāli Buddhist texts (See *PTS Dictionary*, p. 274 for the *chattamaṅgala* "umbrella ceremony" of coronation). Collins lists the coronations from the *Mahāvaṃsa* (p. 269); Bernard S. Cohen and McKim Marriott, "Networks and Centres in the Integration of Indian Civilization," *Journal of Social Research* 1, no. 1 (1958): 1–8.

69. Bharatavarśa, Maturbhūmi, Puṇyabhūmi, Dharmabhūmi, Devabhūmi, Karmabhūmi, Jambudvīpa, Bharatakhaṇḍa, and Bhārata Mātā.

70. The scholiasts called this theme *aracāvakai* (eulogizing the impartiality of a chief or king, as in *Puṟanāṉūṟu* 17, 19–23, 25, 26, etc.).

71. George L. Hart, *Poets of the Tamil Anthologies: Ancient Poems of Love and War* (Princeton: Princeton University Press, 1979), p. 140, translating *Puṟanāṉūṟu* 20.

72. *Puṟanāṉūṟu* 9 in *Ettuttokai: The Eight Anthologies*, vol. 1 of *Tamil Poetry Through the Ages*, trans. S. M. Ponniah (Chennai: Institute of Asian Studies, 1997), p. 357.

73. This list of the *dasa rājadhammā* is found in the Jātaka tales (Collins, pp. 460–61, refers to Jātaka I 260, 399, II 400, V 510, Ja V 377–78, etc. Collins links this *sutta* with mode 1, but it better fits mode 2, I think, because of the inclusion of nonviolence in the list of virtues).

74. Scholars date the development of Mahāyāna sometime between the second and fifth centuries CE. According to Gokhale, "The Cakkavatti (Universal Monarch) has almost all the characteristics of a Bodhisattva like the marks of great men (*mahāpurisalakkhaṇāni*), and on death his funeral is conducted in the same fashion as that of a Buddha" (SN, Sela Sutta; MN, II, p. 134; DN, II, pp.141–42, cited by Gokhale 1966, p. 18, note 33). "As in the case of a Buddha there cannot be more than one Cakkavatti in a world-system at a time. The charisma of a dead Cakkavatti resides in his *stūpa* and a visit to the *stūpa* of a Cakkavatti is described as an act of merit which may lead a person to heaven after death (DN, II, p. 143 in Gokhale, "Early Buddhist Kingship," p. 19, n. 35; MN, III, 65ff. in Gokhale, "The Early Buddhist View of the State," p. 737, n. 38).

75. Collins, p. 420. Gokhale does not see modes 1 and 2 as a paradox but rather that mode 2 serves as an ideal for mode 1.

76. Collins, p. 24. For the origin of this trope, see Collins chapter 5.2.d and 6.5.b on Theravāda kings claiming to be Metteyya. But he also notes that the commentaries specify that the Buddha's role is much greater than that of the great king. They are by no means equal figures. Collins says that the *cakkavatti*'s Dhamma is the ten paths of Good Action. According to Nyanatiloka, in the "tenfold wholesome course of action" (*kusala-kamma-patha*) of a king, three are bodily (non-killing, non-lying, no unlawful sex); four are verbal (avoidance of lying, slandering, rude, foolish speech); and three are mental (unselfishness, good-will, right views). By contrast, a Buddha's path is the nine Transcendental Attainments" (Nyanatiloka, *Buddhist Dictionary: Manual of Buddhist Terms and Doctrines*, 4th rev. ed. [Kandy: Buddhist Publication Society, 1980], p. 146). According to Collins, "The range of a CV's [Cakkavatti's] power, even those who conquer all four islands, is limited, but a Buddha's power reaches from the highest heaven to the Avīci hell. . . . The Buddha's 'power' can refer either, as in the references just given, to the area over which his teaching extends (the same verb, *anusāsati*, and the related noun *sāsana*, are used for both a king's orders and a Buddha's teach), or to the area over which the protection verses (*paritta*) he teaches are effective: this is his Field of Command" (Collins, p. 472). Texts "also say that the Buddha has two wheels of Dhamma: his *āṇācakka*, Wheel of Command, refers to his injunctions to religious practice (using verbal imperatives); his *dhamma-cakka* is the first sermon . . . the Noble Truth concerning suffering" (Collins, pp. 473–74; Collins concludes that the wheel idea is complex and has an underlying tension [p. 474]).

77. Harvey, p. 242, citing Luk 1972: 89.

78. Harvey, p. 253, citing ASP. 206–8.

79. Harvey, p. 135 citing the *Upāya-Kauśalya Sūtra*.

80. According to Joseph M. Kitagawa, "After the reunification of northern and southern China by the Sui dynasty in 581, the first Sui emperor Wen-ti, made this revealing statement: 'With the armed might of a Cakravartin king, We spread the ideals of the ultimately enlightened one. With a hundred victories in a hundred battles, We promotes the practice of the ten Buddhist virtues. Therefore We regards the weapons of war as having become like the offerings of incense and flowers presented to Buddha, and the fields of this world as becoming forever identical with the Buddha-land' (quoted in Wright, 1959, p. 67). The

Dowager Empress Wu (r. 684–705) of the T'ang dynasty claimed equally pretentious honors by allowing herself to be styled Maitreya or Kuan-yin (Eliot 1954, p. 261)" (Joseph M. Kitagawa, "Paradigm Change in Japanese Buddhism," *Japanese Journal of Religious Studies* 11, no. 2–3 (1984): 122.

81. Harvey, p. 254.

82. Rosita Dellios, "Mandala: From Sacred Origins to Sovereign Affairs in Traditional Southeast Asia," The Centre for East-West Cultural and Economic Studies Research Paper No. 10, 2003, http://www.international-relations.com/rp/WBrp10.html. According to Collins, "In Southeast Asia in the first millennium AD polities in which Buddhism existed were on the Indic model—that is rulers supported various schools of Buddhism . . . along with Hindu deities" (Collins, p. 70). Collins then says, "In the Indic model, the use of Sanskrit as the language of trans-localism (as witnessed in the epigraphic record from central Asia to Java) implied nothing about the content of the dominant ideologies—kings would normally support Śaivites, Vaiṣṇavites, Jains, Buddhists and others, with or without one being a favored group. When there is in this part of the premodern world an isomorphism between a single language and a unitary ideology (at least in the case of forms of Indo-Arian) . . . it is Pāli and Theravāda Buddhism, in Sri Lanka from the beginning of the first millennium AD, and in the mainland Southeast Asia from the beginning of the second" (Collins, p. 72).

83. Dellios, p. 10.

84. Dellios, p. 1.

85. Dellios argues that although the *cakravartin* existed as an ideal in Southeast Asia, there were few empires aside from Angkor (which lasted six centuries) and Vietnam (which had to counter Chinese imperialism). Leaders were chosen by merit as a sign of spiritual power rather than by birth. Dellios calls this "a spiritually sourced meritocracy." Political alliance with such a ruler was viewed useful by lesser rulers. "The centre may thus be said to consist of power that is personal and devotional rather than institutional. This is not the power of conquest that is being described (though military power was viewed as a consequence), but the ability of the leader to tap into 'cosmic power,' be it as a Hindu 'devaraja' (king of gods) or a Buddhist 'dharmaraja' through virtuous behaviour. This concept had entered Southeast Asia by the seventh century CE" (Dellios, p. 10).

86. Harvey, p. 262.

87. V. R. Ramachandra, trans., *Tirukkural of Tiruvaḷḷuvar* (Madras: The Adyar Library, 1949), ch. 39.

88. *Tirukkuṟal*, ch. 55–57.

89. Kane, vol. 2, pp. 39, 965.

90. Paula Richman, *Women, Branch Stories, and Religious Rhetoric in a Tamil Buddhist Text*, Foreign and Comparative Studies/South Asian Series, 12 (Syracuse, NY: Maxwell School of Citizenship and Public Affairs, Syracuse University, 1988), pp. 114–17, 120–21. Richman points out that the umbrella is a symbol of shelter and protection, the scepter is a symbol of justice, and the discus represents the extent of the kingdom and royal jurisdiction. Justice, for the author of *Maṇimēkalai*, is preeminently the protection of the monastic community, a tradition established by Aśoka; see R. Parthasarathy, trans., *The Cilappatikāram of Ilaṅkō Aṭikaḷ: An Epic of South India* (New York: Columbia University Press, 1993). The narrative of this epic, in fact, turns on the issue of injustice. The Pāṇṭiya king wrongly condemns the hero Kovalaṉ to death, an event that makes his scepter bend (16.230–233) and his parasol, which usually gives cool shade, radiate heat (19.20–26). It also causes Kaṇṇaki, the wronged wife of Kovalaṉ, to condemn the king for this enormous injustice (after which he dies) and burn the city of Maturai.

91. *Tirukkuṟaḷ*, 734, 151.

92. *Tirukkuṟal*, 49, 485.

93. Here are the first three: "In the story of Mūlarāja they portray a Śaiva king who, while not renouncing his personal attraction to Śaivism, nonetheless is an active builder of

Jain temples as a matter of royal policy. In the story of Jayasimha Siddharāja, we see this support of temples extended to the honoring and patronizing of Jain mendicants. Further, the narrators avail themselves of Jayasimha's personal relationship with Hemacandra to put into the Jain mendicant's mouth a moral metaphysical agnosticism that could provide a theological underpinning to a political policy of impartiality. In the story of Vanarāja Cāvaḍā, the narrators move beyond a portrayal of the best the Jains might hope for in the potentially dangerous political universe of Śaiva and Brāhmaṇical kings to present a king who is ritually infused into his kingship through a distinctively Jain rite, thereby advancing a distinctive Jain ontology of kingship" (John Cort, "Who is a King?" in *Open Boundaries: Jain Communities and Cultures in Indian History*, ed. John Cort [Albany: State University of New York Press, 1998], pp. 102–3).

94. Cort, p. 103.

95. Cort, p. 102.

96. See Jaini, pp. 53–54 for a synopsis of the stories of Bāhabali and Bharata, including the one in the *Triṣaṣṭiśaḷākāpuruṣacaritra.*

97. Jaini, pp. 53–54.

98. Jaini, p. 54.

99. Paul Dundas, "The Digambara Jain Warrior," in *The Assembly of Listeners: Jains in Society*, ed. Michael Carrithers and Caroline Humphrey (Cambridge: Cambridge University Press, 1991), pp. 169–86, 178–80.

100. Ambivalence over the just-war context is apparent in Jaini's discussion. On the one hand, he does not want to acknowledge the Hindu origin of the just-war principles when he says, "The Jaina lawgivers of medieval times *accorded with* customary Hindu law in these matters" (emphasis added), as if the Jains originated the idea, and, on the other, he continues to praise the Jain dislike of dealing with war, bemoaning the fact that "the Jainas were showing great insight into the possibility of building a society that practiced minimal *hiṃsā*. It must still be said, however, that the Jainas lacked either the vision or the organization to translate this precept into a general social philosophy" (Jaini, p. 56). He holds to the moral superiority of Jainism by suggesting that "what distinguishes the Jaina conception of nonviolence from that found in other world religions is that it is truly a personal way of religious discipline. It forbids the taking of all life, however, that might be justified or excused in other religions and warns that nothing short of hell or animal rebirth awaits those who kill or who die while entertaining thoughts of violence" (Jaini, p. 60).

101. Dundas, p. 179.

102. I thank my student Thomas Pokinko for drawing this text to my attention and for many helpful discussions about just war in Jainism.

103. *Sutta Nipāta*: 883 cited in Arvind Sharma, "Truth and Tolerance: Christian, Buddhist and Hindu Perspectives," in *Truth and Tolerance*, ed. E. Furcha (Montreal: McGill, Faculty of Religious Studies, *ARC Supplement*, 1990), p. 113.

104. *Sandaka-sutta,* cited in Sharma, p. 116.

105. Brahmāsakkhidiṭho, D.I.238, cited in Sharma, p. 116.

106. *Ṛg-Veda* I.164.46.

107. Katherine K. Young, "The Classical Indian View of Tolerance with Special Reference to the Tamil Epic *Cilappatikāram*," in Furcha, pp. 83–112.

108. From the fifth century BCE on, the cultural heartland was expanding. In his *Aṣṭādhyāyī*, Pāṇiṇi speaks of Gandhara and Kashmir as well as Andhra and the kingdoms of Tamilnadu: the Cōḻa, Cēra, and Pāṇṭiya.

109. The Śuṅgas acted against foreign incursions of the Yavanas, some of whom became Buddhists; Śuṅga evidence is ambiguous: there is a story in a Buddhist text about the price on the head of a Buddhist. But the story is supernatural; Sanci and Bharut were enlarged under the Śuṅgas. For details, see Lalmani Joshi, *Studies in the Buddhist Culture of*

India (Delhi: Motilal Banarsidass, 1967), p. 416. Lalmani Joshi is pro-Buddhist and has collected a lot of evidence of the persecution of Buddhists.

110. "The new paradigm of Buddhism which emerged may be characterized as blending two levels and structures of meaning, the classical formula of the Three Jewels (Buddha, Dharma, saṁgha) and a second triple schema of the kingship, the state, and Buddhist-inspired morality. According to the new paradigm, the king is not only the political head; he is endowed with religious authority, a claim not made by any previous Buddhist monarch. In Aśoka's own words, 'Whatever the Lord Buddha has said, Reverend Sirs, is of course well said. But it is proper for me to enumerate the texts which express the true Dharma and which make it everlasting' (Nikam and McKeon 1959, p. 66). Not only did Aśoka thus assume as king the prerogative to evaluate doctrines; he also exercised his authority to require monks and nuns to observe the discipline. As Rahula points out . . . 'He was the first king to adopt Buddhism as a state religion, and to start a great spiritual conquest which was called Dharma-vijaya. . . . Like a conqueror and a ruler who would establish governments in countries politically conquered by him, so Aśoka probably thought of establishing the Śāsana in countries spiritually conquered . . . by him' (Rahula 1956, pp. 54–55)" (Kitagawa, p. 115).

111. "13th Rock Edict," in N. A. Nikam and Richard McKeon, eds. and trans., *The Edicts of Aśoka* (Chicago: University of Chicago Press, 1959), pp. 27, 30.

112. Gokhale, "The Early Buddhist View of the State," p. 734; "13th Rock Edict," Nikam and McKeon, pp. 28–29.

113. "6th Pillar Edict," "7th Rock Edict," "12th Rock Edict," in Nikam and McKeon, pp. 36, 51, 52, respectively. Kane also cites examples from inscriptions from the second century CE that attest to this tolerant attitude on the part of Buddhists, Jainas, and those sympathetic to Brahmans (Kane, vol. 5, pt. 2, pp. 1012–1014).

114. "9th Rock Edict," in Nikam and McKeon, p. 46; the myriad ceremonies compare unfavorably with the moral practices he names "ceremonies of the Dharma" (*dharma-maṅgala*)—particularly, the "diverse, trivial, and meaningless ceremonies" of women ("12th Rock Edict," Nikam and McKeon, p. 46). This style of unfavorable comparison was related to the Buddha's virulent attacks on the *brāhmaṇas* and Vedic rituals in the religion's early days.

115. See Hemchandra Raychaudhuri, *Political History of Ancient India with a Commentary by B.N. Mukherjee*, 7th rev. ed. (New Delhi: Oxford University Press, [1923] 1996), part 2, pp. 301, 304, 309, 325. Raychaudhuri notes the state reform and propaganda dimensions of Aśoka's rule but does not see them as a watershed as I do.

116. Brahmins were allowed to take nontraditional occupations in times of crisis. There is some debate over the brahmanical origins of the Śuṅgas. See also Raychaudhuri, part 2, pp. 327, 329.

117. Shu Hikosaka, *Buddhism in Tamilnadu: A New Perspective* (Madras: Institute of Asian Studies, 1989), p. 25.

118. Cited by Hikosaka, p. 37.

119. See, for example, Paul Younger, *The Home of Dancing Civaṉ: The Traditions of the Hindu Temple in Citamparam* (Oxford: Oxford University Press, 1995), pp. 127ff; Hikosaka, pp. 21–22.

120. Younger, p. 127.

121. Whatever its early history in Tamilnadu, Jainism received considerable support from the Kadamba kings—such as Kākusthavarman (430–450 CE), Mṛgeśavarman (475–490 CE), Ravivarman (497–537 CE), and Harivarman (537–547 CE)—of Banavāsi (Karnataka). In the latter part of the sixth century a number of Chāḷukya kings were patrons of Jainism (Jayasiṁha I; Pulakeśī I, and Kīrtivarman I), a tradition that continued into the seventh century. And it remained strong, albeit with varying fortunes, under the Gaṅgās, Rāṣṭrakūṭas, Chāḷukyas, and then Hoysaḷas of the Deccan in the following

centuries. Yuan Chwang declared that Jains were very numerous, the majority belonging to the Digaṁbara sect (and that Buddhism and Brahmanism were about equal). *Sthala-purāṇas* about the temples in Kāñcī indicate that Buddhism was well-established when Jainism gained ascendancy (Ramachandran, pp. 4–5). At least one Pallava king of Kāñcī, Mahendravarman I (600–630) was a Jain. Jainism flourished after the seventh century as well (perhaps because of new groups of Jain monks arriving from Karnataka and Andhra).

122. *Tēvāram* I.75.10.

123. Indira Viswanathan Peterson, "Śramaṇas against the Tamil Way: Jains as Others in Tamil Śaiva Literature" in Cort, pp. 163–86; Indira Peterson, *Poems to Śiva: The Hymns of the Tamil Saints* (Princeton: Princeton University Press, 1989), pp. 12, 296. See also Kamil V. Zvelebil, *The Smile of Murukan* (Leiden: Brill, 1973), pp. 194–97.

124. R. Champakalaksmi, "Religious Conflict in the Tamil Country: A Reappraisal of Epigraphic Evidence," *Journal of the Epigraphical Society of India* 5 (1978): 69–81.

125. Even so, Jainism remained strong in Tamilnadu between the seventh century and the thirteenth according to inscriptions, archaeological evidence, and texts such the *Cilap-patikāram* and *Cīvakacintāmaṇi*. By the thirteenth century, the Jain settlement in Kāñcī—called Tiruparuttikuṉṟam after the region's cotton industry, which had welcomed Jain merchants—was so well-established that it had its own district called Jina-Kāñcī.

126. Peter Schalk, *īḻam<sīhala? An Assessment of an Argument* (Uppsala [Sweden]: Uppsala University, 2004), p. 72.

127. Ananda W. P. Guruge, trans., *Mahanama: the Mahāvaṃsa* (Pondicherry: The M. P. Birla Foundation, 1990), p. 71.

128. Guruge, pp. 73, 79: the monk Thera Moggaliputta sent Buddhist missionaries to many places, as far away as North India.

129. Guruge, p. 158.

130. Guruge, p. 161.

131. Guruge, p. 163.

132. See Schalk, p. 72. See also David Carment, *Force and Statecraft in Medieval South India and Sri Lanka: Synthesis and Syncretism* (Ottawa: Carleton University, 2003), pp. 148–58.

133. Schalk, p. 196.

134. In this context, I should point out that the Liberation Tigers of Tamil Eelam defines itself as secular movement because it wants to unite Tamil Hindus, Christians, and Muslims. Nevertheless, it has many quasi religious rituals. See Peter Schalk, "Beyond Hindu Festivals: The Celebration of Great Heroes' Day by the Liberation Tigers of Tamil Eelam (LTTE) in Europe" in *Tempel und Tamilen in zweiter Heimat: Hindus aus Sri Lanka im deutschsprachigen und skandinavischen Raum*, ed. Martin Baumann, Brigitte Luchesi, and Annette Wilke (Würzburg: Ergon Verlag, 2003).

135. Tessa J. Bartholomeusz, *In Defense of Dharma; Just-war Ideology in Buddhist Sri Lanka* (London: Routledge Curzon, 2002).

136. Bartholomeusz, pp. 57–58.

137. Tambiah, pp. 52–53. Although Tambiah's Tamil sympathies sometimes prevent him from appreciating the enormous stress for Buddhists caused by Tamil ascendancy under colonial rule, this is an important insight.

Part II

Terror

CHAPTER 6

Religion and Terror: A Post-9/11 Analysis

Stephen Healey

In the nineteenth century, Horace Bushnell wrote that

> [M]en undertake to be spiritual, and they become ascetic; or, endeavoring to hold a liberal view of the comforts and pleasures of society, they are soon buried in the world, and slaves to its fashions; or, holding a scrupulous watch to keep out every particular sin, they become legal, and fall out of liberty; or, charmed with the noble and heavenly liberty, they run to negligence and irresponsible living; so the earnest become violent, the fervent fanatical and censorious, the gentle waver, the firm turn bigots, the liberal grow lax, the benevolent ostentatious. Poor human infirmity can hold nothing steady.[1]

Bushnell's Christian account has much to commend it. Since the terrifying acts of September 11, 2001, the relationship of religion and politics—especially purported failures and dangers of Islam—has dominated scholarly and popular discussions. From the ashes of this catastrophe, Islamophobia, an irrational fear of things Muslim, has taken on new urgency. In the last few years, scores of books have been written either denouncing or defending Islam.[2] Authors have insisted that the West and Islam are at war. In the same broad strokes, Islam has been heralded as a religion of peace. When authored by Westerners these claims are often couched in, but not sufficiently critical of, the prevalent Western view that all religions should honor the separation of church and state. When authored by non-Western Muslims, these claims generally reject church-state separation as a secular system devoid of theology, instead of viewing it as an ecclesiology.[3] Beguiled by assumptions entailed within this ecclesiology, Islam's detractors have more often misunderstood than understood the religion, and Islam's defenders have more often misrepresented than represented it. The ecclesiological-theological, and not merely secular, dimension of church-state separation has often gone unrecognized. In the post-9/11 era, renewed conversation and critical theological thinking about religion, politics, violence, and peace is mandated for everyone who wishes to see a peaceful world. In work of this sort, comparative analyses of the major religions that treat social, political, economic, and cultural contexts will be most fruitful. Since the post-9/11 era is fraught with violence, ethical concern to understand and uproot violent tendencies is also a crucial starting point.

Two recently published books—Sam Harris's *The End of Faith* and an edited volume titled *World Religions and Democracy* by Larry Diamond, Marc Plattner, and Philip Costopoulos—are especially worth considering in this respect.[4] Harris reflects ethically on the capacity of religious faith to precipitate acts of madness, and Diamond, Plattner, and Costopoulos examine the capacity of world religions to support development of large-scale social systems, especially democratic politics. On the face of it, the conclusions the authors draw are diametrically opposed. Harris argues that faith is poisonous to the prospect of civility, decency, and peace. Faith, he argues, is identical to irrationalism.[5] In his view, even religious tolerance and liberalism are dangerous, because they conceal the fanaticism lurking in all kinds of religious faith.[6] On the other hand, Diamond, Plattner, and Costopoulos argue that the world religions have multivalent resources that can be marshaled to nondemocratic and dangerous or to democratic and constructive ends.[7] Understanding conditions in which particular religions support democracy and yearn for peace, and those in which they might legitimate oppressiveness and hostility, is more complex than Harris's account acknowledges.

Key differences in the approaches of Harris and Diamond, Plattner, and Costopoulos, however, make synthesizing these works profitable. The two works together suggest important views for thinking about religion and terror in the post-9/11 age. The social-historical and empirical work of Diamond, Plattner, and Costopoulos can be used to broaden Harris's ethical-analytical treatment of religions, and the moral dimensions of Harris's analysis can be used to enrich that of Diamond, Plattner, and Costopoulos. Troubling aspects of Harris's moral analysis (Harris, for example, defends the use of torture as morally equivalent to collateral damage in war) can be addressed by democratic safeguards suggested in the other work.[8] Both Harris and Diamond, Plattner, and Costopoulos raise issues about religiously associated violence and peace, interreligious dialogue, and current politics that are worth pondering in the post-9/11 era.

THE END OF FAITH?

Harris's main contention in *The End of Faith* is that religious belief is generally malicious, and that religions insulate themselves from critical scrutiny by advancing claims that disallow rational analysis. Faith, defined by Harris as irrational assent, provides this insulation. Is there a God? God only knows! Harris denies that reason can answer this question. Instead of rational warrant, religions introduce the ministry of unfeasible certitude. Harris portrays this certitude as a cartoon he believes predominates in the minds of most believers. There is a God; this God revealed a book; he used especially good men as absolute examples; he gives reasons to kill neighbors when they harbor false notions of God (i.e., views that differ from this or that book, or this or that prophet). Harris suggests that religious faith exploits people's gullibility, overrides their basic capacity for sympathy, and leads them to believe incredible (even murderous) assertions. This is downright dangerous, he contends. Our beliefs, no matter how crazy, control our choices.[9] If a group believes that its neighbors are infidels whom God will punish in an eternal lake of fire, that group is likely to see violence toward these neighbors as justified. If a group believes its neighbors are worthy of love, it will love them. The religions, however, admix low and high views of neighbors and provide numerous examples of righteous warriors killing infidels. Human credulousness is easily provoked to a low view of the neighbor; thus, religions breed intolerance and foster violence. Harris points to history to show that this is more or less how it works. His catalog of evidence supporting this idea should give pause to believers and nonbelievers alike.

According to Harris, liberalism seeks to correct this penchant for religious violence. But it develops a view of religious belief, a meta-belief, that Harris argues leads toward the abyss of religiously motivated global-scale destruction. Liberal tolerance, on Harris's reading, insists that religiously motivated choices should always be honored.[10] This essentially leads to winking at insanity. To make this point, Harris describes bizarre belief-based practices. For example, Harris grieves,

> The rioting in Nigeria over the 2002 Miss World Pageant claimed over two hundred lives: innocent men and women were butchered with machetes or burned alive simply to keep that troubled place free of women in bikinis.[11]

But Muslims, Harris shows, are not alone in holding silly ideas.

> We should be humbled, perhaps to the point of spontaneous genuflection, by the knowledge that the ancient Greeks began to lay their Olympian myths to rest several hundred years before the birth of Christ, whereas we have the likes of Bill Moyers convening earnest gatherings of scholars for the high purpose of determining just how the book of Genesis can be reconciled with life in the modern world.[12]

Jesus wept, Harris sighs. Come now, he argues, if something is clearly erroneous, whether it is a religious creed that motivates people to harm their neighbors or one that espouses pure nonsense, it should be judged rather than tolerated. It is unethical not to judge crazy or harmful ideas, because such ideas lead people to dangerous and harmful actions. However sharply Harris makes his points, they are often leavened with humor and wit, and he is motivated by desire to see the world at peace. Without irony, he claims to have written the book "very much in the spirit of a prayer."[13] His prayer, put simply, is that people will start thinking and as a result will stop killing in the name of incredible beliefs.

Harris's criticism of religious faith is more or less ecumenical. All religions that inspire unreasonable thinking, those that make a virtue of irrational faith, come under fire. Especially prominent in his analysis, however, are Islam and Christianity. He gives special attention to the failings (witch burnings, torture ordeals for heretics, anti-Semitism, jihad, to name a few) of these two religions.[14] The evidence, though well-known, is arranged with dark humor to prosecute the case that faith itself is to blame for insane actions of Christians and Muslims. However dangerous these faith orientations are, Harris thinks they nonetheless address real human spiritual needs that science cannot satisfy.[15] The problem is not that religions address needs, but how religions conceive irrational faith as an answer to them. Instead of faith, the current moment requires ethics and spirituality that are aligned to truths about the world and self known through science. Harris presents this mixture of resources as a rational means to address spiritual needs.

Harris's analysis leads him to be *certain* that many religious believers are wrong about important matters. Against the faithful certitude of believers, Harris does not introduce hand-wringing liberal doubt or relativism. Instead, he introduces certitude of his own by combining the convictions that science tells us what reality is like, that we should not harm sentient creatures (unless dictated by very compelling ethical reasons, such as self-defense), and that we can learn about the nature of our own consciousness through spirituality and meditation. Harris is receptive to Buddhism as a source of genuinely rational spiritual insight. Indeed, the final chapter in Harris's book, entitled "Experiments in Consciousness," is the most constructive one. In this chapter, he holds that meditation helps the practitioner distinguish between thinking and consciousness. That, he says, is a key assumption of mysticism, which is rational, in contrast to irrational faith.

Though the issues Harris raises are essential, the constructive point of view he offers will not support development of institutions that will bear pressures in the post-9/11 era. To discover these, Harris's narrow view of religious faith must be complemented by socially informed study of the world religions.

WORLD RELIGIONS AND DEMOCRACY?

Whereas Harris sees the destructive potential of faith, others look to the world religions for their civilization-building potential. The essays collected in *World Religions and Democracy*, many first published from 1995 to 2004 in the *Journal of Democracy* sponsored by the International Forum for Democratic Studies of the National Endowment for Democracy, examine whether the world religions are congenial to the development of democracy. Alongside articles by academic heavyweights such as Peter Berger, Bernard Lewis, Francis Fukuyama, and other significant academics, the volume contains essays by the spiritual leader His Holiness the Dalai Lama and Burma's human rights activist Aung San Suu Kyi. Though authored by a diverse group, the articles are fairly well integrated. Those interested in the plight of democracy in our hyperreligious world will find that these articles challenge and complement the findings of Harris. Whereas Harris focuses on religious beliefs and their implications for action, the authors in *World Religions and Democracy* give more attention to religious institutions and social-historical context.

Diamond, Plattner, and Costopoulos have grouped nineteen chapters into sections on the Eastern Religions, Judaism and Christianity, and Islam. A conceptual framework for the book is set forth in the introduction by Philip Costopoulos and within the first article by Alfred Stepan. The essays are dense with sheer detail and thoughtful analysis. The discussion that follows will illuminate areas in which

Harris's criticism of faith can profitably be engaged from broader social and historical perspectives.

In *World Religions and Democracy*, the conceptual framework raises the concept of "twin tolerations," which presumes the differentiation of "religious and political authority."[16] In short, the idea of twin tolerations (one for each fallen tower?) means that religions should not have the constitutional right to set public policy for democratically elected governments, and that individuals and groups should have the unrestricted right to express their values publicly, so long as they do not "impinge on the liberties of other citizens or violate democracy and the law."[17] However, the authors reject the idea that twin tolerations can be honored only through one model of church-state relations. As such, they critically examine assumptions about this relationship.

Stepan explores how religions have actually interacted with political systems along these lines. He convincingly shows that the idealized separation of church and state so often heralded by Americans is at variance with the historical reality in Western Europe. Five members of the European Union, for example, have established churches, and those that do not nonetheless often divert significant public funds to church agencies. Germans, for example, generally elect to pay *Kirchensteuer* (Church tax), because significant social benefits (the right to be baptized, married, or buried in a church, and to be afforded access to church-based hospitals, for example) accrue primarily to those who pay it. In the EU, only Portugal prohibits political parties from using religious affiliations and symbols. Additionally, an idealized language of church-state separation inhibits understanding of Eastern Orthodoxy, Confucianism, or Islam. In sum, "From the viewpoint of empirical democratic practice . . . the concept of secularism must be radically rethought."[18]

Based upon this study of European democracies, Stepan refutes three commonly held positions. All of the essays in the volume accept these basic premises. First, religions are not reducible to single essences that can be judged, thumbs up or thumbs down. The same religion might well support diverse, even antithetical, objectives, including some that are laudatory (democracy and love, for example) and others that are horrific (antidemocracy or mindless violence, for example). Second, Stepan questions whether the social and religious conditions that prevailed at democracy's origin are necessary to export it to another society. He pointedly questions the idea (propounded by noted political scientist Samuel Huntington, and accepted by many) that societies informed by Eastern Orthodoxy, Confucianism, and Islam will remain uncongenial to democracy. Third, eliminating religion from public and political discussions is shown to be pointless, since religiously based practice is a common part of the world's most established democracies. These perspectives provide a valuable foundation to examine the implications of the world religions in the post-9/11 era.

Harris recognizes the pluralistic nature of religions, and he knows that religions have inspired great people to do great things and base people to do base things. He claims that the latter predominate by a wide margin. Whereas Diamond, Plattner, and Costopoulos work with the assumption that religions are multivalent, Harris focuses on faith and views it univocally. He holds that faith always requires suspension of reason and entails certitude about ridiculous creeds. He is aware of significant theologians (Paul Tillich, for example) who see matters with significantly greater nuance, but he does not engage their work because, in his view, the common believer gives shape to history. The common believer, Harris is convinced, is most likely a fanatic duped by unreason. Against a theological orientation, Harris's turn of mind is sociological; but his argument is a series of theological judgments. Thus, he develops an admixture of sociologically and theologically inclined perspectives. In short, Harris's *theology* is judgmental, too quickly dismissive, and thus unlikely to support the aims he has in mind.

The substantial notes to *The End of Faith* do not engage significant findings of religious studies scholarship. Too bad, because the devil, as they say, is in the details. For example, Abdou Filali-Ansary, who contributed three articles to *World Religions and Democracy,* points out that the influential work of Jamal-Eddin Al-Afghani (1838–97) has led many Arab and non-Arab Muslims to treat the word "secular" as more or less equivalent to "atheism" and "godlessness."[19] This explanation illuminates Muslim resistance to secular democracy, but Harris's analysis does not ponder the issues deeply or broadly enough to get to this level. In his view, which he shares with Samuel Huntington, the West and Islam are at war.[20] Instead of broad-based analysis, Harris relies heavily upon his analytical schema (faith is ruinous; meditative reason is emancipatory), even when the data he presents suggests otherwise. For example, in a lengthy footnote, he states,

> Attentive readers will have noticed that I have been very hard on religions of faith—Judaism, Christianity, Islam, and even Hinduism—and have not said much that is derogatory of Buddhism. This is not an accident. While Buddhism has also been a source of ignorance and occasional violence, it is not a religion of faith, or a religion at all, in the Western sense. *There are millions of Buddhists who do not seem to know this, and they can be found in temples throughout Southeast Asia, and even the West, praying to Buddha as though he were a numinous incarnation of Santa Claus.*[21]

Harris's preconceived (and essentialist) understanding of Buddhism leads him to obscure it.[22] More thorough acknowledgement of the social history of Buddhism would suggest that the simple lens used against the so-called faith-based religions and then used to praise Buddhism distorts the historical realities both of what Harris affirms and of what he denies. Harris lauds an idealized, nonexistent version of Buddhism, which is at variance with most Buddhist practice in the world. The essays by the Dalai Lama and Aung San Suu Kyi in *World Religions* provide examples of how to think about Buddhism as a living reality that is embedded in time, space, and culture. In contrast, Harris's focus on one particular definition of faith distorts the historical realities of the religions he surveys.

Harris believes that religious liberalism leads to suspension of judgment about foolish and dangerous creeds, when we should be willing, ultimately, to judge grotesque foolishness, even if it is dressed up in the pontifical vestment and florid calligraphy honored by a billion believers. Serious theology, in his view, is a mind game that ignores the predominant (and crude) dimensions of faith-based religions. This aspect of Harris's thought is not convincing, because serious theology and religious liberalism have more power to challenge foolishness than nonreligious naturalism does, even if the latter is augmented by spirituality and meditation. Harris's hope for peace is profoundly limited by the tenor and substance of his analysis. Diamond and coauthors show more ably how to engage in analysis of religious propensity to justify harmful practices while remaining open to their contributions.

Harris has noted that Western religions tend to be historically focused and action-oriented. In the histories of Judaism, Christianity, and Islam, it is undeniable that this orientation has been expressed in militant fashion. It is also true, therefore, that the basic texts of these religions contain theological justifications for war and violence.[23] Should a fanatic wish to justify his choices by citing chapter and verse, each of these traditions provides an ample store of references. Harris documents without attempting to understand these tendencies. As a result, he is curiously blind to the fact that his justification of war and torture is essentially analogous to what he condemns in Christianity and Islam. Harris gives no significant attention to wider histories and broader social possibilities entailed by these religions. Were he to do so, the question of ecclesiology would be a profitable beginning place. In this context, Peter Berger's brief article entitled "Christianity: The Global Picture" draws attention to the importance of social differentiation afforded by the Church as an institution.[24] The article by Hahm Chaibong entitled "The Ironies of Confucianism" provides a fascinating discussion of Confucian values, statecraft, and economics. In short, Hahm argues that Confucian values show strong correlation to economic development and growth, but these same values have not provided significant resistance to absolutist governments. Confucianism's main loci are family and state, and thus it lacks "a realm of awareness or action over against the realm controlled by the state."[25] Harris's proposal may eliminate the capacity to build civil society and thus undermines a source of dissent against governments and a resource to challenge fanaticism. This is not to suggest that Harris should engage in detailed analysis of Confucianism, but rather that his critical approach to the Western religions could be augmented by a richer understanding of their social potential.

None of the authors of *World Religions and Democracy* is an apologist for any religious tradition. Further, they are fully aware of the horrors catalogued by Harris. Yet the authors also rightly hold that the potential benefits of religious ideas, communities, and institutions must be weighed against their risks in a context in which religions inevitably exist. Religious communities are here to stay, and they will continue to represent promise and peril because they will guide the choices of billions of people. The best strategy is to work with urgency tempered by patience to encourage their long-term transformation. That process, almost surely, will entail religions engaging in self-criticism. Diamond, Plattner, and Costopoulos set forth examples of religious communities doing just that. Nothing Harris offers will encourage self-critique by religious groups.

Religious traditions need not speak in the idiom of liberalism, but they will need to cultivate their own deepest capacity to inspire tolerance and denounce fanaticism. In one of Harris's more heartfelt criticisms of religious faith, he points out that human beings did not require a prophet to teach them to be sympathetic to one another.[26] Harris believes that when human beings see someone suffer, they suffer along with them unless a religious tradition blunts this capacity. He believes that sympathy is rooted in human nature, which innately understands the golden rule. However true this is in intimate settings (small communities, for example), or in ad hoc settings that spontaneously partake in the intimacy of these conditions (seeing a family in the hospital worry about a sick child, for example), most societal experiences are constituted by impersonal relationships. Globalization is increasing the scope of these impersonal relationships. By their very nature, these impersonal relationships are not and cannot be founded upon sympathy; instead they need to be grounded in principle and abstraction. Prophets did not teach principle and abstraction of this sort, but they did expound religious visions that fueled later societal developments of universalistic significance.

Taken together, Harris and the authors of *World Religions and Democracy* raise questions that religious communities will need to address in the post-9/11 era. Harris's suggestion that religious fanaticism could lead to massive destruction is correct. The terror of 9/11 is a wake-up call to renew the task of theology as a public mode of inquiry. The broad-based analyses in *World Religions and Democracy* support this suggestion as well. In particular, the following recommendations for the post-9/11 era can be derived from synthesizing the works of Harris and Diamond et al. and processing implications of the post-9/11 era.

CONCLUSIONS FOR THE POST-9/11 ERA

In the post-9/11 era, religious traditions must be engaged as multivalent moral institutions capable of inspiring good and evil. To use the term "religion" as an analogue for "good" or "evil" is irresponsible. In addition to being positive resources within civilizations, religions have been sources of profound malice. Nor should there be doubt that religions continue to harbor these potentials. The pressure of teleological pursuit (the need for decisiveness and urgent action) has led members of every religion to challenge, alter, and engage in ad hoc reinterpretation of basic principles that they deem to be absolute. The appearance of doctrinal permanence is usually preserved through theological sleight of hand even as the principles are being fundamentally altered.[27] Some of these compromises have reduced religious malignancy, but others have led to its development.[28] It is an essential task to identify, then reduce or eliminate these tendencies. Harris's work contains examples of compromise that a theological-ethical analysis might well question. He supports the nonviolent tendencies of Jainism and Buddhism, yet he denies that pacifism is a viable political strategy.[29] Further, he criticizes Christians for persecuting witches (with the *strappado,* for example), but on the other hand suggests it would be justifiable under certain circumstance to use the *strappado* against a terrorist.[30] Religious ethical analysis in the post-9/11 era will require examining how religious principles interact with particular social and historical settings to justify some courses of action and discredit others. Such an examination will require making judgments for some religious points of view and against others.[31] This is not the task of one person, but a conversation for communities to inform policies of institutions. This conversation cannot rely upon Harris's judgmental idiom, since no participant will possess enough truth to justify the arrogant assertion of his or her point of view or the callous dismissal of other points of view.[32]

In the post-9/11 era, the capacity to engage in interreligious dialogue must be developed among believers of every religion. At this time, few believers are adequately equipped to engage in interreligious dialogue. Most religious communities have expended enormous energy instilling the basics of their own perspectives, but they have expended almost none teaching about other points of view.[33] Harris is correct to suggest that religious claims are not exempt from the canons of reason, argument, and debate.[34] Some positions of faith, at least the most dangerous extremes, can be shown to be unreasonable through dialogue. Conversations of this sort are important. Harris's criticism is flawed where it renders dialogue impossible, but his view that religious positions require defense is correct.[35] Interreligious dialogue and theology will not bring religiously associated violence to an end, but both are indispensable pursuits in our time. Because they will shape the choices people make, both dialogue and theology have political import. The article by the Dalai Lama in *World Religions and Democracy* demonstrates that a religious leader can benefit from fresh perspectives.[36] However, to engage in fruitful interreligious dialogue, everyday believers will need to learn how to recognize, challenge, and modify malignant tendencies in their own religions, and to engage with others in discussion about this. All religions possess resources to recognize enduring principles, accommodate change, and engage in self-correction, but too few of these resources have been made broadly available. In our time these potencies will need to be fully utilized. In short, rethinking religions in this manner will require theological analysis combined with broad awareness of the social histories of religions. Communities will do well to train specialists and to equip everyday believers in the area of interreligious dialogue.

In the post-9/11 era, renewed attention must be given to the relationship between Islam and the West. A good starting point is to view the post-9/11 era as analogous to the post-Cold War era. A dimension of the analysis ought to question this us/them rhetorical construction. In the new post-Cold War era, "Islam" often is used as a dyadic other that replaces "Communism." If aggregate concepts are used, careful historical analysis is necessary to understand the influence of these entities.[37] All religions have at times inspired terror and violence; Harris's declaration that Islam is especially bloodthirsty is unwarranted.[38] It is true that terror attacks currently waged by Muslim terrorists capture news headlines, but this should be understood in a historical perspective. Most Muslims quietly (some vocally) find terrorist acts un-Islamic, but many Muslims also share the anger that motivates them.[39] Huntington correctly identifies the need to develop a post-Cold War *conflict* paradigm, even though the paradigm he suggests is significantly flawed.[40] The collapse of Soviet Communism and the turn of China to a market-style economy have raised questions in the minds of many Muslims about political economies that have prevailed in the Islamic countries of the Middle East and North Africa, most of which have been Islamic socialisms, dictatorships, monarchies, or an unhappy mixture of these. Leaders in these regimes have emulated Machiavelli more than Muhammad to exploit the construction of faith, world, and identity particular to Islam in order to solidify political power.[41] In the post-Cold War world, the deepest assumptions that prevailed in these regimes and in the minds of their citizens are undergoing rapid change. Whether democracy will prevail in the Middle East and North Africa—the U.S. presence in Iraq is not auspicious—is unclear.[42] But current acts of Muslim terrorists ought to be viewed as the surface-level reaction to an immense ethos shift of which the actors are only dimly aware.[43] The intellectual maps of "the world" that have guided these actors are being dramatically altered, and what the world will become—to put it in other terms, whether Allah will emerge as the victor—is unclear. This ethos shift contributes to deep anxiety, which couples with the youthful demographic of the Arab world and the Islamic notion of divine sovereignty that seems thwarted by recent events, to promote conditions conducive to profound resentment and, for the fanatically inclined, terrorism.[44]

In the post-9/11 era, the role of theology originally promoted by sectarian ecclesiological practices and then later accorded to it by political liberalism must be rethought.[45] In the post-9/11 era, which is the post-Cold War era, the intellectual basis of political liberalism is also changing. The words of and actions sponsored by U.S. politicians show that anxiety about these profound changes is not limited to Muslims. Political liberalism renders politically (and as a normative ecclesiology) the sectarian Protestant account of the relationship of church and state. In this view, the epistemologies of faith on the one side and of politics on the other are viewed as completely separate matters.[46] Faith is viewed as a matter of speculation and opinion or unassailable heartfelt conviction. Harris is correct to criticize the notion that faith is merely private: as he says, "it is time that we recognized that belief is not a private matter."[47] When faith is held strictly separate from other cultural spheres, over time it becomes irrelevant and idiosyncratic. Further, when politics is viewed as a matter of self-evidence, the many normative, religious, and doctrinal dimensions of politics become opaque. To examine the separation of church and state, theological analysis will be necessary, because the separation itself entails many issues that are essentially theological in character. Theology must be renewed as a matter of public, and not simply ecclesial, reflection. This renewal will in turn mean that political science as a discipline will need to be intellectually reconceived, as the strictly secular object of political science is a fiction of political liberalism.

In the post-9/11 era, an important task of theological and comparative religious reflection, then, is to develop principles for dealing with religiously inspired terror. Terror is not simply a concern of political science. Religious communities can and should propose solutions to states that are dealing with terror. Further, they ought to denounce terrorist acts committed in their name; the practice of excommunication may seem a quaint residue of the past, but now is the time to renew it. The post-9/11 era has altered the moral landscape, and standard ethical and legal replies to moral questions are not sufficient. Harris's justification of torture lacks moral basis, but he is correct to encourage articulation of new principles and strategies. The acts of 9/11 contribute urgency to the suggestion that globalization is altering the significance and power of nation-states.[48] The acts of 9/11 were committed by individuals whose creed justifies, even sanctifies, acts of violence against perceived oppressors and idolaters.[49] Nation-states and international agencies will continue to supply police who find and bring terrorists to justice. The nature of justice remains somewhat open, however, since rogue individuals can affect the plight of millions of people. Also open is the question of strategies to employ against terrorists in various religious, political, and legal contexts. Without open, public reflection on these questions, the prevailing spirit of anxiety will foster extremist replies, even by those who mean well.

In the post-9/11 era, Max Weber's empirically based insight that religious strategies often lead to unintended results is worth recalling in the context of religion, terror, and dialogue. Efforts that aim to reduce religiously associated violence may actually increase it, similar to how Protestant attitudes of this-worldly asceticism had the unintended effect of stimulating wealth production. In the case noted by Weber, dualism was at work: the early Protestants feared the temptations of luxury, since they viewed luxuriousness as a tool of the Devil. In seeking to avoid luxury, they created conditions that favored promoting it. In considerations of religion and violence, it seems wise to formulate less dualistic accounts, understanding that a certain level of violence and conflict are inevitable. Instead of seeking to rid the world of religious violence and conflict, it is better to seek ways to manage it and minimize its destructive potentials. This notion of conflict is a key assumption of democratic theory that has distal roots in Protestant theology. Formulating institutions that recognize the inevitability of struggle is prefigured in Protestant ecclesiologies.

The post-9/11 era apparently will be highly religious, and neither secularism nor scientism is likely to replace religious communities in the near or distant future. Thus, in the post-9/11 world, the role of religious institutions and democratic safeguards for them, and against them, are invaluable societal resources. It has become commonplace to observe that religion has not dwindled in significance as predicted by the so-called secularization thesis of early twentieth-century social theorists. According to that theory, the advance of modernity would lead to the decline of religion. In a vein similar to that of the great Enlightenment *philosophe* Voltaire, whose witty dictum was that humanity would not be free until the last king was strangled with the entrails of the last priest, these theorists foresaw a day in which religionless modernity (democracy, urbanity, capitalism, and science) would prevail. In the fully modern, hyperreligious world of today, however, religions show remarkable vitality. In addition to their power to heal, religions possess shocking destructive potential. If anything, to take a phrase from philosopher Jürgen Habermas, it is the "philosophical discourse of modernity" that has declined.[50] An implication of this is that Niebuhrian realism should prevail.[51] The world's religions are aspects of the power struggle that dominates all of life, and this power struggle is an ineradicable part of historical existence. Christianity, Islam, and the other world religions provide adherents something to live for, something to die for, and, under certain conditions, something to kill for. This way of putting it raises the issue of peace and violence in religions and begs for careful analysis. In that respect, the post-9/11 era—an era that began in 1989—will require renewed attention to theology, which itself will need to be transformed. In a theological idiom, willingness to criticize and be criticized must be cultivated. Whether the future ushers in a new dark age, an age of global renaissance, or a combination of these depends upon how well religious communities and individuals accomplish these acts of self-critique and conversation.

Acknowledgment

Originally published in *International Journal on World Peace* by Stephen Healey as "Religion and Terror: A Post-9/11 Analysis," 2005, vol. 24, no. 3 (September 2005), pp. 3–22; reprinted with permission of the *International Journal of World Peace*.

NOTES

1. Cited by Harry Emerson Fosdick in *The Manhood of the Master* (New York: Association Press, 1917), p. 167. The original reference is Horace Bushnell's *The Character of Jesus* (1860).

2. For two shrill denunciations that obscure historical Islam, see R. L. Hymers and John S. Waldrip, *Demons in the Smoke of the World Trade Center: The Invasion of Evil Spirits and the Blight of Islam* (Oklahoma City: Hearthstone Publishing, 2002) and Robert Spencer, *Islam Unveiled: Disturbing Questions about the World's Fastest Growing Faith* (San Francisco: Encounter Books, 2003). For a defense of Islam, see Feisal Abdul Rauf, *What's Right with Islam: A New Vision for Muslims and the West* (San Francisco: HarperSanFrancisco, 2004). In addition, see Tariq Ramadan, *Western Muslims and the Future of Islam* (Oxford: Oxford University Press, 2005); Omid Safi, *Progressive Muslims: On Justice, Gender, and Pluralism* (Oxford: Oneworld Publications, 2003); Khaled Abou El Fadl, *The Place of Tolerance in Islam* (Boston: Beacon Press, 2002). Sam Harris, treated below (see note 5 and *passim*), holds the view that Islam is more reprobate than other religions.

3. For some of the historical reasons behind this, see the articles by Abdou Filali-Ansary in Larry Diamond, Marc Plattner, and Phillip Costopoulos, *World Religions and Democracy* (Baltimore: Johns Hopkins University Press, 2005).

4. Sam Harris, *The End of Faith: Religion, Terror, and the Future of Reason* (New York: Norton, 2004); Diamond, Plattner, and Costopoulos.

5. Harris makes many claims about this. A representative one is that "while religious people are not generally mad, their core beliefs absolutely are" (p. 72).

6. Harris, pp. 16–23, *passim.*

7. In chapter 1, which sets the framework for those that follow, Alfred Stepan criticizes the "assumption of univocality" and suggests that religions are multivocal. See "Religion, Democracy, and 'Twin Tolerations,'" in Diamond, Plattner, and Costopoulos, pp. 9–10. I use the concept of valence (multivalent) to render Stepan's concept of "vocality" (multivocal, univocal).

8. Harris, pp. 192–97.

9. "A belief is a lever that, once pulled, moves almost everything else in a person's life" (Harris, p. 12). See also, Harris, pp. 44–46 and 50–79.

10. Harris, pp. 14–15, *passim.*

11. Harris, p. 46.

12. Harris, p. 47.

13. Harris, pp. 48–49.

14. Harris, ch. 4–6.

15. Harris, p. 16.

16. Philip Costopoulos, "Introduction," in Diamond, Plattner, and Costopoulos, p. xi.

17. Stepan, p. 5.

18. Stepan, p. 9.

19. See Costopoulos, "Introduction," and Abdou Filali-Ansary, ch. 12, 15–16, in Diamond, Plattner, and Costopoulos. For the reference to enduring significance of Al-Afghani, see pp. 154–56 (in ch. 12).

20. "We are at war with Islam" (Harris, p. 109). See Harris, ch. 4.

21. Harris, p. 283, emphasis added.

22. Harris's view that "Buddhism is not a religion at all" squares with the historical and non-essentialist way of thinking about "religion" that derives from the work of comparativist Wilfred Cantwell Smith. See Wilfred Cantwell Smith, *The Meaning and End of Religion* (Minneapolis: Augsburg Fortress Publishers, 1991). However, Harris does not benefit from this theoretical perspective, because he treats meditation as the essence of Buddhism. Harris also does not apply the insight to other religions. Abdou Filali-Ansary shows the importance of this insight for interpreting Islam (see Abdou Filali-Ansary, "Muslims

and Democracy," in Diamond, Plattner, and Costopoulos, pp. 153–67; Bernard Lewis, "A Historical Overview," in Diamond, Plattner, and Costopoulos, pp. 168–79).

23. Readers who share Harris's general approval of Buddhism will benefit from reading the *Mahāvaṃsa* of Sri Lankan Buddhism, Stanley Tambiah, *Buddhism Betrayed? Religion, Politics, and Violence in Sri Lanka* (Chicago: University of Chicago Press, 1992), and Tessa J. Bartholomeusz, *In Defense of Dharma: Just-War Ideology in Buddhist Sri Lanka* (London: Routledge Curzon, 2002).

24. Peter Berger, "Christianity: The Global Picture," in Diamond, Plattner, and Costopoulos, pp. 146–50.

25. Hahm Chaibong, "The Ironies of Confucianism," in Diamond, Plattner, and Costopoulos, p. 34.

26. Harris, p. 172.

27. A classic source for this with respect to Christianity is Ernst Troeltsch, *The Social Teachings of the Christian Churches and Sects* (Louisville, KY: Westminster/John Knox, 1992 [reprint]).

28. This notion of "ethics of compromise" comes from Ernst Troeltsch, *Christian Thought: Its History and Application*, ed. Baron von Hugel (London: University of London Press, 1923).

29. Harris, pp. 199–203.

30. See Harris, p. 81, for a description of this outrageous device; Harris, p. 193.

31. This is a key task of religious ethics. Readers interested in pursuing this can start with the works of Max Stackhouse, David Hollenbach, Mark Heim, Lisa Cahill, Robert Benne, Ronald Thiemann, and James Gustafson. Readers will find in these authors a type of theological analysis (publicly inclined, fair-minded conversation, argument, and debate) that Harris believes impossible.

32. Harris focuses on extremes (burning heretics, for example). It is true that some such extremes will not be overcome through conversation and will require physical resistance. The cause of civilization in the post-9/11 era, however, is not furthered by imputing religious extremism to entire communities. See Max Stackhouse's discussion of religious-ethical judgment in *Creeds, Society, and Human Rights: A Study in Three Cultures* (Grand Rapids: Eerdmans, 1984), ch. 10, for an example of how judgments can be made in a more ecumenical tone. Also see Reinhold Niebuhr, *Human Destiny*, vol. 2 of *The Nature and Destiny of Man* (New York: Charles Scribner's Sons, 1946).

33. In the post-9/11 era, the ideas of religious communitarians and anti-apologists, such as Stanley Hauerwas and John Milbank, will increase this sort of ignorance of the other, should these ideas prevail. Hauerwas and Milbank both publish voluminously, and readers would do well to critically digest their views. But in spite of the erudition of Hauerwas and Milbank, Harris's criticism of the unintelligibility of faith applies to them. Milbank, for example, goes to great lengths to show that Christian doctrines are "baseless" and thus not open to intellectual defense or apologia. See Milbank's *Theology and Social Theory* (Oxford: Blackwell, 1990) and "On Baseless Suspicion: Christianity and the Crisis of Socialism," *New Blackfriars* 69 (Jan. 1988).

34. Harris, pp. 45–46.

35. Harris holds, for example, that the "spirit of mutual inquiry is the very antithesis of religious faith" (p. 48).

36. "Buddhism, Asian Values, and Democracy," in Diamond, Plattner, and Costopoulos, pp. 70–74.

37. Samuel Huntington's *The Clash of Civilizations and the Remaking of the World Order* (New York: Simon and Schuster, 1998) presents the valuable insight that the post–Cold War era is not a dyadic contest but a multi-civilizational one.

38. Harris believes that Jainism might be exempt from this claim. On the whole, that is correct. However, the Jain tradition differentiates between monastics and lay believers and recognizes that the latter may need to use violence in self-defense. Consult the Jaina

Shrävakächär Code. Harris also sanctions violence in such cases; chapter 4 in Harris is titled "The Problem with Islam."

39. Bernard Lewis's controversial book *What Went Wrong? The Clash between Islam and Modernity in the Middle East* (San Francisco: Harper Perennial, 2003) discusses reasons behind current Islamic anger toward the West. A very different analysis is presented by Mahmood Mamdani, *Good Muslim, Bad Muslim: America, the Cold War, and the Roots of Terror* (New York: Doubleday, 2004).

40. For a more convincing analysis, see Bruce Lincoln's *Holy Terrors: Thinking about Religion after September 11* (Chicago: University of Chicago Press, 2003).

41. Criticism of the penchant of Islamic states to adopt secular socialism goes back to Qutb, Mawdudi, and Khomeini. None of these figures were able to see the nonsecular dimensions of democracy. Reasons for that blindness are explored in Abdou Filali-Ansary, "Muslims and Democracy." Also see Lewis for a very different interpretation.

42. See chapters 12–20 in Diamond, Plattner, and Costopoulos.

43. This provision applies to all actors, not only Muslims. It is true, however, that Islam's place in the newly emerging world is especially problematic, especially given the wager the Islamic world made on the socialistic aspects of modernity, which seem to have been refuted.

44. Most Muslims live outside of the Arab world, but Muslim terrorism is largely the product of Arab Muslims or their non-Arab Muslim converts; it goes without saying that this analysis does not suggest that terrorism is caused by these factors. The issue is considerably more complex.

45. Among theologians working on this, in my view the most important are those who champion so-called public theology. (See the authors listed in note 31.)

46. This portrait of liberalism is, of course, drawn from John Locke's *Letter Concerning Toleration*. Few contemporary liberals engage in the kind of religious disputation supported by Locke. He encouraged vigorous (but nonpolitical) interreligious argument. The primary contribution of *World Religions and Democracy* is the questions it raises about this view.

47. Harris, p. 44.

48. For a thoughtful treatment of this issue, see David Held, Anthony McGrew, et al., *Global Transformations: Politics, Economics and Culture* (Stanford, CA: Stanford University Press, 1999).

49. The acts of 9/11 were not by Islam, but by certain fanatical Muslims. Harris profoundly errs when he suggests the West and Islam are at war. "The West" and "Islam" are categories, not actors. It is also important to focus on how global forces allow individuals to have dramatic results. An important treatment of this issue is Thomas Friedman's *The World Is Flat: A Brief History of the Twenty-first Century* (New York: Farrar, Straus, Giroux, 2005); this point is made by Bruce Lincoln in *Holy Terrors* (see note 40).

50. Jürgen Habermas, *The Philosophical Discourse of Modernity: Twelve Lectures* (Cambridge, MA: The MIT Press, 1990).

51. For the question of democracy, a good resource is Reinhold Niebuhr's *The Children of Light and the Child of Darkness* (New York: Charles Scribner's Sons, 1960).

CHAPTER 7

The Approach of Muslim Turks to Religious Terror

Ramazan Bicer

DEFINITION OF TERROR

Terrorism is an expression of conflict. It operates within a political construct in which one or both parties refuse to recognize the other's legitimacy. In fact, one goal of a legitimate political entity, when it is fighting a political movement seeking legitimacy, is to disallow negotiation. "Terrorism" and "terrorist" are thus significant legal constructs. Successfully labeling a group, a movement, or even a state as terrorist denies its political legitimacy. It can then be dealt with as a merely criminal organization. One doesn't negotiate with criminals; one simply brings them to justice. We know from history that the attempt to criminalize authentic political movements has often failed. Terrorist conflicts end up being just as much about negotiation as any legal war is. Many terrorist entities have been awarded political legitimacy, often after a long conflict, and often by the very parties that sought to destroy them.[1]

Terror is a kind of dissension; in Islamic terminology it is called *fitnah*. Dictionaries give various meanings for *fitnah:* temptation, misguidance, commotion, sedition, confusion, affliction, torture, and strife.[2] Among the juridical meanings, of immediate concern, are seditious speeches that attack a government's legitimacy and that deny believers the right to practice their faith.[3] Simultaneously, the correct meaning of *fitnah* here is aggression that seeks to eliminate freedom of belief.[4] Freedom of expression should not be used to justify corrupt views and influences that violate Islamic principles. Such offensive speech and conduct may be penalized, although the precedents of the Prophet's four immediate political successors suggest that punishment should be severe only if the conduct in question amounts to blatant disbelief. Although Islam forbids the use of coercion by those seeking to spread the faith, it also takes measures to protect Muslims against aggression that would deny them their own freedom.

Terrorism is a complex phenomenon. Therefore, it is not easy to describe clearly. Terrorism, which possesses a global dimension today, does not possess a single definition. There is no prevailing consensus on what terrorism includes and excludes. The meaning of terror depends on the time and place, such that a so-called terrorist act could be regarded at one place and time as a struggle for freedom, yet proclaimed a terrorist act at another.[5] Acts considered terrorist in nature in some countries may be considered only political crimes in others. Was not Gandhi hastily labeled a terrorist by the United Kingdom, and Mandela imprisoned for years? Even UNESCO has awarded some of its peace prizes to those who were once called terrorists.[6]

REASONS FOR TERRORISM

In fact, terror does not exist and survive without external support. Major factors that shed light on and nurture the phenomenon of terrorism in a given country can be broadly placed in four categories. They can be listed as follows:

- Economic reasons
- Sociocultural reasons
- Educational reasons
- Religious reasons [7]

Socioeconomic and Cultural Reasons

Emile Durkheim's dictum that "social events/phenomena can only be explained by social events/phenomena"[8] helps us to solve the problem here. Terrorism as a social phenomenon has many dimensions and aspects to it.

Social change involves every kind of change in society, and in its institutions and organizations. Social division involves the departure of society from its national culture to the maximum extent. Societies are constantly changing. If social change makes the institutions in society unable to perform their activities and causes defects in the system, then change results in division.

A major reason for social change is urbanization. Urbanization involves a rapid change of lifestyles and cultures in society as a whole, but city life is not the only source of violence. Nonetheless, uneven opportunities, unequal levels of income, and different life patterns in urban and rural areas, and likewise differences within city areas caused by insufficient urbanization planning, have fed tendencies toward violence in society in the case of Turkey.[9]

According to research on reasons behind the rise of terror in Turkey, economic conditions and matters of education appear as primary factors. Research clearly indicates that most members of what may be perceived as Turkish terror organizations come from layers of society with low income and education. A noticeable observation is that individuals, and groups of individuals, with higher education and income are infrequently participants in such organizations.[10]

Financial problems affect people not only materially but also psychologically. That is why terror organizations exploit disparities in income and social equity in a society. It is used as material for propaganda and as a tool of exploitation. Consequently, uneducated and ignorant people are easily subject to manipulation.[11]

According to research on terrorism, militant actions in terror operations are mostly performed by people of low income and education. The main item of propaganda for communism is poverty. Communist ideologists exploit the economic conditions of the people. For instance, a militant gave his personal reason for being impressed by the leftist organizations as follows: "I could not own anything I wanted in my childhood and youth because of having a very poor family. While the young people of my age were having fun in summer holidays, my family and I were obliged to go to Cukurova to work under the scorching heat in cotton fields for the summer. I had to work while studying. The condition I was in caused me to get interested in the approach to those organizations."[12]

Another member, who joined a terrorist group because of hard living conditions, and not due to ideological beliefs, proclaims: "I went to somewhere far from home because of economical difficulties. I did not have any occupation. That's why I started to work as a building constructions worker. It was impossible to make a living with the amount of money I earned."

Despite many positive consequences, rapid development in economic and social life can produce inharmonious and destabilizing effects on a group of young people in their most sensitive period of development. A lack or insufficiency of basic institutions for dealing with such problems among young people is unfortunately aggravating the situation. A system cannot work properly if economic development and growth are not supplemented by social integration.

Educational Reasons

These terrorists are people who grew up in Muslim families before our eyes. We thought they were Muslims. What kind of process have they undergone, such that they turned out to be terrorists? Aren't we all guilty? Our guilt is the guilt of a nation. It is the guilt of an inadequate educational system. A real Muslim, who understood Islam in every aspect, cannot be a terrorist. It is hard for a man to remain a Muslim if he gets involved in terror. Religion disapproves of using manslaughter to reach a goal.

Education begins within the family and continues in school, at the workplace, and so on. Political parties, civil associations, nonprofit organizations, mass media, and other social organizations are part of this educational process. If one neglects the role played by non-school educational processes, one cannot penetrate into the reasons why some join a terrorist group or participate in terrorist acts. As a matter of fact, leaders of terrorist groups in Turkey generally either never had or discontinued their higher education. They are not uneducated.[13] If the number of higher-educated people who are involved in terrorist acts is relatively high, then this is a warning that the education system should be examined. Therefore, one might argue that student movements should be taken seriously into account, in order to understand the possible relationship between them and the violence occurring in Turkish society.[14]

Education has the power to thoroughly change the thoughts and minds of individuals and society. Education gives opportunity to shape people according to a set of goals, even if all of the goals cannot be attained. Philosophers such as Herbert Spencer believe that education makes people become more reasonable, more decent, and less greedy. The psychologist Gustave Le Bone asserts that education is an act of constructing and understanding relations of reason and result and not a matter of only memorizing and being able to repeat material. It is unfortunately true that education in Turkey brings people up as civil servant individuals, bound to desks at which the students are expected to sit rather than act, create, and produce. As a result, a person henceforward rising to a leading position at a high rank in, for example, government services, will be incapable of comprehending necessary democratic aspects of social management and, further, real-life problems in his or her society.[15]

Peace in society depends on thoroughly tested and positive education being imparted to its members. Briefly, the better and the more sufficient and affirmative the education is, the more useful the educated individuals are to the society, or vice versa. The role and duty of families, schools, institutions, and media are to cultivate character, leading people to serve society. The role of a society's government is to make this education possible, at the same time supervising and controlling it. A basic feature of education today is mere parroting, making students memorize without directing them to think.

A leading member of the MLAPA (Marxist-Leninist Armed Propaganda Association), having participated in 184 operations involving 117 murders, states the following about his life: "I joined leftist groups at the age of 17, when at high school. Because the people around me were in different political groups, I felt obliged to take part in one of these. At the time, I believed that the method for correcting defects in the social structure was the revolution of proletarians, aiming directly at dominant government control as in the Marxist-Leninist doctrines." The former general secretary of a terrorist group also says the following: "We were interested in social issues, as we were youngest leaving the childhood behind. We were not satisfied with what we learned from our families or people we lived with in our environment. The communists made use of this period of our youth, manipulating our inexperience and excitements, weakening religious and national senses into annihilation through time. They tried to substitute nationalism and national morality with internationalism and proletarian morality."[16]

Clearly, relative weakness of a country's inner structure provides an opportunity for interests prone to make use of terrorism.

The problem of terrorism will be solved once economic and educational problems are solved; these are, as pointed out earlier, the main reasons behind terrorist acts in Turkey. It should be kept in mind that counterviolence is not a historically proven solution to stop terrorism, because violence always gives birth to violence. In addition, the continuation of the possibility of violence is also violence.[17]

Religious Reasons

First of all, we may mention the existence of various religious opinions, and lack of tolerance is one among them. Thus, many think that they can deliver religious judgments on the basis of God's will. However, almost all of those who use this religious message miss the main point, namely, that no one has the ability to know the exact will of God. We also cannot disregard the fact that some religious leaders lead their followers astray. Clearly, ordinary people consider these men as religious leaders; people tend to think that the views of their leaders reflect the judgment of God. Consequently, the worldly opinions of these leaders come to be taken as constituting the essence of religion. Another important reason for intolerance is fanaticism existing in the subconscious of many people. This fanaticism cannot bear to endure the existence of other opinions. Thus it produces people who stand against God and also produces people who behave harshly and violently against their fellow men.

It should be explained that Muslims couldn't possibly be terrorists. The Qur'an says, "Killing one is the same as killing all" (V:32). Ibn Abbas, a companion of the Prophet, says, "a killer of a man will stay in hell for eternity."[18] This judgment is also true for unbelievers. This means that any man in Islam is subject to the same worldly judgment as an unbeliever. That is, the killer of a human being is equivalent to an atheist and thus someone who does not accept Allah and the Prophet. Now, if this is fundamental to religion, then it should be taught through education. This is not done. After September 11, we saw that Muslims tended to indulge in convolutions. Does it always have to be the "others" who are guilty? Does it always have to be that they want us to be the bagman? Why is there no culture of self-criticism in Islam? Now, it is necessary to correct the statement that "Islam does not have a culture of self-criticism." There is self-criticism in Islam. Muslims question everything, except for the holy messages. To my knowledge, such self-criticism does not appear to exist in other religions: "If you are not right, we will do this to you." Scholars and ethnologists have discussed and debated Islamic issues so many times that these discussions fill countless volumes. Anybody may criticize another in Islam. These criticisms have been met with sensible tolerance. For example, Ghazali wrote a *tahafut* (a critique on a philosopher's incoherence of teaching). Subsequently, another scholar was free to reply to this. Had there been an Islamic state at the time, these people would have been severely punished. However, no offense was involved and the respondent did not come to grief: "There are many different thoughts."[19]

The Sources of Religious Terror

Nevertheless a most arresting and unexpected development has taken place during recent years, namely, the emergence of the theological justification of terrorism, a phenomenon that makes it possible to label terror "holy" or "sacred." Put another way it is *jihad*. Some radical religious groups use the term of *jihad* to describe a sacred and holy war.

Jihad in Arabic is both a verb and a noun. Its singular past tense verb is *jahada* or *jahadat*. The singular active participle of *jihad* is *mujahid* or *mujahida*. The verb *juhd* means exertion. Another related word is *ijtihad*, which means to struggle hard or assiduously.

Jihad is simply the process of exerting one's best in some form of struggle and resistance to realize a particular goal. In other words, *jihad* is the struggle against, or resistance to, something with the goal in mind. The meaning of the word is independent of the nature of the effort or the intended goal.

As a term, *jihad* is used by the Qur'an to indicate striving against something, as, for instance, in the following passage: "And We have enjoined on man goodness to parents, but if they *jahadaka* (do *jihad* against you) to make you associate [a god] with Me, of which you have no knowledge [being a god], do not obey them. To Me is your return [O people!], so I shall inform you of your past deeds" (XXIX:8).

Additionally, the Qur'an defines *jihad* as a system of checks and balances, as a way that Allah set up for one group of people to act as a check on another. When one person or group oversteps the limits and violates the rights of others, Muslims have the right and the duty to intervene and bring them back in line. There are several verses of the Qur'an that describe *jihad* in this manner, such as "And did not Allah check one set of people by means of another, the earth would indeed be full of mischief; but Allah is full of Bounty to all the worlds" (II:251).

The term *jihad* has acquired a number of meanings, which include the effort to lead a good life, to make society more moral and just, and to spread Islam through preaching, teaching, or armed struggle. Such a definition has virtually no validity in Islam and is derived almost entirely from the apologetic works of nineteenth- and twentieth-century Muslim modernists. To maintain that *jihad* means "the effort to lead a good life" is bathetic and laughable. In all the literature concerning *jihad*—whether militant or internal *jihad*—the fundamental idea is to disconnect oneself from the world, to die to the world, whether bodily (as in battle) or spiritually (as in internal *jihad*). The semantic priorities of *jihad* in Islam are here exactly reversed from the point of view of historical and religious realities: the armed struggle—aggressive conquest—came first, and then additional meanings became attached to the term.[20]

Historically speaking, *Kharijites,* a well-known Islamic sect, gave primary importance to this idea when they spread pernicious views and doctrines against Islam. They were not exercising legitimate freedom of expression in pursuit of either truth or knowledge, but were bent on destruction and abuse. Their activities threatened to disintegrate their community. The *Kharijites* acted in concert and had enough power to jeopardize the security of the nascent Islamic state.

Thus ancient authority on *jihad* has modern force. For example, the thirteenth-century Mamluk scholar Ibn Taymiyyah reached out through the centuries to mold today's radical Islamist thinking about *jihad.* Hillenbrand explains why Ibn Taymiyyah's ideas have been embraced enthusiastically by modern Islamic reform movements: To him *jihad,* both spiritually and physically, is a force within Islam that can create a society dedicated to God's service. But although stressing the prototypical religious importance of the Prophet's career for those who wish to wage *jihad,* Ibn Taymiyyah is sufficiently a man of his own age to draw parallels between Mohammed's time and contemporary events. Ibn Taymiyyah sees the Muslim world assailed by external enemies of all kinds and the only solution is to fight *jihad* so that "the whole of religion may belong to God."[21] There are several important insights here. First, the mid-thirteenth century was a time of danger and crisis for Islam. The danger was not simply from external enemies—in the *Dar al'Harb*—but from enemies within—in the *Dar al'Islam* itself.[22] Second, *jihad* is the path to renewal in Islam, but that renewal requires both armed struggle and spiritual struggle. Third, no one is exempt from the struggle, when Islam is threatened at its very heart. Finally, this collective *jihad* is in itself a form of celebration, creating a current of collective piety that in effect moves history forward.

A detailed exposition of *jihad* is given by the Ottoman Hanafite legist Ebu's Su'ud (d. 1574). His views reveal the conservative nature of the Islamic legal tradition and how little the theory of *jihad* changed over the centuries. Indeed, there is very little difference in content and structure between Islamic law books composed in the tenth century and those composed in the nineteenth. According to Ebu's Su'ud, *jihad* is not incumbent on every individual, but on the Muslim community as a whole.[23] Fighting should be continual and should last until the end of time. It follows, therefore, that peace with the infidel is impossible, although a Muslim ruler or commander may make a temporary truce, if it is to the benefit of the Muslim community to do so. Such a truce is not, however, legally binding. Hillenbrand is saying many things here. First, the implication is that Islamic law, especially in terms of *jihad,* has not really evolved over the centuries. Second, centrality is accorded to perpetual struggle: it is a condition of the religious life. Third, its existential rules for living—the heart of Islam's ethos—do not apply to relations with the infidel. This is not the radical ideology of Islamists. Such is the very nature of Islam.[24]

Many of the books and ideas of the classical period involve *jihad* and importance of *jihad*. All of the books are especially interested in their times. The authors mean to take care of their people, and consequently these books define the term *jihad* strategically in accordance with their times, their adversaries, and associates. So *jihad* is, more often than not, defined politically.

It is clear that, at the same time, the definition and understanding of classical Muslim scholars do not transcend their historical contexts and events.

It is clear that, according to the views regarding *jihad* found in classical books, the normal state of affairs, and peaceful relations between the Islamic and non-Islamic states, are contingent on the acceptance of Islam by the non-Islamic states, and on their payment of annual tributes to the Islamic state.

Contemporary Understanding of Jihad

Radical movements striving for the purification of Islam and the establishment of a purely Islamic society have proclaimed *jihad* against their opponents, both Muslim and non-Muslim, throughout the history of Islam, although this is a particularly marked feature of the eighteenth and nineteenth centuries. In order to justify the struggle against their Muslim adversaries, they brand them as unbelievers for their neglect in enforcing the strict rules of Islam.

In the case of some intellectuals, the colonial experience affected their outlook on *jihad*. Some would argue, in view of the military superiority of the colonizer, that *jihad* was not obligatory anymore, on the strength of Qur'an (II:195). Others, however, elaborated new interpretations of the doctrine of *jihad.*[25]

Contemporary *jihad* theory begins from the time when overt military resistance to Western incursions ceased and the need arose to radically redefine the meaning of *jihad*, either for apologetic reasons or because the definition was no longer relevant to new circumstances. By the early twentieth century, most of the Muslims world was ruled over by Europeans, who imposed their laws and norms upon Muslim societies. In some cases the Europeans ruled directly (as in India and Algeria); in others they ruled through proxies (as in Morocco, Tunisia, and Iran) or through local elites that were clearly subservient to their dictates.[26]

Historical reasons required a redefinition of *jihad*. Most Muslim scholars now exhibit new thinking about *jihad*. Besides these powerful writings themselves, a major factor in the success of the movement may be attributed to the very method Said Nursi (1878–1960) chose, which may be summarized in two phrases: "manevi *jihad*" (that is, "*jihad* of the word" or "non-physical *jihad*") and "positive action." Nursi considered the true enemies in this age of science, reason, and civilization to be materialism and atheism, and their source, materialist philosophy.

He combatted and "utterly defeated" these with the reasoned proofs offered in *Risale-i Nur*. He also strengthened the belief of Muslims and raised it to a new level of sophistication. *Risale-i Nur* thus served as a most effective barrier against the corruption of society initiated by these enemies. Nursi insisted that his students avoid any use of force and disruptive action in order to be able to pursue this *jihad* of the word. Through positive action, and the maintenance of public order and security, the damage caused by the forces of unbelief could be repaired by the healing truths of the Qur'an. And this is the way they have followed.[27]

Moreover, in Nursi's view, the essential enemy of the Muslims in this age was not the outside enemy but the enemy within, in the form of ignorance, poverty, and conflict—the antithesis of Islam. These pitiless enemies and their consequences had brought about the Islamic world's decline, and prevented Muslims from performing the duty of upholding the Word of God.[28]

As far as the *jihad* against poverty is concerned, he first defined poverty as the material and technical backwardness of Muslim communities. He also included need, hunger, and want in his examination of poverty. Nursi always stressed hard work and thrift. The third enemy was conflict. Nursi asked Muslims to cooperate with all other religious groups to avoid conflict. He identified ignorance as one of the key sources of conflict and suggests education and constant exchange with all groups as a way of overcoming suspicion in society.

Nursi regarded such words as *dissension*, *disorder*, and *enmity* as synonyms of conflict and offered a general solution by translating religious ideas into everyday life practices to build a more just society. According to Nursi, it was ignorance that brought about the decline of the Muslim world. He called upon all Muslims to withdraw from the darkness of ignorance, poverty, and conflict through self-contemplation. *Jihad*, for Nursi, means to kill the inner enemy and to do good work to please God.[29]

Another contemporary Islamic scholar, Mawdudi, advised Muslims "not to establish secret organizations in order to spread Islam, and not to appeal for the use of force or violence in order to change the conditions. Such methods are detrimental to both religion and society. Call people to Islam openly. Be broad-minded and try to change the hearts and minds of people. Make people approve of you by your morality and virtue."[30]

According to those who share the thinking of Bruno Etienne, the term *jihad*, heavily referred to in Western media, is reduced to a single meaning. However, the term *Guerre Sainte* has other meanings in theological and hermeneutic senses; for example:

1. The war made to spread Islam.
2. The war waged against Muslims who deviated from Islam later on, as atheists or *mushriks* (idol worshippers).
3. Defensive wars.[31]

According to Etienne, *jihad* in general means to struggle to attain religious and moral excellence. In addition, lately Muslim scholars have warned people not to engage in activities that may be defined as "terrorist."[32]

Some radical Islamist approaches, like those of Al Qaeda and Taliban ideology, might seem archaic or even unacceptable to most Muslims. Ibn Taymiyyah here has done a disservice to today's Islamist cause. Again, as Hillenbrand explains: his implacable diatribes against all kinds of innovations in Islam—against mystical practices, philosophy, theology, and veneration of tombs—are all motivated by his desire that the true religion should not resemble in any way the practices of non-Muslims.[33] Ibn Taymiyyah's interpretation of *jihad* in effect has created a historical precedent for approaching non-Muslim innovation solely in terms of its potential theological impact on Islam. Thus, some radical Islamists today judge Western technology on theological grounds as potentially corrupting, as exemplified by the Taliban's rejection of TV. Mohammed and original Islam, in contrast, welcomed innovations of all kinds, whole-heartedly adopting such as were useful.

MUSLIM TURKS AND RELIGIOUS TERROR

There is today a prevailing view that the world is witnessing a resurgence of Islam. It is therefore important to determine whether this view is justified or well-founded. In order to do so, an understanding of what Islamic resurgence means is needed. Is it a revival of Islamic teachings, or is it a radical religious movement that aims at making Islam the basis of temporal power through the establishment of a theocracy? Or is it both at the same time?[34] If this is a reasonable and plausible characterization of the causes and motives of Islamic resurgence today, then it suggests that the problem it reflects is not so much one that concerns the rest of the world, but Islamic society itself. Nor is it a new problem.

Before going in detail, it is better to give some historical information about the role of religious people in Turkish society. The Ottoman religious elite could offer no effective response either to European intervention or to the determination of the state elite to create a secular national state. The religious elite in effect consisted of subordinate functionaries of the state, committed to the authority of a regime, which for centuries had been a warrior state, and protector of Muslim peoples. Throughout the nineteenth century, Ottoman sultans continued to stress their credentials as caliphs and defenders of Islam. With their base of power crushed by the liquidation of the Janissaries in 1826, and ambivalent about reform because of their desire to see a revitalization of Muslim life, the *ulama* were unable to resist the program of the state intelligentsia. Whatever the opinion of the *ulama*, and whatever the shock to the feelings of masses of Turkish Muslims, the voice of the Westernized political establishment was the only one heard at the foundation of the Turkish modernization.

Thus, from its inception, the Turkish republic was aggressively committed to a cultural revolution and to state-sponsored economic development. The heritage of strong state control as well as nineteenth-century circumstances induced the country's political elite to implement Western-type reforms and to subordinate the religious establishment, allowing the state elite to pursue policies of economic and cultural development. These processes seem to have broken inherited institutional patterns and created a more differentiated and pluralistic society.[35]

Another consideration in assessing the credibility and prospects of the current movements of militant Islam is the effectiveness of Islam as a political ideology. In the recent past (since the nineteenth century), Islam as a political ideology was tried briefly as a defense against the onslaught of the West and was quickly abandoned in favor of borrowed secular ideals of nationalism, progress, and modernity.[36]

Religion is a fact of life. Thus, even when the first human being came into being, he always felt the need to worship a superior power. The fact is that religions change according to people's cultures, traditions, and understandings. In this manner, in such a state as ours, in which Islam is the common belief, there are bound to be some misinterpretations and misunderstandings about religion. However, when we search the roots of radical ideas, we may find the Middle East countries to be their source.

Radical thoughts are easily adopted by the people of underdeveloped countries, who are economically weak. The people of such countries could easily rebel against the existing administration, as they have lost their confidence in the government institutions, but they find themselves demoralized because of political and economic pressures.

Although radical Islamic thoughts are opposed to the Turkish culture, they have been adopted by some marginal Turkish groups through Iran's influence. Geographical closeness could be considered the reason for the diffusion of Iran-originated religious thoughts in Turkey. Islamic policies became a topic of discussion for the first time after the revolution in Iran, and unfortunately Iran became a role model for reactionary Muslims in many countries.

However, Iranian Shiite Islam and Turkish Sunnite Islam differ in many ways. Essentially, Islamic scholars are convinced that Turkey is a country in which Islam is lived freely. On the other hand, Iran always sees Shiism as its most important government institution. Thus, Muslims in Iran are in many ways stricter in following their religion than Muslims in Turkey are. Generally speaking, Islam is not a religion of wars and bloodshed, but a religion of tolerance, eternal love, and peace. The translations of the works that identify Islam with revolution, blood, and wars have affected some groups in Turkey. The Qur'an says, "The one who killed another is as guilty as if he killed all, the one who saved another's life is as precious as he gave life to all" (V:32).

The vast majority of the Turkish people are opposed to terrorism. According to research carried out in Turkey, the Turkish people are against terrorism and violence.[37] It is known that most Turkish people are Muslim. In any case, according to Islamic thought, "nobody can be killed unjustly" (V:32).

For this reason Muslims, Christians, and Jewish people have been all living together in the same region without conflict. In other words, in Turkey they have lived together peacefully for ages in the same neighborhoods and still do so. As a matter of fact mosques, churches, and synagogues have existed side by side through centuries in Istanbul and in other Anatolian cities. The people in Turkey have lived in this way through history, although they believe in different religions. No one is accused or denounced for his or her belief.

The fact is that terrorism has no religion; it means that all terrorists are criminals, regardless of who they are, or what cause they claim to serve.

For this reason, all moderate Muslims in Turkey condemned the terrorist attacks in November 2003 on the British embassy, HSBC, and on synagogues in Istanbul. Among the people who died in these unfortunate events were Muslims; actually, a greater portion of the lives lost were Muslim, which further shows to the world and the Turkish public that the terrorists, who carried out these attacks, were not trying to serve the cause of Islam or the Muslims.

Consequently, the shopkeepers and businessmen in the districts of Istanbul, who were attacked by terrorists, reopened their shops and offices the next day, as a reaction to the terrorist attack. By doing so, they declared and proved that they are not afraid of terrorists and that they are actively opposing terrorism.

Turkey and Turkish people suffered a lot for a very long time from terrorism, especially in the eastern part of Turkey. More than thirty thousand people and military personnel have been killed by terrorists. This is one of the reasons why the Turkish public is so sensitive toward the subject of terrorism. Turkish people, who have experienced terrorism in this bitter way, condemn and reject terrorism of all sorts, including the fatal attacks on the synagogues, the British embassy, and HSBC headquarters.

Generally, Muslims, and in particular religious people from Turkey, have been associated with various terrorist attacks and organizations in the world media, and as a result of this, Western societies misunderstand Muslim people and sometimes incorrectly identify Muslims with terrorists. These misunderstandings and incorrect views about Muslims in the Western public arise because of the way in which the media represents Muslims to the world. The media is reluctant to investigate the issues and the events, and their reluctance to pursue the truth of news stories results in incorrect, if not fictitious, news coverage and reports. This creates grave misunderstandings and misrepresentations, which further create prejudices about Muslim people in the West, as a result of which various discriminative behavior patterns emerge in Western societies with regard to Muslims.

It is a fact that some terrorists present themselves as Muslims, but what they have done is incompatible with the principles of Islam. Islam, just like other major religions of the world, has many different branches and sects. Some heretical branches or sects might preach terrorism to their followers, but orthodox Islam opposes "the killing of a person unjustly," and hence opposes terrorism. Terrorists who present themselves as Muslims live isolated from everybody; their thoughts and mentality do not coincide with reality. At the same time, according to those terrorists, "dissimulation" (*taqiya*) is the most important belief.[38] Radical thoughts like these may be found in any religion or movement. Although this is definitely incorrect according to Islam, people with such radical tendencies might be found among the followers of any religion.

We should think very deeply about the Muslim terrorists. Is religious anxiety its source? Terrorism as a phenomenon is a complex entity. Like other forms of violence, there is no single reason why people engage in acts of terrorism, and no simple solution to the problems this poses. But if we wish to move beyond vengeance and seek a solution, we must try to understand and effectively address the conditions that give rise to terrorism and help it grow. In our search for a solution, there is no doubt that economic and political development play a critical role. They do not constitute the whole answer, but they are an important part of it.[39]

Finally, one of the leading Muslim organizations, along with several other Muslim outfits owing allegiance to different sects and ideologies in India, issued a "fatwa" against terrorism at the Anti-Terrorism Global Peace Conference. But Islam is a religion of peace and security. In its eyes, rioting, breach of peace, bloodshed, killing of innocent persons, and plundering are the most inhuman crimes irrespective of where they are practiced. At this event, delegates from various Islamic sects, numbering around 10,000, were administered an Islamic pledge to stay away from terror.[40]

We can be sure that the Turkish people are opposed to terrorism like the fatwa. It would be unjust to claim that any existing terrorist group originated in Turkey.

NOTES

1. *The Oxford English Dictionary*, 2nd ed., s.v. "terrorism"; Michael E. Vlahos, *Terror's Mask: Insurgency within Islam* (Laurel, MD: Johns Hopkins University Applied Physics Laboratory 2002), p. 2.

2. *Macma al-luga al-arabiya: Mustalahat al-ilmiya wal-fanniya* (Kahire: Mecmaü'l-Lugati'l-Arabi, 1967), s.v. "fitnah."

3. Thomas P. Hughes, *A Dictionary of Islam* (London: W. H. Allen & Co., 1895), p. 129, s.v. "fitan."

4. M. H. Kamali, "Freedom of Expression in Islam: An Analysis of *Fitnah*," *American Journal of Islamic Social Sciences* 10, no. 2 (1993): 178–201.

5. Y. Tacar Pulat, *Teror ve Demokrasi* (Ankara: Bilgi Yayinevi, 1999), p. 30.

6. Hannah Arendt, *On Violence* (New York: Harcourt Brace & Co., 1970), pp. 46–56; Antony Arblaster, "Terrorism: Myths, Meaning and Morals," *Political Studies* 25, no. 3 (1977): 414–21.

7. M. S. Denker, *Uluslararası Teror ve Turkiye* (Istanbul: Boğaziçi Yayınları, 1997), pp. 9–15.

8. Emile Durkheim, *The Elementary Forms of Religious Life*, ed. Mark S. Cladis (Oxford: Oxford University Press, 2001), p. 308.

9. Orhan Turkdogan, *Sosyal Siddet ve Tirkiye Gerçegi* (Ankara: Mayas Yayinlari, 1985), p. 122; Necati Alkan, *Genclik ve Terorizm* (Ankara: TEMUH Dairesi Baskanligi, 2002), p. 46.

10. Cihat Ozunder, "Terorun Sosyo-Kulturel Yonleri", Dogu Anadolu Guvenlik ve Huzur Sempozyumu, Elazig 1998, p. 292; Abdülkadir Aygan, "Bir Itirafcinin Kaleminden PKK ve Terorun Sosyal Temelleri", Cilginliktan Sagduyuya, Itirafcilar Anlatiyor, Ankara 1987, pp. 101–2.

11. Aydin Yalcin, *Demokrasi, Sosyalizm ve Genclik* (İstanbul: Ak Yayinlari, 1969), pp. 238–42; Denker, pp. 10–12.

12. www.teror.gen.tr (May 23, 2006).

13. Alkan, pp. 50–51.

14. Pulat, p. 49; Olivier Mongin, "Les Engrenages de la Terreur: Une Renonciation Politique," *Esprit*, 1994–1995, p. 48; Lawrence Hamilton, "Ecology of Terrorism: A Historical and Statistical Study" (Ph.D. diss., University of Colorado, 1978), pp. 91–92.

15. Yalcin, pp. 246–48.

16. www.teror.gen.tr (May 12, 2006).

17. Leslie Macfarlane, *Violence and the State* (London: Thomas Nelson & Sons Ltd., 1974) p. 46.

18. Nasai, "Qasāma," 48; "Tahrim," 2; Ibn Maca, "Diyat," 2; Ahmad b. Hanbal, al-Musnad, I, 222.

19. Nuriye Akman, "A Real Muslim Cannot Be a Terrorist," http://www.fgulen.org/index.php?id=1727&option=content&task=view (June 11, 2008).

20. David Cook, *Understanding Jihad*, (University of California Press. 2005), p. 42

21. Carole Hillenbrand, *The Crusades: Islamic Perspectives* (New York: Routledge, 2000), p. 243.

22. See Halil Inalcik, "The Question of the Emergence of the Ottoman State," *International Journal of Turkish Studies* 2 (1980): 71–79.

23. See Bernard Lewis, "The Significance of Heresy in Islam," in *Islam in History* (Chicago: Open Court, 2001), pp. 293, 351, 361.

24. Hillenbrand, p. 99.

25. Rudolph Peters, *Jihad in Classical and Modern Islam*, (Princeton: Markus Wiener Publication, 1996), p. 324.

26. Cook, p. 93.

27. Sukran Vahide, "Jihad in the Modern Age: Bediuzzaman Said Nursi's Interpretation of Jihad," http://www.nur.org/en/nurcenter/nurlibrary/Bediuzzaman_Said_ Nursi_s_ Interpretation_of_Jihad_168 (April 12, 2008).

28. Said Nursi, *Hutbe-i Samiye*, (Istanbul: Sinan Matbaasi, 1960), p. 86.

29. M. Hakan Yavuz, "The Sufi Conception of Jihad: The Case of Said Nursi," at International Conference on "Jihad, War and Peace in the Islamic Authoritative Texts," Georgetown University, November 2–4, 2002, http://forum.talktopics.com/2983/sufi-conception-jihad-case-said-nursi (May 16, 2008).

30. Cevdet Said, *İslami Mücadelede Siddet Sorunu*, trans. H. I. Kaçar (Istanbul: Pinar Yayinlari, 1995), p. 98.

31. Bruno Etienne, *L'Islamisme Radical* (Paris: Hachette, 1987), pp. 21–22.

32. Etienne, p. 177.

33. Hillenbrand, p. 243.

34. M. Sami Denker, Uluslararası Terör ve Türkiye (İstanbul, 1997), pp. 5–7; P. J. Vatikiotis, "Islamic Resurgence: A Critical View," in *Islam and Power*, ed. A. Cudsi, H. Dessuki, and E. Ali (London: Croom Helm, 1981), p. 169.

35. Ira Marvin Lapius, *Contemporary Islamic Movements in Historical Perspective* (Berkeley: University of California, 1983), p. 54.

36. Vatikiotis, p. 170.

37. Ozer Ozankaya, "Türkiye'de Terorun Etkenleri ve Cozum Yollari," SBF Dergisi, XXXIV/I–IV (1979): 51–61; Denker, p. 5; Mustafa Gunduz, *Basin ve Teror* (Izmir: Saray Medikal Yayıncılık, 1996), pp. 54–57; Suat Ilham, *Teror: Neden Turkiye* (Ankara: Nu-Do Yayın Dağıtım, 1998); Doğu Ergil, *Turkiye'de Teror ve Siddet* (Ankara: Turhan Kitabevi, 1980), pp. 26–48; Pulat, pp. 47–48.

38. Mehmet Dalkilic, "Critiques of Dissimulation in Islamic Sects," *Review of the Faculty of Divinity of Istanbul University*, 5 (2003): 113–39.

39. J. Lloyd Dumas, "Is Development an Effective Way to Fight Terrorism," in *War after September 11*, ed. Verna V. Gehring (Lanham, MD: Rowman & Littlefield Publishing, 2003), pp. 74–75.

40. http://www.twocircles.net/2008jun01/indias_islamic_scholars_issue_fatwa_against_terrorism.html (02/07/2008).

CHAPTER 8

Is It Relevant to Talk about Democracy in Lebanon in the Aftermath of the Summer 2006 Conflicts?

Pamela Chrabieh

I was in Lebanon during the summer 2006 conflicts and came back to Montreal to attend the World Religions Conference. My main tasks consisted of organizing the panel session on *Religion, Democracy and Human Rights in the Arab World* (September 12, 2006), and introducing the results of the work I have conducted so far for my postdoctoral research entitled *Voices—Paths of Reconstruction in Lebanon: Contributions of the 25–35 Lebanese Age Group.*[1] This chapter is a point of departure that could contribute to the debate on the religion-politics-society relations in Lebanon; but the answers proposed here are far from complete. To be more precise, Lebanon has continuously been driven by intermingling conflicts and status quo for several decades, and the analysis of its social-political situation has always been an arduous task to undertake. However, the staggering blow of the last conflict with Israel and its aftermath reveals a reality that appears to be far more complex to grasp, adding new wounds, war memories, and intricacies to old ones, weakening an already fragile Lebanon that found itself in the arena of proxy wars. In this context marked by disastrous damages in housing and public infrastructure and by terrible toll on civilian life leading to suffering and survival quest, one may ask the following: Is it relevant to talk about democracy? In other terms, is democracy a priority in the process of national reconstruction?

IS IT RELEVANT TO TALK ABOUT DEMOCRACY IN LEBANON?

The assassination of the former Lebanese Prime Minister Rafiq Hariri on February 14, 2005, unleashed a series of fundamental political changes: a big part of the Lebanese population united in an unprecedented outpouring in favor of independence in March 2005, and the Syrian army and intelligence services left after thirty years of occupation. Several car bombings led to the killing of elites and political leaders such as Samir Kassir and Gebran Tuéni, and activists within the Lebanese civil society and diaspora tried to capitalize on these changes and overcome the diverse challenges in order to construct-reconstruct a sustained democracy and a pluralistic society.

These activists were backed up by analysts who focused on democratic prospects, religious reforms, and human rights promotion, and who saw Lebanon as a "promising Arab democratic project in the making," a view shared by international media reports that praised Lebanon as a "positive" regional example that has been given a great opportunity by regaining its sovereignty, by the U.S. and French governments, and by U.S. institutions such as the Foundation for Defense of Democracies—which promotes democracy in the Middle East as a long-term weapon in the war against "Islamic terrorism"—and the Freedom House in New York.[2] According to the findings of this institution presented in "Freedom in the World 2006"—an annually issued index of global political rights and civil liberties—Lebanon experienced the most significant improvement in both political rights and civil liberties among the countries of the Arab Middle East in 2005. Its status changed from "Not Free" to "Partly Free." Consequently, it seemed to have the potential to build a "truly" democratic and prosperous society.

Nevertheless, the parliamentary elections of May 2005 did not lead to a renewal of the Lebanese leadership or to reforms in the political system. According to Ghassan Rubeiz:

> The parliamentary elections going on now are not likely to bring significant reforms or ensure stability for long. For better or worse, Lebanon has become a typical Arab regime, in which political wisdom is suppressed, reform is inhibited, triumphal rhetoric is encouraged, religious authority is supreme, and minorities are marginalized. The first three rounds of the four-part elections have failed to produce important new leaders with practical ideas for building a modern and unified state. Politically, the same old wine is packaged in new electoral bottles.[3]

The Cedar Revolution did not result in a long-lasting democratic change in Lebanon. Despite the promises of the government, the country suffers from an inability to institute deeply needed social-political reforms. "Lebanon has not embarked on new political adventure or experiment, but rather a process of reinforcing existing institutions and behavior patterns."[4] Furthermore, the summer 2006 conflicts and their impacts seem to have turned the attention of many analysts, politicians, and members of the Lebanese civil society from important internal issues to focus on the Arab-Israeli conflict. In other terms, these conflicts demonstrated that the Arab-Israeli conflict remains an inescapable reality in the region. The horror of a regional war resurfaced, along with a polarizing dichotomy of resistance (i.e., survival, self-defense, and even revenge) versus surrender. According to Amr Hamzawy, senior associate at the Carnegie Endowment for International Peace in Washington:

> Arabs [and Lebanese in particular] feel they have to choose between resisting American and Israeli hegemony in the Middle East or giving up the right of the Arab and Muslim *Umma*, or community, to exist. More troubling is that the positions of

> putatively democratic Arab opposition movements on the war in Lebanon have exposed their totalitarian and populist tendencies. There is a great difference between adopting a rational discourse that rightly condemns the Israeli military for its crimes against civilians and criticizes unconditional American acceptance of the war, and cheering the death of Israeli civilians as a step toward the destruction of the "Zionist entity." The regional shadows of the war in Lebanon will persist for many years. They may well be a long and painful reminder that the hope for any near-term democratic transformation of the Arab world was perhaps the greatest loser in a war that produced tremendous damage on all sides.[5]

At first sight, one may agree with Amr Hamzawy. Nevertheless, based on my personal experience and research while in Lebanon during this gruesome summer, I cannot endorse either his generalization or his pessimism. Being present in the field helped me realize that despite an obvious shift of issues in the official political and media arenas, democracy is still a matter of deep concern that is closely linked to the process of the national reconstruction, especially among the young Lebanese generations in Lebanon and abroad.

THE CULTURE OF RESISTANCE: CONTRIBUTIONS OF THE 25–35 LEBANESE AGE GROUP

My statement is based on participatory observation in Beirut and Montreal since September 2005, the collection and analysis of published data (press releases, scientific articles, and electronic and multimedia material), and on contacts and interviews with twenty Lebanese aged between 25 and 35: journalists, poets, novelists, artists, bloggers, psychologists, and movie and documentary producers, in addition to activists in NGOs (nongovernmental organizations) (e.g., *Nahwa al-Muwatiniya* [Towards Citizenship] and *Tadamon* [Solidarity]), transnational organizations (e.g., *Art of Living Foundation* and *Helem* [Dream]), and groups for interreligious dialogue.[6] Since September 2005, I have been asking young Lebanese numerous questions summarized as follows: How do they define the wars in Lebanon? How do they remember and memorialize these wars (or how do they construct personal war memories)? How do they use their personal war memories to define their identity? Do they find it significant to construct or reconstruct a national war memory as part of a national reconstruction process?[7] How do they link their personal memories to the construction-reconstruction of this national memory? How do they link the construction-reconstruction of a national war memory to other pending issues such as the religion-politics-society relations, and especially the issues of confessionalism—a system of managing diversities or structures of governments, modes of political governorship, and social strategies adopted to ensure social-political cohesion between different confessions—and democracy? What are the strategies, discourses, or actions addressing these issues that they develop and promote on the individual and collective levels in Lebanon and Canada?

The data collected from the first stage of this fieldwork allowed me to identify many characteristics of this 25–35 age group.[8] Individuals within this age group who are part of the "lost" Lebanese generation of war—"la génération des perdus de la guerre," in the words of Wadih al-Asmar from SOLIDA Movement[9]—survived, while having been deeply marked by, the 1975–1990 period of conflict. Most of them use informal, alternative, or even underground strategies of testifying, rather than traditional demand-making actions: publishing articles and independent media reports on the Internet; launching alternative websites and blogs; producing alternative radio programs, short movies, documentaries, trauma plays, or dramas of survival; organizing home movie screening events, artistic exhibitions, round tables, and debates using new media resources (video, interactive installation, Internet, and virtual reality); and mixing literary and artistic genres.[10]

The testimonies of the individuals I interviewed during the first three weeks of the Israeli invasion focused on its horrific impacts, and many let go of their anger and fear without restraint. "Bomb Tel Aviv" was a common reaction out of despair among some young individuals, whether Muslims, Christians, or atheists. Once the shock effect was absorbed, many began analyzing the causes and impacts of previous conflicts and linking them to the most recent ones. A very interesting example lies in the Lebanese blogosphere, of which I am part. A blogosphere is the collective term encompassing all blogs (a type of website that often functions as a personal online diary) as a community or social network. Many blogs are densely interconnected; bloggers read others' blogs, link to them, and reference them in their own writing, and many post comments on each other's blogs. Because of this, the interconnected blogs have grown their own culture.[11]

The recent conflict with Israel has sent the Lebanese blogosphere into hyperdrive, with a litany of personal experiences, explanations, and exhortations crisscrossing the Internet along with disturbing pictures of the violence. Since July 2006, I have identified more than eighty blogs for young Lebanese in their twenties and thirties living in Lebanon and abroad, battling against war through the Internet. Most of these bloggers illustrate old invasions and massacres through their personal souvenirs. They also comment on recent conflicts using anecdotes, photographs, video footage, and drawings, while showing that the construction-reconstruction of a national war memory begins with the representation of wartime events lived by ordinary people and the promotion of social conditions that are conducive to creativity and innovation.

The Lebanese blogosphere culture is part of a "culture of resistance" that is not ephemeral and that has been evolving since the mid-nineties within the vibrant Lebanese civil society, a mix of traditional, communally based associations and more advanced civic groups "that helped bring the country through all the years of war without the dramatic collapse that we have seen in Iraq, Afghanistan, and elsewhere."[12] According to Paul Salem, these associations and institutions provide "strength" and "durability" to the society, "even at times when the state is in great flux or has all but disappeared."[13] The resistance in that case does not only focus on survival, and is not driven by hatred or by revenge. It is a multilevel process that deals with the regional conflicts and the national problems.

PRIORITIES ON THE NATIONAL LEVEL

On the national level, the culture of resistance aims not only at ending the conflicts, but also at breaking the internal status quo. Breaking this status quo requires a first priority: to deconstruct the "invisible" or nonphysical war, a gigantic symbolic and psychic conflict that involves the whole population; it is the war of fantasies and representations run by "passive fighters" who fail to understand the nature of their complex memories and identities. This war is the usual counterpart of the visible or physical war—conflicts, negotiations, and treaties run by "active fighters."[14] According to many young activists and bloggers (e.g., caricaturist Wassim Mouawad, blogs: "Shlon" and "Les niouzes: des infos du Liban"; movie and documentary producer Nada Raphael) I interviewed, the deconstruction of the invisible or nonphysical war begins with the treating of the trauma, by expressing, creating, and transmitting a national war memory that could be nourished by the diverse personal and collective memories. The main objective is to move from ancient and recent wounds to the most important duties as citizens: mutual respect, conviviality, and the exploration and understanding of similarities and differences.

This first priority calls for a second one: constructing-reconstructing a long-term conviviality between the diversity of memories and identities; a conviviality that is not only interreligious or interconfessional as the mainstream media tended to portray the relief campaigns and social solidarity in July and August 2006, but also between generations, nationalities, social classes, and genders—an inter-human conviviality in all its dimensions. For example, in the blogs that I have reviewed so far, we find many testimonies of solidarity and conviviality between Lebanese notwithstanding their religious or nonreligious affiliations.[15] It is also the case of new NGOs and social movements/networks run by young activists such as Nahwa al-Muwatiniya, Amam 05, Haya Bina, Kafa, Sawa Group, Samidoun, and Tadamon. This inter-human conviviality can be generated through these individuals and collectivities, but it would be insufficient. That is why the idea of a national dialogue is being promoted, a dialogue that is not reduced to political and religious leaders, and that allows individuals to think about the complex spaces in which democracy extends beyond the realm of electing rulers. This dialogue should integrate private-sector leaders, academics, technocrats, and young activists, whose expertise would help balance the needs of all Lebanese citizens and that would allow Lebanon to tackle the significant challenges it faces in fields such as confessionalism or sectarianism, also called consociate democracy.[16] Indeed, for most of my interviewees, the conflicts of summer 2006 forced them, more than before, to ask what kind of nation and what kind of society they want to live in.

For some interviewees, Lebanon is the most democratic Arab state.[17] Its confessional system has spared Lebanese the twentieth-century totalitarian regimes of most Arab countries. It allows basic human rights to be promoted and offers a model of confessional coexistence between Christians and Muslims, Sunnis and Shiites; this is a model that has problems in its application but cannot be replaced because it strengthens the balance between multiple confessional components and constitutes a barrier against the emergence of dictatorship. However, many activists, artists, and bloggers believe that confessionalism is one of the main reasons why Lebanon's central government never constructed a coherent long-term national policy that focuses on the public good. Whatever its merits, this social-political system is inherently discriminatory because it does not take into account the various components of the Lebanese society. Citizens have no opportunity for representation outside the boundaries of their sect; thus, there is no institutionalized citizen-state relationship. Also, this form of power sharing (half the parliamentary seats for Christians and half for Muslims) is not likely to work forever, given the country's changing population profiles. Furthermore, it is a constrained democracy that is imbued with potential instability because it always requires external involvement to stabilize it.

For some interviewees, the ideal system has to be secular as in Western countries and has to promote human rights as stipulated in international conventions. For others—even the most secular and liberal activists—advocating a secular Lebanon at this time is unrealistic.[18] Furthermore, the ideal system should not be based on imported visions and values of democracy, human rights, and management of diversities—including the religious diversities. Democracy in Lebanon must be tailor-made in order to respond to the various religious, cultural, and social backgrounds of the populace. Therefore, in the view of most of the interviewees, Lebanese should make a greater effort to manage or readjust their confessional system or consociate democracy in the short run, so that in the long run it safeguards the rights of all citizens equally without sacrificing public interests for private interests—whether religious, ethnic, cultural, or economic. Such a system would also allow the blooming of a society in which the public has the means to participate in a meaningful way in the management of its own affairs and the means of a more open and free information and knowledge transmission.

Still, any changes will be greatly affected by regional and international dynamics. Even the "proper exercise" of constitutional democracy in Lebanon will have to wait for a balance of power between "the conflicting parties competing for regional hegemony."[19] No lasting cure for Lebanon will be effective outside a comprehensive solution to the Arab-Israeli conflict and the resolution of the U.S.-European-Iranian crisis over the issue of nuclear enrichment. Also, this cure requires the delineation of borders, thus regularizing the diplomatic exchanges with an eye to preserving Lebanese sovereignty. That does not prevent most of my interviewees from taking "baby steps" in the internal process of the national reconstruction, since the Cedar Revolution remains half-finished, "un projet en gestation."[20] Certainly, weapons have to be silenced, independence has to be accomplished, and the "truth" about the Hariri assassination has to be revealed, but a serious and comprehensive dialogue on the country's past and future is a must. This dialogue, a pillar in the construction of a better-quality democracy, is a permanent day-to-day conquest. It is a dynamic order that is perfectible through citizen action. It will never be independent from a lively public sphere because "the latter nurtures the former and provides the setting in which Democracy can expand and enrich itself."[21]

NOTES

1. The importance of this panel sponsored by the Canada Research Chair of Islam, Pluralism and Globalization consists of rethinking the widespread belief in Western media and public opinion that the Arab world is incapable of implementing democracy and promoting human rights because of religious totalitarianism and oppressive systems of governance; see Sheri Berman, "Islamism, Revolution, and Civil Society," *Perspectives in*

Politics 1, no. 2 (2003): 257–73, reprinted in Bernard Brown and Roy Marcridis, eds., *Comparative Politics: Notes and Readings* (New York: Harcourt, Brace, 2005); Barry Rubin, *The Tragedy of the Middle East* (New York: Cambridge University Press, 2002); Fatima Mernissi, *Islam and Democracy: Fear of the Modern World* (New York: Perseus Books Group, 2002); Eva Bellin, "The Robustness of Authoritarianism in the Middle East," *Comparative Politics* 36, no. 2 (2004): 139–57. In fact, this belief confines the discussion to the narrow limits of the political regimes; see Laith Kubba, "The Awakening of Civil Society," *Journal of Democracy* 11, no. 3 (2000): 84–90; United Nations Development Programme, *Arab Human Development Report 2003* (New York: UNDP, 2003), pp. 31, 171; Urdan Al-Jadid, "Civil Society and Governance: Case Study of Jordan," Country Report (Sussex: Institute for Development Studies, Civil Society and Governance Programme, 1999), p. 78; Lebanese Center for Policy Studies, "Civil Society and Governance: Mapping Society and Its Connection with Governance," Country Report (Sussex: Institute for Development Studies, Civil Society and Governance Programme, 1999), pp. 4–8. Furthermore, it conceals the complex realities of the Arab World societies.

The first phase of my research took place in Montreal and in Beirut from September 2005 to May 2006. It was financed by the Canada Research Chair of Islam, Pluralism and Globalization (University of Montreal) and consisted of literature analysis, participation in many encounters and events organized by Lebanese and transnational NGOs, and encounters with young activists, artists, and journalists in Lebanon and Canada. The second phase of my research is currently being pursued at the same Chair and at the Institute of Islamic-Christian Studies (Université Saint-Joseph, Lebanon), from June 2006 to May 2008. This phase is financed by the Social Sciences and Humanities Research Council of Canada (Government of Canada). Given the lack of data, this second phase is based on qualitative analysis of field interviews—individual, collective, group focus, field notes, and different materials collected during fieldwork (press reviews and articles, multimedia reports and documentaries, electronic material, educational material, reports of meetings and workshops, statements and reports designed for fundraising, and unpublished documentation). See Denise Jodelet, "Aperçus sur les méthodologies qualitatives," in *Les méthodes des sciences humaines*, ed. Serge Moscovici and Fabrice Buschini (Paris: Presses Universitaires de France, 2003), pp. 139–62; Jorge Vargas Cullell, "Democracy and the Quality of Democracy: Empirical Findings and Methodological and Theoretical Issues Drawn from the Citizen Audit of the Quality of Democracy in Costa Rica," in *The Quality of Democracy: Theory and Applications,* ed. Guillermo O'Donnell, Jorge Vargas Cullell, and Osvaldo M. Iazzetta (Notre Dame, IN: University of Notre Dame Press, 2004), pp. 93–162; Patrice Brodeur, "Pour faire place à l'étude critique appliquée de la religion," *Religiologiques*, 29 (2004): 61–78; Patrice Brodeur, "From Postmodernism to 'Glocalism': Towards a Theoretical Understanding of Contemporary Arab Muslim Constructions of Religious Others," in *Globalization and the Muslim World*, ed. Birgit Schaebler and Leif Stenberg (New York: Syracuse University Press, 2004), pp. 188–205; Patrice Brodeur, *Building the Interfaith Youth Movement,* with co-editor Dr. Eboo Patel (Walnut Creek, CA: AltaMira Press, 2005).

2. Democratization in the Arab World has received much attention in the wake of the Gulf War of 1991. See John O. Voll and John L. Esposito, "Islam's Democratic Essence," *Middle East Quarterly*, September 1994, pp. 3–11; David Garnham and Mark Tessler, eds., *Democracy, War and Peace in the Middle East* (Bloomington, IN: Indiana University Press, 1995); Augustus Richard Norton, ed., *Civil Society in the Middle East,* 2 vols. (Leiden: E. J. Brill, 1995–96). However, according to Habib C. Malik, "Western analysts and leaders then realized that greater freedom and real elections could destabilize some of the oil-rich authoritarian regimes in the region, and interest waned. Lebanon, the only Arab state with an enduring democratic experience and an impressive track of record on freedom, was somehow neglected during this discussion" ("Is There Still a Lebanon?" *Middle East Quarterly,* December 1997, http://www.meforum.org/pf.php?id=371).

3. Ghassan Rubeiz, "Shaping Lebanon's Future," *The Christian Science Monitor,* June 16, 2005, http://www.csmonitor.com/2005/0616/p25s02-cogn.html.

4. Paul Salem, "Lebanon at the Crossroads: Rebuilding an Arab Democracy," *Saban Center Middle East Memo,* no. 7, May 31, 2005, http://www.brook.edu/fp/saban/salem memo20050531.htm.

5. Amr Hamzawy, "The Big Loser after Lebanon: Democracy," *The Daily Star*, August 22, 2006.

6. Other Lebanese NGOs, groups, and movements dealing with the issues of war, conflict resolution, peace building, and dialogue will be contacted through this year: *Permanent Peace Movement, Amam 05, Haya Bina, Kafa, Sawa Group, Solida.*

7. I describe the war memory in Lebanon as "an ongoing process of interactions between individual and collective readings of the diverse pasts and presents; a plural and dynamic process to which the constructions-representations-expressions of all actors of the Lebanese Civil Society and Diaspora contribute" ("processus en devenir d'échanges-interactions entre des relectures individuelles et collectives des divers passés et présents; un processus pluriel et dynamique auquel contribuent les constructions-représentations-expressions de tous les acteurs de la société civile et de la diaspora libanaises" [Pamela Chrabieh, *Pour une gestion médiatrice des diversités au Liban. Une théorie du plurilogue, au-delà du confessionnalisme* (Thèse doctorale, Bibliothèque des Lettres et des Sciences Humaines, Université de Montréal, Montréal, Juin 2005), pp. 12–13]).

8. The second stage, which began in 2007 and continues in 2008, aims at expanding the research in order to identify these contributions as the work of important social-political actors in the national reconstruction. It also aims at showing changes in issues of religion, identity, and citizenship in the topography of the Lebanese social-political context.

9. Interview with Wadih al-Asmar, Beirut, 2006.

10. Asef Bayat, *Social Movements, Activism and Social Development in the Middle East*, Civil Society and Social Movements, Programme Paper Number 3, United Nations Institute for Social Development, November 2000, http://www.unrisd.org/80256b3c005bccf9/(httpauxpages)/9c2befd0ee1c73b380256b5e004ce4c3/$file/bayat.pdf; Karam Karam, "Associations civiles, mouvements sociaux et participation politique au Liban dans les années 90" (draft paper presented at conference "ONG et Gouvernance dans les Pays Arabes," March 29–31, 2000, Cairo, http://www.unesco.org/most/karam.doc).

11. See http://www.wikipedia.org.

12. Karam, p. 1.

13. Salem, p. 1.

14. This terminology was identified by the Lebanese Psychiatric Adnan Houballah in *Le virus de la violence* (Paris: Albin Michel, 1996). The two wars mingle and nourish each other, thus creating a vicious cycle that drags along all individuals within a society.

15. See http://pchrabieh.blogspot.com for the list of Lebanese blogs against war.

16. Antoine Messara, *Le modèle libanais et sa survie. Essai sur la classification et l'aménagement d'un système consociatif*, Publications de l'Université Libanaise, Section des études juridiques, politiques et administratives, no. 7, Beirut, 1983.

17. According to Michel Touma, "among Arab states, Lebanon is the only that combines a history of extensive political pluralism with a culture that is hospitable to personal and communal freedoms. The fact that different minorities—including a strong indigenous Christian community—were not reduced to a subjugated status under Muslim rule was an important element in this process" (p. 3).

18. "The usual option called for in Lebanon—deconfessionalizing political life—is unworkable because it ignores the socio-communal indicator realities on the ground. For better or worse, religion remains a strong, indeed the leading indicator of identity on the sub-state level in Lebanon and throughout the Middle East" (Malik, p. 1). According to Ghassan Rubeiz, "if Lebanon is to gain long-term stability, power sharing must be secularized.

A more realistic alternative, in the short term, would be to rotate leadership positions among the different communities. Currently, Muslims are not allowed to hold the position of president or head of the army; nor can a Christian become a prime minister. An additional reform would be to allow Lebanese emigrants to vote in Lebanese parliamentary elections" (Rubeiz, p. 1).

19. Ghassan Tuéni, "Democracy in Lebanon: Anatomy of a Crisis," *The Beirut Review*, no. 6, Fall 1993, http://www.lcps-lebanon.org/pub/breview/br6/tuenibr6.html.

20. Michel Hajji Georgiou, "Entretenir la flamme du 14 mars," *L'Orient-le-Jour* (Beirut), March 17, 2006.

21. Guillermo O'Donnell, Jorge Vargas Cullell, and Osvaldo M. Iazzetta, eds., *The Quality of Democracy: Theory and Applications* (Notre Dame, IN: University of Notre Dame Press, 2004), p. 6.

Part III

Peace

CHAPTER 9

9/11 and Korean American Youth: A Study of Two Opposing Forces

Heerak Christian Kim

The Korean American community has been deeply impacted by 9/11 and its aftermath. For many Koreans, these terrorist attacks brought to the fore questions about communal safety in the American context because the previously held assumption as to the safety of America was broken and the concept of North Korea as an axis-of-evil power became more relevant and real. Many began to question how this would impact South Korean immigrants in the United States. The question regarding the safety of Koreans in America as an immigrant community came to be externalized in two completely opposing tendencies. One trend was an aggressively conservatizing trend among the churchgoers, pushing even historically left-leaning Korean churches closer toward the evangelical/fundamentalist direction. The other trend went the other direction, with many individual Korean Christians leaving the church and abandoning institutional Christianity altogether, thereby leaving many Korean local congregations empty. This latter post-9/11 trend is most noticeable among those in the late teens and in college. In this chapter, I will describe the sociological phenomena of the two opposite forces that have impacted Korean American Christianity after 9/11, particularly focusing on late-teen and college-age Koreans. Specific examples will be provided from Korean American youth movements (parachurch) and Korean American youth group studies.

The starting point of any discussion on Korean Americans must be with their perception of themselves or their understanding of their group identity. It is difficult to generalize about Korean American identity because there is a wide spectrum of who belongs to this group. On the one hand, you have the FOBs, which stands for "fresh off the boat." They are Korean immigrants who recently came from Korea and retain all traits that are distinctively Korean in nature. They generally speak in Korean. They subscribe to Korean fashion in clothing. Their mannerisms and way of behaving is traditional Korean and not what would normally be described as American or Western. On the other far end of the spectrum are what Koreans refer to as Bananas. Bananas are Korean Americans who have lived in America for a long time and consciously work toward integrating into the American way of life. Put another way, Bananas are those who consciously work toward divesting themselves of what they perceive as Korean culture or Korean ways. Not all Bananas are American-born. In fact, some Bananas are quite recent immigrants; some may even have immigrated to the United States three or four years ago, or even less. Whereas FOBs are identified by their perpetual use of the Korean language and resorting to visible Korean customs and dress, Bananas are identified primarily by the company that they keep. Because the term Banana in colloquial discourse stands for those who are "yellow on the outside but white on the inside," it would not be surprising to find that the label of Banana applied to Koreans who have mostly white friends. Evidence of a person's Banana status continues to be having a white spouse or significant other, such as a white girlfriend. Of course in both cases—that of the FOB and the Banana—identity markers are more complex than that. But certainly, on a popular Korean American discourse level, these are the simplistic ways to identify FOBs and Bananas—by the language they speak, the clothing they wear, and the friends they keep.

Most Korean Americans do not neatly fall into the group of the FOBs or the Bananas. The majority of Korean Americans fall somewhere in between. Of course, depending on where on the spectrum a Korean American falls, he or she will identify other Koreans as FOBs or Bananas slightly differently. However, the general rule still applies. A Korean American who speaks mostly in Korean and has mostly Korean American friends tends to be considered a FOB, and a Korean American who has predominantly white friends and speaks only in English is considered a Banana. The fact that most Korean Americans fall between these two antipodal ends is recognized by most Korean Americans, although they may not verbalize it in such terms. In a sense, we can describe this understanding as culturally innate or a sublimated part of the Korean American consciousness. The reality is assumed to be fact, and this reality is rarely questioned.

The fact of Korean American assumptions regarding the linear spectrum between the FOB and the Banana is visible in the way Korean Americans describe themselves. Korean Americans have developed a decimal point system to describe themselves. For instance, a Korean who just emigrated from Korea is first-generation Korean American. A Korean who came from Korea at the age of about thirteen years old is a 1.5-generation Korean American.[1] And a Korean who came from Korea at the age of seven years old is a 1.75. A Korean who emigrated from Korea at the age of seventeen is a 1.2. Although the decimal point has not been systematized per se, there is a popular understanding of what a 1.5 is, what a 1.75 is, and what a 1.2 is. The guideline is set by unspoken communal consent that assumes the spectrum between the FOB and Banana.

What is a second-generation Korean American? A second-generation Korean American in the Korean American cultural context is a Korean who was born in the United States to parents who immigrated to the United States. Interestingly enough, children born to first-generation Korean Americans and children born to 1.5-generation Korean Americans are both said to be second-generation. The reason that the distinction is not made between the two can be attributed to the relative newness of the majority of Korean Americans in the United States. Most households have parents who are first-generation. Rarely will one find third-generation Korean Americans—Korean Americans born in America to parents who were born in America. The Korean American immigrant experience is about one generation (calculated at thirty-five years) old or less.[2] The 1970 census found about 70,000 Koreans residing in the United States. But the number has increased rapidly since then by about 30,000 Koreans every year. In 1976, about 290,000 Koreans were resident in the United States. And the 1980 U.S. census numbered Koreans at 354,529.[3] Furthermore, a demographic study of Los Angeles in 1979 revealed that almost 81 percent of Koreans living in the Los Angeles area had been living there for 7 years or less. And the mean was 6.5 years.[4] Tae-Hwan Kwak and Seong Hyong Lee note that in 1990, the Korean American population was estimated to be 1.3 million. The majority of them immigrated to the United States since 1965, when the U.S. government lifted its prohibition of immigration from Asia. Kwak and Lee state in the introduction to their edited book, *The Korean-American Community: Present and Future,* that most of the 1.3 million Koreans in 1990 represent the wave of immigration in 1970s and 1980s.[5] And Won Moo Hurh in his 1998 book states: "More than two-thirds of the current Korean population in the United States are foreign-born, and the majority of them arrived after 1970."[6] It is clear how recent Korean immigration in the United States is. The majority of Korean Americans living in the United States were born in Korea or had parents born in Korea. This is the current reality. Because of the relative newness of Korean immigration, the language is limited in terms of the decimal point system applied between the second generation and the third generation. One will find many Korean Americans who are 1.5 or 1.7 or 1.2, but one will never find Koreans who are 2.5.[7] This is not a part of the Korean American discourse on a popular or academic level. There is only the second generation and the third generation; there is no decimal point between these two spectrums.

Korean Americans have developed this system instinctively without any academic dictating of the point system. No one knows who started the discourse. It just became completely adopted by Korean Americans all over the United States. It can be seen as an integral part of Korean American culture. It became normative spontaneously. Won Moo Hurh writes regarding the term "the 1.5 generation": "The term was coined in the Korean community around 1980. Although the Japanese terms for first-, second-, and third-generation immigrants—*issei, nisei,* and *sansei*—are found in *Webster's Dictionary,* a term such as "1.5 generation" has not been used with reference to other immigrant groups."[8] I would argue that the reason for this is the spectrum between the FOB and the Banana that operates distinctively in the Korean American context. In a way, the reality of the FOB and the Banana explains the innate tensions within the Korean American community, wavering between the mother country that they left behind and the new land they now live in.

The Korean American decimal point system is innately Korean American. Most ethnographers do not even know of the point system. Generally, anthropologists and sociologists refer to first American-born immigrants as first-generation Americans, with whichever ethnic title attached. Thus, if a couple emigrated from Ireland, their baby born in America would be first-generation Irish American. The parents would be immigrants and would not really have a generation attached to them. This assumption is based on the fact that sociologists and anthropologists attribute the identity of the parents to the country they emigrated from. So, the Irish immigrant couple is Irish and not really Irish American per se. They are Irish immigrants in America. Even American laws seem to support this presupposition. As powerful as Governor Arnold Schwarzenegger is, he is treated by a different set of laws than are his children, who were born in the United States. Governor Schwarzenegger is not American per se by the standards of anthropologists and sociologists. He is an Austrian immigrant in America who has been naturalized and became an American citizen. Thus, if Governor Schwarzenegger breaks a law, he can be extradited to Austria. He is not really American the way his children are. They cannot be extradited to Austria because they are not seen as Austrian in any legal sense of the term or sociological sense of the term. They are first-generation Americans. In contrast, Governor Schwarzenegger is not really American and that is why he cannot become U.S. president by law. Not only can he be extradited to Austria, the American law fundamentally assumes that he is not loyal to the United States by the virtue of his immigration.

American custom, academia, and laws perceive first-generation Americans as those who are born in America to immigrants from another country. Only the Korean Americans in the United States view things differently and utilize their own system of attaching generation designators within the community. What are we to make of this? I would argue that this reality points to the way Korean Americans view themselves in the American context. First of all, they rebel—whether they are aware of it or not—against the cultural, academic, and legal mores of America in the way they perceive themselves. This can be approached from various angles. I would like to emphasize that the reason for this approach is that they were concerned more with the spectrum between the FOB and the Banana.

Why were Koreans so concerned about this spectrum? It goes to the history of the Korean people. Korea is called the Hermit Kingdom for a reason. It has remained radically isolationist. Although China called white people "white devils," they gave white people access to China relatively early. This was the case with Japan as well. Despite the highly anti-Western and anti-white sentiment floating around in Japan, Japan welcomed white individuals into Japan relatively early in its history. In contrast, Koreans intentionally held off welcoming in Westerners. Korea was the last nation in East Asia to establish normalized relations with the United States. This was done in 1882 through the signing of the Korean-American Treaty in 1882.[9] The fear of the Banana factor is a part of the conscious fear of the Westerner in the Korean community.

Every Korean American will tell you that their parents wanted one thing from them—that was to marry a Korean.[10] Most Korean-American parents have historically threatened to disown their children if they married a white person.[11] This cultural standard is operating still in many Korean families. Chon S. Edwards, a Korean who married a white American, states that even reputable Koreans with high social status living in the United States would be ashamed if their children married white. Often, the wedding will be done in secret and their close Korean friends will not be invited to the wedding.[12] Perhaps Ji-Yeon Yuh's comments about Korean women who married white American soldiers best explain the situation. Yuh writes regarding these Korean women who intermarried: "For second-generation Korean Americans, they were the women sitting alone, without husbands, during church service and fellowship, the ones they'd ignored because everyone else did."[13] It is this anti-white sentiment that has developed the Banana system, or the 1.5 system of identification. The sentiment of the Korean immigrant parents has been internalized in their children. It is not surprising, therefore, that even second-generation Korean Americans in California refuse to marry non-Koreans and often ostracize Koreans in their midst who marry non-Korean. The Banana fear is an integral part of the Korean-American experience that is connected to Korean historical experience.

A part of the reason for the phenomenon is due to what Won Moo Hurh and Kwang Chung Kim call "adhesive" adaptation of Korean Americans to the American context.[14] What that means is that Korean Americans tend to keep the Korean core—such as Korean traditional culture and Korean social-networks—while being Americanized culturally and socially. The Americanization is surface and for public consumption in the American context. However, on a fundamental level Korean Americans tend to value their Korean identity and culture. What is quite relevant in this regard is the conscious sentiment in the Korean American community that Korean Americans should be closely tied to things Korean regardless of how long they have been in the United States. Sang-O Rhee expresses this sentiment: "What we desire most is that the second generation should identify with the Korean society in America and Korea and develop positive attitudes towards them. If this can be successfully accomplished through the Korean education system, we can develop responsible citizens of a pluralistic society of multi-language and culture. This type of adaptation is called 'harmonious self-identity of love America and love Korea.'"[15] Sang-O Rhee is voicing a normative desire in the Korean American community, desiring preservation of Korean culture among Korean Americans born in the United States. This is quite visible in the Korean American church context. It is not surprising, therefore, to find Korean American churches that have thousands of members in Los Angeles, Anaheim, Baltimore, New York, and other cities who speak only Korean and preserve Korean ways. No other ethnic group in the United States has had this phenomenon. German Americans are Christians. But there are no churches with thousands of German Americans. The same goes for Chinese Americans. There are many Chinese-American Christians but it is hard to find a Chinese church in any city that numbers over a thousand.

The Korean-American church functions as a cultural center of the Korean American people as well as its religious center. This was the case from the beginning of Korean immigration, which was in 1903 in Hawaii.[16] Early Korean settlers made Christian worship their first major social event after immigrating to the United States. For instance, early Koreans (some 300 Christians and 30 preachers who followed the immigrants everywhere) set up a Christian church on July 5, 1903, in Mokolia, Oahu, and another Christian church on River Street, in Honolulu, on November 10, 1903.[17] This trend of setting up Korean churches as both a Korean cultural center and a place of religious worship for Koreans still characterizes the Korean American community. Hurh and Kim write: "The Korean immigrants appear, therefore, to crave both types of fellowship—spiritual (Christian) fellowship *and* ethnic fellowship. . . . The Korean ethnic church provides best both fellowships for the immigrant."[18] Thus, it would not be surprising that if any Korean American clergy adopts a Banana stance, he will lose his church membership like dust in the wind.[19] For instance, if a Korean American church of 3,000 members hires a senior pastor who prefers Banana ways and encourages marrying white people, Korean-American members will leave that church and find a Korean American church that is more dedicated to Korean ways.[20] The Korean-American church is a cultural center for the Korean-American people, and the central thrust of the Korean-American culture tends to be anti-Banana.[21]

Thus, even third-generation Korean Americans are ashamed if they cannot speak Korean.[22] And those who speak even a few sentences boast and lie and say that they can speak good Korean.[23] In the Korean American cultural matrix of the Korean American church, the Banana factor is feared, shunned, and hated. It is not surprising, therefore, to see that many Korean Americans actually see teaching of the Korean language and culture as an integral mission of the Korean American church. Yong Choon Kim writes: "The education of the second generation of Koreans is one of the most important tasks of the Korean church for the healthy progress of the Korean American community. For this task Korean churches in America should make a special effort to continue teaching the Korean language along with Christian education."[24] One of the reasons why Korean American churches have been so successful in America in contrast to other Asian ethnic churches is simply because of the fact that Korean American churches have been aggressively pro-Korean and anti-white.[25]

The anti-white sentiment persisting in the Korean community was enhanced by the L.A. riots in 1992 when white American leaders (who controlled most of Los Angeles, including the police, government agencies, and the media) ignored pleas for help by Koreans. Koreans had given a lot of donations to police charities, election campaigns funds, and other types of support for white leaders of Los Angeles.[26] Most Koreans felt betrayed, and pro-white factions in Korean communities were silenced for the foreseeable future. This fueled greater anti-white sentiment in Korean American churches. As a corollary, more Korean American churches embraced things Korean, more aggressively. It would be difficult to find a Korean American church that does not sing the Korean national anthem on Korean Independence Day. In contrast, one will almost never find a Korean American church singing the American national anthem, ever. One of the reasons why Korean Christianity combined with Korean nationalism is that those who attacked Koreans attacked Korean Christianity. This was the case during the Japanese Occupation, when Korean nationalism became identified with Korean Christian martyrs. And this was the case during the Korean War when anti-communism became identified with Korean Christianity. It was a fact that Korean Christians were sought out by communists and killed for their Christian faith. For many Koreans, their religion became an integral part of their national identity as Koreans in the Japanese Occupation period and South Korean identity in the Korean War.

It does not really matter how accurate the perception is. The fact is that the communal memory hinges on this perceived reality. It may in fact not be completely the case in true Korean history. But this perception has been perpetuated within Korean Christianity and in Korean Christian pulpits. And thus, it is an integral part of the Korean collective memory and communal consciousness. If one does not understand this reality of the Korean Christian experience, which cannot be separated from Korean historical experience for Korean Americans, then one will not understand the Korean American experience. Unfortunately, not much study has been done on this aspect of Korean American identity. I hope to rectify this error in academia through a more in-depth study in the future.

The extent to which this reality is fact for Korean Americans is attested by the fact that almost 100 percent of Korean American college students will say that they have been to a Christian church in their youth.[27] Even parents who are non-Christians often sent their children to Korean churches for Korean cultural experience. It is only a very recent phenomenon that some Koreans have started to rally around the Buddhist temple. This reality is evident when we look at the case of Chicago. In 1997, there were estimated to be 100,000 Koreans in the Chicago area. There were 196 Korean American churches, primarily conducting their programs in the Korean language. In contrast, there were only five Buddhist temples.[28] Chicago actually has one of the largest Korean Buddhist communities, in terms of percentage, but still only about 4.2 percent of Korean Americans in Chicago are Buddhist. In Los Angeles, only about 1.5 percent of the Korean Americans are Buddhist.[29] For Korean Americans, Buddhism was a non-factor for much of their immigration history.

The beginning of Korean Buddhism in the United States is dated to 1964, when Soh Kyongbo, a Korean Buddhist monk, arrived in Philadelphia to pursue his Ph.D. studies at Temple University. Soh Kyongbo led a small Buddhist meditation group while he was a Ph.D. student at Temple University. Much of the Buddhist movements were scattered away from major Korean population centers, including Los Angeles, Chicago, and New York. For instance, Kim Samu, a Korean Buddhist monk, set up Zen Lotus Societies in Toronto, Canada, and Ann Arbor, Michigan, in the 1970s. There were hardly any Koreans in these cities at the time. Another Korean Buddhist leader, Sungsan, set up a Son Center in Providence, Rhode Island, in 1972.[30] There were hardly any Koreans there at the time. Eventually, Buddhist movements spread to population centers of Korean immigration, such as Los Angeles and New York. But it is significant that Buddhism started in the fringes of the Korean American community.[31] In this sense, Korean historical experience in America is vastly different from other immigrants from Buddhist lands, such as China and Japan, which had a visible Buddhist population in the United States from the very beginning. Korean Americans were completely different. Many Koreans abandoned Buddhism when they immigrated to the United States. They saw their immigration as immigrating to Christianity. Although parents may not have actively converted to Christianity, those who left Korea and Korean Buddhism behind were willing to attend the church and subscribe to the Christianity of America. The fact that Korean American churches functioned as Korean American cultural centers[32] made the transition easy, and many Korean Americans readily converted to Christianity in the context of the Korean American church.

Current high-school students and college students who are Korean Americans must be understood in light of this historical experience of Korean Americans. The majority of them have been to a Christian church in America and many of them have been active participants. For many Korean American youths, their

Korean American identity is closely tied to their experience in a Korean American church. In this light, it is understandable why the Korean American church experienced a great shock to the system with 9/11. The terrorist attacks of 9/11 shocked Korean Americans, and the shock manifested itself in the setting of the Korean American church.

What happened? In terms of the Korean-American experience, Korean American immigrants were shocked in religious terms. Most Korean Americans not only changed countries but also religions when they immigrated to the United States. Most Korean Buddhists abandoned Buddhism and many actively converted to Christianity. It is not surprising to find some churches with something like 80 percent of its members being converts to Christianity. They converted after they came to the United States as immigrants. This seems to be in line with Korean immigration to the United States since the first immigration of 1903. Regarding the first wave of Korean immigrants, Bong-Youn Choy writes that 40 percent were Christians but most Korean immigrants—including non-Christians—eventually became Christian churchgoers.[33] For many of these Korean American immigrants, they identified America with a Christian land. They identified the blessings of America in the areas of economy and military in terms of its Christian identity. For Korean immigrants, the United States was a great country because it was Christian. They immigrated to America, the great nation, and they adopted Christianity, the great religion. The Korean American church with its focus on Korean cultural identity made the transition in religious identity that much more smooth. They could be Koreans and be Christians and live in the Christian land as Korean Christians. In fact, it would not be wrong to say that Koreans did not really see themselves as becoming naturalized as American citizens—rather, they perceived themselves as being Koreans in America who became Christians. For many of them, Christianity was their identity that they shared with Americans. If one were to ask a Korean today what nationality he has, a typical Korean would say "Korean" even though he holds a U.S. passport and had to give up his Korean passport and Korean citizenship. One would be hard pressed to find a Korean, even a second-generation Korean, who will refer to himself as an American.

Within the Korean American experience, American identity meant being Christian. This allowed Koreans to maintain their Korean heritage and continue the Hermit Kingdom ways while being fiercely loyal to the United States. This is a reason why Korean Americans comprise the greatest percentage of Asian Americans at West Point and other U.S. military academies. Every Korean American clergy member will pray for America as a Christian nation that God should protect. Korean Americans are patriotic to America not because they see value in their American citizenship but because their Korean American identity became a Korean American Christian identity and so they found solidarity with America the Christian nation on a religious level.[34] There was never confusion among Korean Americans regarding their loyalty to America the nation. Korean Americans were and remain loyal to Korea as their nation despite their U.S. citizenship. They do not see the contraction of being loyal to Korea "their nation" and being loyal to American "the Christian nation."[35] In fact, given the persecution that Korean Christianity suffered in the last 100 years, if push comes to shove, they would be more loyal to the Christian nation over Korea. This was the case in the Korean War. Communists were killing Korean Christians, so Koreans in the South chose to die as Christians at the hands of their relatives from North Korea.

9/11 changed a lot of things. First of all, for many Korean Americans, it proved that God no longer protected America. How could God allow a small band of unsophisticated terrorists to highjack American planes right under the noses of American security and the most highly safeguarded place in American public life—the airport system—and use the American planes against American buildings? Surely, God took away his protection of the country for such a thing to happen.

9/11 imbued Korean Americans with doubt about America as a nation blessed by God. Because the identity of America as a Christian nation was firmly fixed in the Korean American consciousness, doubting America's divine protection encouraged doubting the veracity of Christianity itself.[36] Unlike white evangelical Christians who have questioned the Christian identity of America since the 1920s and even chose to separate themselves from American politics in pursuit of Christian holiness and Christian identity, Korea-American Christians identified America with Christianity.

Korean American clergy encouraged this identity. Korean Americans frequently pray for the United States, and every time, they would pray that God protect the Christian nation of America. Korean American pastors frequently preach about American missionaries bringing Christianity to Korea. When Korean American clergy chastise Korea, they will not use any other nation on earth except for America to chastise Korea with, because America was a Christian nation, "founded by the Puritans." Thus, Korean American church teachings along with individual understanding of what America is—a Christian nation—encouraged the doubt that was created among Korean Americans after 9/11. For many, it was as conclusive evidence that Christianity was not true and that the God of the Americans was false.

Of course, evangelical Christians who are white in America have been clamoring for decades that America is a secular nation with a secular agenda and not a Christian goal. But they are a part of the American society, experience, and discourse. Korean Americans choose to be outside of that. Not everyone would say that Koreans had a choice in the matter. Sang Hyun Lee writes that by being nonwhite, Koreans in America are permanent outsiders even if they are more westernized than many of the white immigrants.[37] This applies to Korean Americans born in the United States and their descendants as well. Whether Korean Americans are outside of the American mainstream by choice or not, the effect is the same. Korean Americans view America through the lens of Korean American identity and society. In other words, most Korean Americans know only the America that the Korean American church painted in rosy colors, through the lens of Korean Christianity.[38]

Thus, 9/11 encouraged a mass exodus of Korean Americans from Christianity. Korean American churches became empty as Korean Americans chose to abandon Christianity, which 9/11 proved to be a false religion in their minds. Many of them in fact went back to their old religion of Buddhism.[39] And throughout Los Angeles and elsewhere, there was a revival of Buddhism among Koreans. This trend also manifested itself among the Korean American youth. Korean American high-school students and college students started to leave the Christian church in massive numbers. In some Korean American churches, the college group became nonexistent as high-school students who went to college refused to go to church.

However, for the younger generation, the departure from Christian churches created a different reality than for their parents. Their parents were originally Buddhists, so they traded in their Christian identity card for a familiar Buddhist one. Thus, they participated in the revival of Korean Buddhism in America. Unlike their parents, Korean teenagers and college students, many of them having been born in the United States, had no experience with Buddhism. They did not know what it was. They had never practiced a single Buddhist ritual in their lives. Thus, when they left Christianity, they did not see Buddhism as an alternative. Many Korean American teenagers and college students did not know what the alternative to Christianity was. Many of them blended into general secular culture without knowing what it is or what it meant for them. What 9/11 did for many Korean teenagers and college students was to push them away from Christianity without any clear direction. So, they left Christianity. Most of them did not adopt another religion. Since 9/11 is relatively recent, we can describe the point where they currently are as a state of flight. They just wanted to abandon Christianity.

It was not too difficult for Korean American youth to abandon Christianity, which they saw as a part of the oppressive white culture. The majority of Asian Americans believe that they are marginalized in the United States. And Asian-American youth in the United States do not fit in with cultural institutions tied to the Old Country, either. Thus, it is not difficult to see how an event such as 9/11 can easily unglue Korean American teens from Korean American churches and the Christianity they were taught in these churches. Since 9/11, many Korean American youths have been drifting away from the Korean American church without any clear direction. Interestingly enough, many Korean American churches are abandoning the pro-American position they held before 9/11. Since 9/11 was relatively recent, it is hard to assess completely the nature of the Korean American exodus from Korean American churches and the new direction of Korean American churches. Some churches are reporting over 90 percent of their youth leaving their church, currently.

What this has done is create a very destabilizing reality for the Korean American community. The mass exodus away from Christianity without any clear direction has created a communal vacuum. The Korean American church still is the only real Korean cultural center. Sang Hyun Lee emphasizes the importance of Korean American churches: "Without them, for example, a communication with our second generation will not be possible."[40] Korean American churches tend to be conservative, evangelical churches. But their religious Christian conservatism is matched by their conservatism about Korean culture. When Korean Americans leave the Korean American church, they are not only leaving Christianity. They are in fact leaving the only real connection to Korean culture and the Korean American community available to them as an institution in America. It is still too early to tell what kind of impact this will have on individuals, the Korean American community, and the larger American society as a whole.

The separation from Christianity was not the only reaction caused by 9/11. 9/11 created another extremist reaction among Koreans. Whereas some Koreans chose to abandon Christianity altogether and the only Korean communal center available to them, some Koreans became more aggressively conservative as

Christians and held more firmly to the Korean cultural center of the Korean American church. Thus, it became more and more possible to hear Korean pastors preach from the pulpit against alcohol consumption and dancing. Korean clergy who had been moderate in their preaching tended to become more fundamentalist. And churchgoers followed this trend. Thus, in the past, they may have been willing to overlook certain things such as drinking among their churchgoing friends, but now Korean American laity has taken on almost a witch-hunting stance toward those who engage in drinking, gambling, or dancing. For many Korean American churches in Los Angeles, for instance, drinking came to be equated with being a non-Christian. If you drank alcohol, you could not be a Christian. Such a fundamentalist position came to dominate the popular Korean Christian discourse since 9/11.

Such a fundamentalist trend is not present only among older generations of Korean Americans. Many Korean American teenagers and college students came to adopt aggressively fundamentalist positions. Formerly evangelical Christian groups became fundamentalist. Thus, it would not be surprising for Berkeley Korean Christians to say that a person who was not willing to take the bus 40 minutes to go to a conservative church was not a Christian at all. A person who drinks cannot be a Christian. This kind of fundamentalist Christian discourse came to dominate formerly moderate settings such as UC Berkeley and UCLA among parachurch and church groups.

Some have complained that there was a legalistic dualism developing among some of these fundamentalist Christians. Korean Americans who emphasized that a person who did not take a bus 40 minutes to go to a Bible-believing church was not a Christian were often caught not being able to live up to the fundamentalist Christian standards they set for their communities. Thus, the bars were set aggressively high and the communities that established those rules often were seen as not observing those rules. This worked to create a greater dichotomy within the Korean American community. Korean Americans who left the church used this discrepancy to justify their departure from Christianity. Those in the fundamentalist Christian communities emphasized fundamentalist Christian rules even more to ensure that the violators come into line with the rules set for the Christian community.

Before 9/11, Korean American Christians tended to exist in a broadly evangelical setting, but those days ended with 9/11. Many Korean teenagers left the Korean American church and Christianity altogether. Those who remained in the church did not know what to do and reacted by going in the opposite direction of fundamentalist Christianity. The dichotomized trend is continuing in the Korean American community. It seems that the trend will not stop in the foreseeable future.

In terms of loyalty to America, this has had two divergent results. Those who tended toward fundamentalist Christianity tended to be loyal to the United States as a country. It is not surprising to find those who remained in Christianity joining the FBI and CIA, applying to West Point and the Naval Academy, and enlisting in ROTC programs. Christianity has been identified with the United States in Korean American churches for a long time, so this Korean American perception is the reason for these aggressive acts of loyalty to the United States. Of course, white evangelical Christians will be the first ones to tell them that

America is not a Christian nation. As John MacArthur says, America is not the kingdom of Christ; the kingdom of Christ is in heaven. For Korean American Christians, this is an oxymoron. America is a Christian nation, so to be a Christian means to be loyal to the United States of America.

Whereas Korean American Christians who were becoming more and more fundamentalist Christian became more and more loyal to the United States, those Korean Americans who left the church went the opposite direction. Typically, Korean Americans who left the church also silently renounced their allegiance to the United States. Thus, many Korean Americans who left the Korean American church ally themselves with China politically as well as philosophically. Whereas Korean American Christians tend to be anti-China and pro-America, Korean Americans who left the Christian church tend to be aggressively pro-China and tacitly anti-America. In an unprecedented way, many Korean Americans are drifting into socialist and communist ideologies right now, whereas such a phenomenon was practically nonexistent before 9/11. Thus, we have a situation where some Korean Americans will not think twice about betraying the United States to a foreign power because they do not identify with America. They have left Christianity and with it their fundamental loyalty to the United States of America, which they believe were founded on Christian principles, which they left behind. Thus, whereas it would have been impossible to see a Korean American abet China or North Korea in attacking the United States before 9/11, now there is a young generation of Korean Americans who despise Christianity and all that is related to it who may find themselves allying themselves with China or North Korea, lands they have never even visited. Of course, the trend is relatively new—less than five years old—so it is difficult to say with certainty. But the trend away from pro-America and toward pro-China is continuing among this group of Korean American youth, and the real significance will be felt in the next five to ten years.

NOTES

1. Won Moo Hurh defines the 1.5-generation Korean American in this way: "At this point of discussion, however, the 1.5 generation can ideally-typically be defined as bilingual and bicultural Korean American who immigrated to the United States in early or middle adolescence (generally between the ages of 11 and 16). Simply put, the adolescent immigration, bilingualism, and biculturalism constitute a unique sociocultural and existential context of Korean Americans whose life course appears to be quite different from that of the first and second generation immigrants" (Won Moo Hurh, "The 1.5 Generation: A Cornerstone of the Korean-American Ethnic Community," in *The Emerging Generation of Korean-Americans*, ed. Ho-Youn Kwon and Shin Kim [Seoul: Kyung Hee University Press, 1993], p. 50).

2. The greatest wave of Korean immigration started in the late 1960s and in the 1970s because of two factors: (1) Korean President Park Chung-Hee's positive emigration policy, and (2) the 1965 revision of United States immigration laws (P.L. 89-236) (Ji-Yeon Yuh, *Beyond the Shadow of Camptown: Korean Military Brides in America* [New York: New York University Press, 2002], p. 66).

3. Won Moo Hurh and Kwang Chung Kim, *Korean Immigrants in America: A Structural Analysis of Ethnic Confinement and Adhesive Adaptation* (Rutherford, NJ: Associated University Presses, 1984), p. 21.

4. Hurh and Kim, p. 57.

5. Tae-Hwan Kwak and Seong Hyong Lee, *The Korean-American Community: Present and Future* (Seoul: Kyungnam University Press, 1991), p. 1.

6. Won Moo Hurh, *The Korean Americans* (Westport, CT: Greenwood Press, 1998), p. xv.

7. June Ha, "1.5 and 2.0 Generation of Korean Women," in Kwon and Kim, p. 229.

8. Hurh, p. 164.

9. Hurh and Kim, p. 39. The Korean-American Treaty of 1882 is also known as The Chemulpo Treaty or The Treaty of Amity and Commerce.

10. Sunok Chon Pai, "The Changing Role of Korean-Americans," in Kwon and Kim, pp. 218–19.

11. It would not be wrong to describe anti-white sentiment as historical for Korean Americans. Of the Korean males in the United States during 1912–24, those who could not find Koreans remained single until their death—some 3,000 males. Only 104 Korean males married non-Koreans during this period, and they married Asian-looking women (Romanzo Adams, *Interracial Marriage in Hawaii* [Montclair: Patterson Smith, 1937], pp. 336–37).

12. Chon S. Edwards, *I Am Also a Daughter of Korea* (Seoul: Mi-Rae-Mun-Wha-Sa, 1988), p. 111 [in Korean].

13. Yuh, p. 3.

14. Hurh and Kim, p. 27.

15. Sang-O Rhee, "The Leaders of 21st Century Korean Communities in America: The Role of Second Generation Education," in Kwak and Lee, p. 172.

16. Hurh and Kim, p. 47.

17. Warren Y. Kim, *Koreans in America* (Seoul: Po Chin Chai Printing Co. Ltd., 1971), p. 28.

18. Hurh and Kim, p. 134.

19. A study of Korean American Christians in Chicago revealed that 97 percent, regardless of Christian denomination, preferred an ethnically Korean church. Only 3 percent attended an American church that was not specifically ethnic Korean (Hurh, p. 107).

20. A 1979 survey shows that Koreans value their Korean identity. 94.7 percent of males and 94.4 percent of females were proud to be born ethnically Korean. Furthermore, 90.4 percent of the males and 89.2 percent of the females state that Korean language should be taught. Furthermore, over 60 percent were against intermarriage. And the majority of those who approved of intermarriage approved of it only on the basis of true love and understanding (Huhr and Kim, p. 79).

21. In this regard, the statement of Hurh and Kim is significant: "In sharp contrast to the findings on acculturation, most of the dimensions of ethnic attachment are *not* related to the length of residence in the United States. . . . [R]egardless of the length of residence, a high proportion of our respondents subscribe to Korean newspapers, prefer to associate with Koreans, and prefer to attend the Korean ethnic church. Almost all of them also indicate their strong sense of family priority, ethnic pride, and preference for teaching Korean language to their children. . . . The educational statuses also have no bearing on the degree of ethnic attachment. . . . Generally, most of the respondents show strong feelings of ethnic attachment regardless of the levels of their education." (Hurh and Kim, p. 84). Anyone who visits a Korean church today can attest to the lasting impact of this reality as an integral Korean American experience. Furthermore, a visit to UCLA and UC Berkeley will prove most of this to be true for the youngest generation of Korean Americans, today.

22. A part of the reason for the emphasis in speaking Korean relates to Korean history during the Japanese period when Koreans were forbidden to speak Korean. Regarding this period, Sunny Che writes: "As one of the first colonial acts, Japan took the five-year-old crown prince of Korea to Japan to be reared in the Japanese imperial household and

eventually married to a Japanese princess. She banned the Korean language and national symbols—flag, flower, and anthem—and instituted the Japanese laws and Japanese as the official language. The government bureaucracy, commerce, and schools were conducted all in Japanese" (*Forever Alien: A Korean Memoir, 1930–1951* [Jefferson, NC: McFarland and Company, 2000], p. 7).

23. Speaking Korean is very important to the Korean American community. According to the 1970 Census, 91 percent of the foreign-born Koreans stated that Korean was their primary language. And in the 1973 Asian-American Field Study of Koreatown, Los Angeles, 98 percent of Korean Americans said that they used Korean as their primary language (Eui-Young Yu, "Koreans in America: Social and Economic Adjustments," in *The Korean Immigrant in America*, ed. Byong-Suh Kim and Sang Hyun Lee [Montclair: The Association of Christian Scholars in North America, Inc., 1980], p. 88).

24. Yong Choon Kim, "The Protestant Church and the Korean-American Community," in Kwak and Lee, p. 198.

25. This comment by Hurh and Kim is very important to understanding the experience of second- and third-generation Korean Americans: "Simply put, the more closely Korean immigrants identify themselves with their WASP peers, the more they will experience heightened feelings of relative deprivation, social alienation, and identity ambivalence. At this point, the degree of the immigrant's life satisfaction (psychological adaptation) and their desire for assimilation (sociocultural adaptation) may start to decline. To mitigate the problematic situation, some immigrants may shift their reference group back to their own ethnic group (Koreans) or some may seek their identity and reference group elsewhere . . . the relationship between the length of sojourn and the degree of adaptation (life satisfaction) may not be linear but rather quasicurvilinear." (Hurh and Kim, p. 140).

26. Hurh, p. 121.

27. A recent survey shows 70 percent of all Los Angeles Koreans and 77 percent of all Chicago Koreans are active Christians (Hurh, p. 107).

28. Hurh, p. 106.

29. Hurh, p. 114.

30. Grant S. Lee, "The Future of Korean-American Buddhism," in Kwak and Lee, p. 233.

31. In fact, Kim Samu and Sungsan worked primarily with white Americans and not Korean Americans (Lee, "The Future of Korean-American Buddhism," p. 233).

32. In contrast, Korean Buddhist centers were not Korean cultural centers in America. Almost all major Korean Buddhist centers not only targeted white Americans, but Korean Buddhist monks trained white Americans to be their successors. In some Buddhist centers, 90 percent of the followers were white and 10 percent Asians (Lee, "The Future of Korean-American Buddhism," p. 245).

33. Bong-Youn Choy, *Koreans in America* (Chicago: Nelson Hall, 1979), p. 77.

34. The fact that Korean American identity became integrally intertwined with Christian identity is highlighted by *Korea Week* of February 1978. Only 12 percent of the total population in South Korea was affiliated with a Christian church. In contrast, 70 percent of Korean Americans at the comparable time were affiliated with a Christian church in the United States (Hurh and Kim, pp. 129–30). Many of the Korean Americans who were affiliated with a Christian church were recent converts to Christianity after their immigration.

35. This contrasts with the generic anti-American sentiment that has dominated South Korea for decades, especially as South Korea views the United States as its economic rival (Chongho Kim, "Temptation to Conform and Call to Transform," in Kwon and Kim, p. 257).

36. From the earliest period of Korean immigration to the United States, there was the perception that the United States is a Christian country. This perception became ingrained in the Korean American consciousness. Hyung-Chan Kim criticizes this perception and

even blames it as having had a negative impact on the Korean people. Kim writes: "It is tragic, particularly in view of the fact that so much of the energy and resources of the church were diverted to an unrealistic and naïve notion that the leaders and followers of 'Christian America,' when sufficiently supplicated by their fellow Korean Christians, would assist the Koreans in their fight against Imperial Japan" (Huyung-Chan Kim, "The History and Role of the Church in the Korean American Community," in *The Korean Diaspora: Historical and Sociological Studies of Korean Immigration and Assimilation in North America*, ed. Hyung-Chan Kim [Santa Barbara: ABC-Clio, Inc., 1977], p. 60).

37. Sang Hyun Lee, "Called to Be Pilgrims: Toward a Theology within the Korean Immigrant Context," in Kim and Lee, p. 40.

38. Sang Hyun Lee describes the nature of Korean Christianity: "Under the influence of the westernized Christianity, Korean cultural past has been thought of as something that we must leave behind us. We were brought up perhaps with a greater familiarity with such names as Moses, Joseph, Noah, and Santa Claus than with such names as Won Hyo, Lee Toi Ge, and even Tan Gun. I remember the shocking experience I had a few years ago when I realized that I do not know enough Korean religious and philosophical personages even to count on my fingers! Now here in America, our four thousand year old history is almost totally invisible" (Sang Hyun Lee, "Called to Be Pilgrims," p. 53). Lee's comments highlight the pro-Christian and pro-American (by extension) influence on Korean Christianity, which is even willing to abandon some of its cultural past and historical heritage in support of Christianity or what is perceived as a Christian culture by Korean Christians.

39. Although the Yi Dynasty of the Choson period (1392–1910) pushed Confucianism and persecuted Buddhists, Buddhism actually grew among the people more so than it did in times of peace. Even now, Buddhism claims the largest number of the Korean population (Yong-Joon Choi, *Dialogue and Antithesis: A Philosophical Study on the Significance of Herman Dooyeweerd's Transcendental Critique* [Cheltenham: The Hermit Kingdom Press, 2006], pp. 276–78).

40. Lee, "Called to Be Pilgrims," p. 65.

SUGGESTED READINGS

Abelmann, Nancy, and John Lie. *Blue Dreams: Korean Americans and the Los Angeles Riots.* Cambridge, MA: Harvard University Press, 1995.

Alexander, Jeffrey C., and Steven Seidman, eds. *Culture and Society: Contemporary Debates.* Cambridge: Cambridge University Press, 1990.

Baldassare, Mark, ed. *The Los Angeles Riots: Lessons for the Urban Future.* Boulder, CO: Westview Press, 1993.

Barringer, Herbert, Robert W. Gardner, and Michael J. Levin. *Asians and Pacific Islanders in the United States.* New York: Russell Sage Foundation, 1982.

Berger, P., and T. Luckman. *The Social Construction of Reality.* New York: Doubleday, 1966.

Bernal, M., and G. Knight, eds. *Ethnic Identity: Formation and Transmission among Hispanics and Other Minorities.* Albany: SUNY Press, 1993.

Blalock, Hubert M. *Power and Conflict: Toward a General Theory.* Newbury Park, CA: Sage Publications, 1989.

———. *Toward a Theory of Minority Relations.* New York: Wiley, 1967.

Bonacich, Edna, and Lucie Cheng, eds. Philadelphia: Temple University Press, 1994.

Cohen, Nathan. *The Los Angeles Riots: A Sociological Study.* New York: Praeger, 1970.

Douglas, Jack D. *American Social Order.* New York: Free Press, 1971.

Eriksen, Thomas. *Ethnicity and Nationalism.* London: Pluto Press, 1993.

Feagin, Joe R., and Clairece Booth Feagin. *Discrimination American Style.* Malabar: Robert E. Krieger Publishing, 1986.

Franklin, John H., ed. *Color and Race*. Boston: Beacon, 1969.
Gamson, William A. *The Strategy of Social Protest*. Belmont, NY: Wadsworth, 1990.
George, Lynelle. *No Crystal Stair: African-Americans in the City of Angels*. London: Verso, 1992.
Goffman, Erving. *The Presentation of Self in Everyday Life*. New York: Doubleday, 1965.
Goldberg, David Theo. *Racist Culture: Philosophy and the Politics of Meaning*. Oxford: Blackwell, 1993.
Gooding-Williams, Robert, ed. *Reading Rodney King/Reading Urban Uprising*. New York: Routledge, 1993.
Gordon, Milton M. *Assimilation in American Life: The Role of Race, Religion and National Origins*. New York: Oxford University Press, 1964.
Green, Charles. *The Struggle for Black Empowerment in New York City: Beyond the Politics of Pigmentation*. New York: Praeger, 1989.
Hing, Bill Ong. *Making and Remaking Asian America through Immigration Policy, 1850–1990*. Stanford, CA: Stanford University Press, 1993.
Hodges, Harold M., Jr. *Conflict and Consensus: An Introduction to Sociology*. New York: Harper and Row, 1974.
Kasinitz, Philip. *Caribbean New York: Black Immigrants and the Politics of Race*. Ithaca, NY: Cornell University Press, 1992.
Kim, Illsoo. *New Urban Immigrants: The Korean Community in New York*. Princeton, NJ: Princeton University Press, 1981.
Kinloch, Graham C. *The Dynamics of Race Relations: A Sociological Analysis*. New York: McGraw-Hill, 1974.
Kitano, Harry L. *Race Relations*. Englewood Cliffs, NJ: Prentice-Hall, 1974.
Kurokawa, Minako, ed. *Minority Responses*. New York: Random House, 1970.
Kwon, Ho-Youn, ed. *Korean Americans: Conflict and Harmony*. Chicago: North Park College and Theological Seminary, 1994.
Lee, Dae Kil, ed. *The Current Status and Future Prospects of Overseas Koreans*. New York: Research Institute on World Affairs, 1986.
Lee, Shinyoung. *Impact of Ethnic Identity on Psychological Well-Being among Korean Americans in the United States*. Ph.D. dissertation, School of Social Welfare, State University of New York at Albany, 2001.
Lewy, Thomas, and In Chul Choi. *The Korean American Entrepreneur's Guide to Franchising*. Chicago: Columbia College, Chicago, and Korean American Community Services, 1994.
Light, Ivan, and Edna Bonacich. *Immigrant Entrepreneurs: Koreans in Los Angeles, 1965–1982*. Berkeley: University of California Press, 1988.
Madhubuti, Haki R., ed. *Why L.A. Happened*. Chicago: Third World Press, 1993.
Mangiafico, Luciano. *Contemporary Asian Immigrants: Patterns of Filipino, Korean, and Chinese Settlement in the United States*. New York: Praeger, 1988.
Marger, Martin N. *Race and Ethnic Relations: American and Global Perspectives*. Belmont, NY: Wadsworth, 1991.
Massey, Douglas, and Nancy A. Denten. *American Apartheid: Segregation and the Making of the Underclass*. Cambridge, MA: Harvard University Press, 1993.
McCarthy, Cameron, and Warren Crichlow, eds. *Race, Identity, and Representation in Education*. New York: Routledge, 1993.
Min, Pyong Gap. *Caught in the Middle*. Berkeley: University of California Press, 1996.
———. *Ethnic Business Enterprise: Korean Small Business in Atlanta*. Staten Island, NY: Center for Migration Studies, 1988.
Muhlmann, Wilhelm E. *Rassen, Ethnien, Kulturen: Moderne Ethnologie*. Berlin: Luchterhand, 1964.
Myrdal, Gunnar. *An American Dilemma: The Negro Problem and Modern Democracy*. New York: Harper and Row, 1944.

Omi, Michael, and Howard Winant. *Racial Formation in the United States: From the 1960s to the 1980s*. New York: Routledge, 1986.
Park, Andrew Sung. *Racial Conflict and Healing: An Asian-American Theological Perspective.* Maryknoll, NY: Orbis Books, 1996.
Park, Robert E. *Race and Culture*. Glencoe, IL: Free Press, 1950.
Petersen, William. *Japanese Americans.* New York: Random House, 1971.
Roedinger, David R. *The Wages of Whiteness: Race and the Making of the American Working Class*. London: Verso, 1991.
Roosens, Eugeen E. *Creating Ethnicity: The Process of Ethnogenesis*. Newbury Park, CA: Sage Publications, 1989.
Rosald, Renato. *Culture and Truth*. Boston: Beacon Press, 1993.
Rothschild, Joseph. *Ethnopolitics: A Conceptual Framework*. New York: Columbia University Press, 1981.
Schermerhorn, R. A. *Comparative Ethnic Relations: A Framework for Theory and Research.* New York: Random House, 1970.
Scott, A. J., and E. R. Brown, eds. *South Central Los Angeles: Anatomy of an Urban Crisis*. Los Angeles: The Lewis Center for Regional Policy Studies, University of California, Los Angeles, 1993.
Shaw, Marvin E., and Jack M. Wright. *Scales for the Measurement of Attitudes*. New York: McGraw-Hill, 1967.
Shibutani, Tomatsu, and K. M. Kwan. *Ethnic Stratification*. New York: Macmillan, 1965.
Simpson, George E., and J. Milton Yinger. *Racial and Cultural Minorities*. New York: Harper, 1972.
Sleeper, Jim. *The Closest Strangers: Liberalism and the Politics of Race in New York*. New York: Norton, 1990.
Smith, Anna Deavere. *Twilight: Los Angeles, 1992*. New York: Anchor, 1994.
Sonenshein, Raphael J. *Politics in Black and White: Race and Power in Los Angeles*. Princeton: Princeton University Press, 1993.
Stone, John. *Racial Conflict in Contemporary Society*. Cambridge MA: Harvard University Press, 1985.
Terkel, Studs. *Race: How Blacks and Whites Think and Feel about the American Obsession*. New York: Anchor Books, 1993.
Totten, George O., III, and H. Eric Schockman, eds. *Community in Crisis: The Korean Community after the Los Angeles Civil Unrest of April 1992*. Los Angeles: Center for Multiethnic and Transnational Studies, University of Southern California, 1994.
Turner, Victor. *The Ritual Process: Structure and Anti-Structure*. Chicago: Aldine, 1969.
West, Cornel. *Race Matters*. Boston: Beacon Press, 1993.
Wilson, William Julius. *The Truly Disadvantaged: The Inner City, the Underclass, and Public Policy*. Chicago: University of Chicago Press, 1987.
Wolf, Eric. *Europe and the People without History*. Berkeley: University of California Press, 1982.
Yu, Eui-Young, ed. *Black-Korean Encounter: Toward Understanding and Alliance*. Los Angeles: Institute for Asian American and Pacific Asian Studies, California State University, 1994.
Yu, Eui-Young, and Edward Chang, eds. *Multiethnic Coalition Building in Los Angeles*. Los Angeles: Institute for Asian American and Pacific American Studies, California State University, 1995.
Yu, Eui-Young, Earl H. Phillips, and Eun Sik Yang. *Koreans in Los Angeles*. Los Angeles: Koryo Research Institute and Center for Korean-American and Korean Studies, California State University, 1977.

CHAPTER 10

Sacrificing the Paschal Lamb: A Road toward Peace

Jean Donovan

This chapter will address one of the ways in which the Catholic Church and its membership can help achieve the goals of the World Congress on World's Religions after September 11, namely, to build bridges among the world's religions so as to create a safer, more peaceful community on this earth. It will address questions raised by Professor Leo Lefebure, of Georgetown University in Washington, D.C., concerning the relationship between Christian worship and the ongoing violence prevalent in society. Dr. Lefebure presented a paper recently in which he noted that the theological arguments by Melito of Sardis in the second century, portraying Jesus as the paschal lamb, became the rationale used over the centuries to justify the violent Good Friday rituals directed toward the Jewish community.[1] This chapter will explore the implications of the Catholic Church's incorporation of the rituals of Passover as a foundation for our theology of worship, in particular the use of imagery of sacrificing the innocent lamb, Jesus, for the sins of many. Embedded in the rituals of Passover is the killing of innocent children.[2] Where are we at this point in Christian history, that we must find our salvation by exacting the suffering of the innocent? And by permitting this violent symbolism to remain as a central expression of Catholic self-understanding, to what extent are we perpetuating the religious hatred and violence that exists in the world today? We need to refocus our imagination on the union of the divine and human in Jesus, and the promise that holds for the entire human race. It seems to me that we have to consciously and willingly sacrifice the paschal lamb imagery and symbolism, and redefine Christian worship in ways that are more life-giving, on behalf of global peace.

THE CHALLENGE: RECONSIDER OUR ACCEPTANCE OF VIOLENCE IN RELIGIOUS RITUAL

In his plenary address to the North American Academy of Liturgy in January 2004, Professor Leo Lefebure raised the issue of the relationship between religious rituals and violence. He presented a series of examples of the way in which Christianity, Islam, and Judaism incorporate rituals that both remember the victims of violence and provoke new acts of vengeance and reprisal. He stated:

> . . . rituals are mimetic in a two-fold sense; first, they often re-present acts of violence, making them present in symbolic form and thereby vivid in the consciousness of participants. But second, they often call forth more violence in imitation of the original injury. Ritual responses to violence are tragically ambiguous. They have proclaimed paths of peace and visions of social and cosmic harmony, but in practice rituals have repeatedly offered justifications for attacks on other groups deemed to be enemies. In the present global context of continuing conflict inspired at least in part by religions, I think it is worthwhile to explore the more problematic aspects of violence.[3]

When he gave this address, I would describe the response of the people around me as stunned. Professional liturgists, musicians, pastors, priests, and theologians who spend their lives facilitating prayer and communion with God in worship are inclined to see the positive value in the experience. And yet, the buzz in the room was that Professor Lefebure was saying something important, and the participants were listening. I, too, was stunned by what he was saying.

In June of that same year, Professor Lefebure continued to pursue this line of thought with a paper he gave at the meeting of the Catholic Theological Society of America. He asked me to respond to his paper at that conference. This personal invitation to engage the issues with him eventually led to a paper I wrote for a theological conference at the University of Leuven, in Belgium, in November 2005.[4] The immediate impetus for that paper came from an email from my seventeen-year-old daughter Kate. She and her high-school friends were studying the story of the Passover in their religion class and were having some problems.

> I have a question for you. We are discussing the story of Moses in Religion class right now. One of my friends, Meg, is struggling with the 10th plague. God killing children is an upsetting thought for her. We were talking about it on our free [period] today, but no one could come up with a good answer. I figured you would be a good person to ask (since after all, you know just a little about theology). What are your thoughts?[5]

It became clear to me that it was time to reconsider the way in which we have tolerated violence, especially violence against the innocent, as an acceptable, even laudable dimension of our religious ritual. And I came to see that the use of the image of Jesus as the paschal lamb and our ready acceptance of the Passover rituals as expressive of Christian self-understanding were embedded in the religious practices that Dr. Lefebure criticized. I would invite the reader to consider Dr. Lefebure's challenge in his or her own religious practices.[6]

TO SACRIFICE ONE'S LIFE ON BEHALF OF THE OTHER

To begin, a story. It was the first weekend of summer. The weather was warm, the river inviting. Grieving over the loss of their mother and wife, this small family, fishing poles and lunch in hand, heads out to play and laugh, live and enjoy the day with their friends. A father, two six-year-old twin boys, and Helen, a family friend, stand in the muddy riverbank, fishing poles in hand. It is the last weekend of May, the water still cold, the underwater currents running fast and strong. One of the twin boys, Eddie, slips and falls into the river. Almost in an instant, he's pulled under the water and bobs downstream. Screaming, scrambling, people run back and forth along the bank. Bill, his father, jumps into the water. Helen follows him. Both are pulled along in the strong currents. Bill grabs Eddie, and lifts him over his head. Pushed down river, they float toward a pier. Quick hands grab Eddie. Bill has lost consciousness and slips under the water. John Hanson dives into the water, and brings him back to the surface. With the help of others on the pier, Bill and Helen are pulled from the water. Bill is not breathing. Mr. Hanson begins CPR. The paramedics arrive, but it's too late; they can't revive him. Bill is dead. Helen is taken to the hospital, in critical condition.

Not with idle curiosity, but sincere sympathy, news of these events spread throughout the community. The local newspaper reported the story, and interviewed family and neighbors. One friend of Bill's said, "What parent wouldn't risk their own life for the life of their child? There's no thought behind that action. He cared for them very much, and he did what he could to provide them a good life. Like any parent, he did what he had to do."[7] *He did what he had to do.* This heroic act of self-sacrifice seemed self-evident to many: what parent would not risk, even give up, their own life to save their child?

This powerful image of self-sacrifice as a virtue, an ideal, is deeply embedded in Christian sensibilities and spirituality. Jesus preaches about not just loving one's child, but loving one's enemies.[8] And in the powerful moments when he was gathered with his disciples at table shortly before his arrest and death, he inaugurated the rituals of the Eucharist, the bread and wine that became his body and blood. He proclaimed his death as salvific, effectively transforming evil and sinfulness into blessing and healing.[9] For Catholics, the celebration of the ritual of the Eucharist has been a central aspect of worship throughout the centuries. But the true birth of Christianity did not come with Jesus's death, for his followers scattered; rather it came with the glory of the resurrection, when Jesus overcame the very power of death itself. And the command to do as Jesus did was clear, "I give you a new commandment: love one another. As I have loved you, so you should also love one another."[10]

Because we can readily understand the holiness of self-gift, when one human being loves another beyond self-interest, even to the point of accepting death for the other, and we can see how powerful an image the self-sacrifice of Jesus was to the early church, we need now to examine the nature of the Passover imagery to see what problems lie within it.

IMAGE IN QUESTION: JESUS AS THE PASCHAL LAMB

Why has the Christian community incorporated the story of the Passover as integral to the Christian message? And at what cost have we come to use the image of Jesus as the paschal lamb? How often do we think seriously and consider the actual content of the narrative that we have embraced? The experience recorded in the book of Exodus is centered on the conflict between Moses and the Pharaoh. God unleashes ten plagues on the people of Egypt, on behalf of Moses and the Israelites. The plagues begin when the rivers and waterways are turned to blood, polluting them and killing the fish. Then frogs emerge from the river and swarm their homes, then gnats, then flies. A pestilence kills the Egyptians' livestock, and then boils cover their bodies. Hail rains down, beating down plants and splitting trees. Locusts eat whatever vegetation was not destroyed by the hail. The whole land is covered in darkness for three days and then, finally, the first-born child of every family in Egypt is killed. The righteous Israelites are protected from these plagues, and through the ritual of Passover, as the blood of a lamb is shed, then poured onto the doorposts and lintel, their children are saved. Repeated throughout is the relentless "hardening" of Pharaoh's heart purportedly inflicted by God as part of this Passover event ("The Lord hardened Pharaoh's heart"[11]).

How did this ritual of Passover become incorporated into Christian self-understanding, and celebrated within the Christian liturgy? Why has Jesus been named the paschal lamb? Biblical scholars can point to its inclusion in the New Testament.[12] Lefebure notes the influence of *On Pascha* by Melito of Sardis (late second century).[13] As part of the Office of Readings for Holy Thursday, a portion of the text reads:

> There was much proclaimed by the prophets about the mystery of Passover: that mystery is Christ, and to him be glory for ever and ever. Amen. . . . He was led forth like a lamb; he was slaughtered like a sheep. He ransomed us from our servitude to the world, as he had ransomed Israel from the hand of Egypt: he freed us from our slavery to the devil, as he had freed Israel from the hand of Pharaoh. He sealed our souls with his own Spirit, and the members of our body with his own blood.
>
> He is the One who covered death with shame and cast the devil into mourning, as Moses cast Pharaoh into mourning. He is the One who smote sin and robbed iniquity of offspring, as Moses robbed the Egyptians of their offspring. He is the One who brought us out of slavery into freedom, out of darkness into light, out of death into life, out of tyranny into an eternal kingdom; who made us a new priesthood, a people chosen to be his own for ever. He is the Passover of our salvation.[14]

What does it mean to say that the mystery of Passover is the mystery of Christ? Does he argue for the necessary suffering of Jesus to redeem sinful humanity? Or does it mean the necessary suffering of the other, the nonbeliever, whose death brings about new life? Or both?

If we revisit the story of Bill, and the way in which he saved the life of his son, the impact of what I am saying may be clearer. In order to save Eddie, Bill is not going to jump into the water. Rather, forces will be unleashed to punish the river for its coldness, the people on the banks for enjoying themselves. Fish will choke as the waters become polluted, and all of the children playing there must die. All this must happen, for Eddie to survive. And Bill, his father, will readily agree to the spread of this evil, for what matters only is saving his own son.

What an outrageous, absurd claim. Right? And yet, are we not proclaiming the death of the innocent and the destruction of the earth's inhabitants, when we embrace the story of the ten plagues of Egypt? As Catholics, when we proclaim the centrality of the Paschal Mystery, are we not accepting this narrative as revelatory of our beliefs? And the question for us today is, considering the times we live in, can we in good conscience allow this violent ritual remembering of Passover to define our Catholic understanding of the sacrifice of the mass, in the emphasis on the innocent suffering of Jesus as salvific, and in the structure of the Sunday liturgy? Especially if we recall Professor Lefebure's line of thought, that ritually revisiting this violence actually engenders new violence. I would argue that this Passover narrative is dangerous to the people who live today.

To understand how dangerous this narrative, and others, can be, it would be worthwhile to take time to consider the power of stories to affect identity, opinion, and emotional commitments, and to instigate trouble.

THE POWER OF DESTRUCTIVE NARRATIVES

Embedded in the ritual of Passover lies a story. When retold, that story takes on new life, new importance, to the people present at the retelling. Stories tell us about things that have happened, and what they should mean to us today. What are the possible messages that could be learned from the retelling of the Passover stories? It seems to me that they are destructive narratives permitting wholesale violence against those deemed to be "the enemy." I would turn your attention to Robert Schreiter's text, *Reconciliation.*[15] He is a professor of doctrinal theology at Catholic Theological Union in Chicago. In his work in Latin America and South Africa, Bob Schreiter began to build a theology of reconciliation that would help heal communities torn apart by violence. As he explores the way in which narratives undergird the power of oppression, he identifies "narratives of the lie."

> Violence tries to destroy the narratives that sustain peoples' identities and substitute narratives of its own. These might be called narratives of the lie, precisely because they are intended to negate the truth of a people's own narratives. . . . The assumption is that the lie will come to be accepted as the truth if the original narrative can be suppressed or at least co-opted. Any attempt on the part of a population to return to its older, favored narratives is met with violence or the threat of violence. Random violence also may be used to punctuate the fragility of a population's safety. . . . How do we actually overcome the suffering caused by such violence and move to reconciliation and forgiveness? . . . overcoming the narrative of the lie, a narrative that insinuates its way into our individual and collective psyches by coiling itself around our most basic senses of security and self. It is only when we embrace a redeeming narrative that we can be liberated from the lie's seductive and cunning power.[16]

The narrative of the people of Egypt, their culture, history, religious beliefs, their place in God's world, in God's loving embrace, in God's plan for the human race, is eradicated by this narrative of the lie. God so hated the people of Egypt that

God would reign down terror and destruction and heart-wrenching sorrow on them to punish them. And Moses and the Jewish people must accept and believe this Passover narrative as good, in order to secure their place in God's eyes, their place in the Promised Land. How can the Passover stories be anything but destructive of human life, love, and community? And once again, why would the Christian community allow this narrative to define the way in which Christ becomes united with the human race, and with the people he chose to serve? This question is particularly poignant since biblical scholars point out that the events recorded in Exodus of the Passover may very well have no basis in historical fact.[17]

It would be best to let this narrative die. The responsible thing to do is to move away from this destructive narrative, and move toward those that will heal the wounds of religious hatred, racism, and violence. Christine Smith, Associate Professor of Preaching at Union Theological Seminary, writes in an article entitled "Sin and Evil in Feminist Thought," "in my own work, *resistance* has become the guiding word. Part of our resistance to evil must be our work that is theological in nature and content. To provide critiques of theologies of the cross that justify and condone human suffering of every description is an act of resistance."[18] On behalf of my daughter, her friends, and her generation, I choose to resist the narratives of Passover as in any way expressive of my Christian faith. I will not support the destruction of a people, their homes, crops, animals, and children as the path to salvation. And in our worship, rather than to focus on Jesus as a lamb to be slaughtered, I would argue that the theological foundation of the liturgy needs a different focus: that of the incarnation.

LITURGICAL REFOCUSING: THE WORD MADE FLESH

The challenge for Catholics seems clear: sacrifice the imagery and symbolism of the paschal lamb, on behalf of global peace, on behalf of the children born today who need a better world than the one we are giving them. I would not say that this is an impossible task. In fact, just this past week I presented this challenge to a group of Catholic priests, all of whom are engaged in full-time ministry, leading parishes filled with ordinary and extraordinary people, all struggling to find meaning, purpose, and happiness in their lives. These priests, given some time to assimilate the depth of the problems and the faith and imagination needed for solutions, seemed willing and able to take up the charge. Find a life-giving way to celebrate the gift of God's own self in Jesus to the world. None of them seemed angry with me for challenging ancient and well-known symbols.

Last year when I wrote the paper for the Leuven conference, I suggested that perhaps the Western tradition needs to be inspired by the spirituality of the liturgy of the East, and the centrality of the incarnation in worship. The gift of the incarnation is the redeeming gift of God, uniting humanity with the divine. St. Athanasius, a fourth-century bishop, considered the question of the meaning of Jesus's life on earth in *On the Incarnation.* In many ways, Melito and Athanasius faced the same hostile world, wrote apologetically about their faith in Christ with the same fervor, and focused on Jesus's suffering as instrumental, but Athanasius declared the salvific importance of the incarnation.

> We have seen that to change the corruptible to incorruption was proper to none other than the Savior himself, Who in the beginning made all things out of nothing; that only the Image of the Father could re-create the likeness of the Image in men, that none save our Lord Jesus Christ could give to mortals immortality.[19]

The gift of God is immortality. Modern-day Orthodox theologian Father George Dion Dragas, drawing inspiration from St. Athanasius' statement, that Jesus "became human so that we may become divine," argues that "the Son's inhomination is an eschatological (i.e., final and irreversible) but also saving event."[20] Father Dion emphasizes the holistic nature of the celebration of the life, ministry, death, and resurrection of Jesus within the Orthodox liturgy.

> In the Divine Liturgy, the central act of Orthodox worship, we celebrate the whole saving economy of the Incarnate son of God. His descent from heaven and his birth at Bethlehem is represented liturgically by the Prothesis. His public ministry is represented by the Liturgy of the Catechumens. His entry into Jerusalem, followed by his Last or Mystical Supper, his death, burial, resurrection and ascension, are represented by the Liturgy of the Faithful. These three parts constitute the context of the mystery and glorification of the Triune God. Here we have the celebration or representation of the twin mystery of the faith, which rests on the two realities of the Trinity and the Incarnation.[21]

Father Dion argues for the embodiment of incarnational theology in the liturgy. What if the celebration of the incarnation would take on a more prominent role in Roman Catholic worship?

If the incarnation became central to the worship, it would be reflected throughout the liturgy. In the opening prayers as the liturgy begins, not only would voices be raised in praise of God, and in expressions of humility in face of one's failings, but words of gratitude should and would be spoken. The community should celebrate, truly celebrate, the gift of life, family, friends, work, and leisure. The ability to think, and breathe, and smile, to laugh and talk—the gift of life itself would be recalled with fervor. And not only laments for our failings, but our words would ring out with what we actually did right this week. We are silent about the good in our lives. This should change.

To celebrate the incarnation we would have to remember that the homily is a reflection on the good news of salvation, not a critique of our sinfulness, or a plea for the financial needs of the parish. The prayers of the faithful should include all of humanity, not only in its suffering, but in its joy. Most churches pray for the church leadership, the incidents of the week that caused harm, for vocations, the sick, and the dead. During holy week, we mention non-Catholics, and pray for them. Let's pray for the whole human race every week. And why not add a thought or two of celebration, for the ecumenical movement, for social movements that build ties and help neighborhoods? And after the consecration and consumption of the body and blood that Jesus has given to us, why not reflect on the union and communion that have been achieved through this act of faith? God becomes united with us in Jesus. And that work of divinizing the human being is taking place. Since the Catholic Church celebrates the Eucharist each and every week, the possibility of reflecting on the transformative power of the incarnation within the

Eucharist is readily available. Seeing the good in ourselves and others, seeing us as part of the human race, seeing what we share in common, what binds and holds us together as a community no matter the diversity, these would be words and actions that bring healing. And maybe help to end the culture of violence that surrounds us.

CONCLUSION

It seems to me that in today's world, we need to refocus our imagination on the union of the divine and human in Jesus, and the promise that holds for the entire human race. We have so emphasized the suffering of the cross in our liturgical expressions that we may very well be falling into the trap of encouraging the imitation and reenactment of violence in real life. To take Leo Lefebure's challenge seriously calls us to reconsider our narratives, especially our association with the Passover narratives of Exodus.

NOTES

1. Leo Lefebure, "Memory, Mimesis, Healing: Ritual Responses to Violence in the Abrahamic Traditions," *Proceedings of the North American Academy of Liturgy* (2004), pp. 41–63.
2. Exodus 12:29–36.
3. Lefebure, p. 42. In his address, Professor Lefebure focuses on the Christian use of the Passover imagery to blame Jews for the death of Jesus, leading to violence during Holy Week against Jews, to the violence between Moslem sects during the day of remembering the martyrdom of Husayn, the grandson of Mohammed, and the hatred of the other evoked in the Jewish feast of Purim.
4. "The Incarnation in Hiding: Must Our Worship Be Built on the Suffering of the Innocent?" (paper presented at the Leuven Encounters in Systematic Theology Conference V, November, 2005)
5. January 13, 2005.
6. It is not my place to in any way comment on the way the Jewish community interprets and incorporates the violence against the Egyptians within their celebration of Passover. A simple survey of some current articles shows, though, that it is an issue that is being addressed. For example, Thomas Mann points to a Haggadah, "Our triumph is diminished by the slaughter of the foe," from *A Passover Haggadah*, 2d rev. ed., Central Conference of American Rabbis, ed. Herbert Bronstein (New York: Penguin, 1982), pp. 48–49, in his article "Passover: The Time of Our Lives," *Interpretation* 50, no. 3 (July 1996).
7. Nate Guidry, "Father drowns trying to save son," *Pittsburgh Post-Gazette*, May 30, 2006, A-1, A-6; and Jonathan D. Silver, "Boater missing in 3rd incident," *Pittsburgh Post-Gazette*, May 31, 2006, A-1, A-8.
8. Luke 6:27.
9. Matthew 26:26–30.
10. John 13:34.
11. Exodus 11:10.
12. Norman Theiss points to 1 Peter 1:17–21 in "The Passover Feast of the New Covenant," *Interpretation* 48, no. 1 (January 1994).
13. Lefebure, p. 43.

14. "The Lamb That Was Slain—Melito of Sardis," from the website of Dr. Marcellino's The Crossroads Initiative, www.dritaly.com. Dr. Marcellino refers to this excerpt as a "wonderful homily," apparently immune to the significance of Melito's praise for the killing of Egyptian children.

15. Robert Schreiter, *Reconciliation* (Maryknoll, NY: Orbis, 1992).

16. Schreiter, pp. 34–36.

17. Carroll Stuhlmueller, C.P. wrote in his chapter "The Foundations for Mission in the Old Testament": "If a pivotal or key position of Israel's religion, such as the exodus out of Egypt or the acquisition of the Promised Land, left no trace in the archives of Egyptian or Canaanite nations, can we honestly characterize these events as 'historical?'" (Senior and Stuhlmueller, p. 11).

18. Christine Smith, "Sin and Evil in Feminist Thought," *Theology Today* 50, no. 2 (1993): 208–19.

19. St. Athanasius, *On the Incarnation*, 20, http://www.spurgeon.org/~phil/history/ath-inc.htm.

20. Father George Dion Dragas, "The Incarnation and the Holy Trinity," *Greek Orthodox Theological Review* 43, no. 1–4 (1998): 257. St. Athanasius, *De Incarnatione*, 54, in Dragas, p. 257.

21. Dragas, p. 272.

CHAPTER 11

Seeking the Peace of the Global City of Knowledge of God after 9/11

Aaron Ricker

The confluence in 2006 of a Conference on World's Religions after September 11, a (CSSR/CTS) Conference on The City: A Festival of Knowledge, and a (CETA) Conference on Seeking the Peace of the City set me thinking.[1] These efforts to relate theological/religious knowledge to urban life on the one hand, and national disaster on the other, made my thoughts turn toward Augustine's *Civitate Dei.* What might a post-9/11 North American city of God look like? How might the peace be kept in that city? The more I thought about it, the less quixotic the question seemed, because (as I will suggest below) Augustine's situation was, in many ways, not so very different from our own.

SEEKING PEACE IN AUGUSTINE'S POLEMICAL *CITY*

Augustine's *City of God* is like a long-burning match. It owes the lasting heat and light of its inspiration to kindling contradiction—the right question "striking" the right mind, and "rubbing it the wrong way," at the right time. The question, famously, was this: as a Christian and a Roman citizen, how could Augustine explain the fact that dignified, civilized *Roma* had been exposed by her new divine patron, Israel's "Mighty King, Lover of Justice," and Jesus Christ his "Prince of Peace," to the humiliating rape of barbarian conquest? Augustine's answer—his *City*—was therefore conceived in controversy and contradiction. This fact is partly responsible for, and not a little exacerbated by, his decision to address the question of Christian theodicy and the sack of Christian Rome *in the form of* a contradiction—a polemic "Against the Pagans," in the words of his subtitle. P. R. L. Brown writes that "[a]bove all, *De*

Civitate Dei is a book of controversy," and concludes that this simple fact has complex consequences when it comes to describing and discussing the book's political arguments:

> It should never be treated as though it were a static, complete photograph of Augustine's thought. It reads like a film of a professional boxing championship. . . . Augustine is a really stylish professional: he rarely relies on the knock-out; he is out to win the fight on points. It is a fight carried on in twenty-two books [over more than] ten years. . . . To try to extract from this infinitely flexible book a rigidly coherent system of political ideas is like trying to square the circle: it is a problem that has fascinated many great minds, and baffled all of them.[2]

As if to perfect the dynamism—not to say confusion—of this picture, Augustine's *City* was published *serially,* which most likely exacerbated its tendency to digression, and it was written with widely varying audiences in mind.[3] At this point a scholarly excuse presents itself, and I accept it gladly: I have no particular reason to try to cultivate a great medievalist mind for myself and then baffle it. I will not, therefore, attempt to make Augustine systematic where he has chosen to be occasional—I will not try to square Augustine's circular boxing ring. I will instead take advantage of the para-scholarly context of this volume, and simply point out *general currents* of thought in the *City of God* that look particularly relevant to any discussion of religion and peace in a post-9/11 world.

The most obvious point of contact has just been touched upon: Augustine wrote his *City* because Christian Rome had been seriously wounded by the Visigoths, a visibly similar (i.e., Christian) but equally visibly alien (i.e., Arian) and hostile group. The great city's entire colonial satellite system had been destabilized, and its devotees disillusioned. Augustine wrote at the time that some of his contemporaries "began to blaspheme . . . more ferociously and bitterly than before."[4] The political event of Rome's humiliation involved, in short, a serious "psychological impact," and some serious theological distress.[5] "Rome [was] suffering, it was thought, because she ha[d] forsaken the gods of her fathers in favour of a God Who counsel[led] meekness and submission."[6]

To religion scholars, this story of a time long, long ago in a land far, far away has a surprisingly familiar ring. The imperial Rome of our time, the United States, has been wounded by a splinter religious group that, like the U.S. majority, lays some claim to the heritage of Abraham—a monotheistic "people of the book" like themselves, but that is nevertheless identifiably "other." The U.S. umbrella of control and confidence has been visibly shaken by this cruel and humiliating attack, and part of this destabilization is, as with ancient Rome, to be found in the religious/theological sphere. "How could God let this happen?" many people asked, and some concluded, like their ancient Roman counterparts before them, that corrupt and/or meek religion was to blame. They blamed anti-religious secularism, or sinful complacency in the name of tolerance, or both.

Faced with ideas like these, I am found, like Augustine, in the position of a latter-day Deuteronomist, trying to defuse and counter claims that disaster has come because "that old-time religion" has been wrongly neglected. Just as Jeremiah had to defend against the idea that abandoning Ishtar had opened Israel to harm and want, and Augustine had to defend against the idea that abandoning Mars had exposed Rome to attack, anyone writing a *City of God* for today would, in my opinion, need to defend against the idea that the slow death of state-sanctioned prayer and creationist teachings in schools, the banning of religious texts such as the ten commandments from secular courthouse walls, and the decline of "one Christian nation over all" thinking in general is to blame for the tragedy of September 11. Undertaking such a project would thus inevitably, in my opinion, force its writer into arguing that the many and various religious and so-called irreligious groups of our world can and should coexist peacefully. That is, at least, what I would do.

At this point, many discriminating readers will begin to suspect that I am comparing myself to Augustine, and that I am suggesting that we can all just get along. Please let me clear away those doubts: I *am* comparing myself to Augustine, and I *am* saying that we can all get along. There are, obviously, crucial distinctions to be made: in comparing myself to Augustine, for example, I do not pretend to have his abilities or his authority. I do, though, find myself, like him, in the position of a religion scholar and religious thinker, intimately connected in political and cultural terms to the wounded imperial power in question and yet a foreigner with various loyalties of my own. Perhaps more to the point, I find myself, like him, writing about the disaster years later in retrospect, and find myself answering questions about the ups and downs of so-called real and earthly cities with questions about ideal and spiritual cities. As for suggesting that we in North America (and by extension the world) can all get along, it must be understood that I am not (and this is crucial) asserting that we can do so because we are all really saying the same thing. I will explain what I am saying soon enough, but for the moment it is enough to understand that my belief that we *can* all get along even though we are *not* all saying the same thing would make my *City of God* somewhat different from Augustine's.

A DIFFERENT APPROACH TO DIALOGUE WITH "THE PAGANS"

Although my *City of God* would, like Augustine's, naturally find it necessary to address the question of how Christianity related to other forms of religious wisdom and practice, it would not treat them as hostile systems opposed to, or well-meaning but inferior substitutes for, Christianity as I understood that faith.[7] Augustine's idea of Christian identity led him to spend a great deal of time and energy opposing heretics, and to build his *City* as a bulwark "against the pagans," in the words of his famous subtitle.[8] He was careful, for example, to mock the wisdom of the Egyptians as well as that of the Greeks.[9] Might it not have been possible, though, for him to build a city of God *for* the pagans instead? I consider myself to be as Christian as Augustine, but I wonder: even if Christians must continue to imagine "pagans" in the etymological sense of anyone who through some inexplicable backwardness manages to be happy outside our city, can we not imagine cities of God that are built in such a way as to help us go out to meet them, or at the very least invite them in? I wonder if we might even have a special in, or an edge, as we consider ourselves to be living in a global village, in imagining/building cities of God *for* the "pagans."

Of course, any such modern attempt would seek and find ample ancient resources. It would perhaps find justification in traditional material such as Isaiah

19:25: "Blessed be Egypt my people, and Assyria the work of my hands." A post-9/11 *City of God* might well ask its audience to imagine a prophet presenting such an oracle today. Imagine a priest delivering a message to the White House, wherein Jesus blesses Iran and Iraq, and calls them "my people." Imagine an imam delivering a message to the Saudi court or to some little al-Qaeda cell, in which Allah coos over "America the work of my hands." At best, such prophets would be dismissed as unrealistic bleeding hearts. At worst, they would (like Isaiah) be violently attacked themselves, as traitors. My post-9/11 *City of God,* on the other hand, would seek to understand and apply the scandalous optimism (dare I say the pluralist hope?) of Isaiah 19:25.

What, for instance, are we to make of the offerings "the nations" bring to the God of Israel in the new holy cities of Isaiah's vision?[10] Could not some of these offerings be thought of as philosophical or theological offerings? The Jewish and Christian Bibles are emphatic about the need for, indeed primacy of, such offerings. The gospels tell us, for example, that Jesus quoted Israel's *shema* when asked to name the most crucial requirement of God, and that when he did, he specifically added/underlined the need for a loving offering of "all one's *mind.*"[11] Could not a vision that expected the "other" of the "pagan" nation—including even the often-demonic figure of Egypt and Assyria—to be accepted by God along with their offerings allow respect or at least openness when considering the offerings of its "pagan" and "other" mind?

It is true that Isaiah's vision has a pronounced tendency toward theology that we would call eschatological, but I do not consider that a reason to exclude its picture of Zion from theological imagination and analysis directed toward my own time. I am, in this way, not straying far from Augustine. He viewed his city of God as being one of two spiritual cities that transcended time and space, and found themselves "intermingled" in this life.[12] Now, for me at least, this image of human life as a choice between the citizenships of two timeless cities is reminiscent of the "two cities" Barbara Rossing has identified in the theo-ethical exhortation of another eschatological work, that is, the book of Revelation.[13]

I admit that the decision to bring Revelation into my discussion of Augustine and the *City of God* has its ironies, given that in Revelation Rome *is* the pagan *and* the destroyer. I know, too, that every generation thinks Revelation is talking about them. I wonder, though: what if that is Revelation's aim? Many of the book's most remarkable strategies, such as its insistently vague symbolism, its constant toggling between future realities and liturgies in the present tense, and so on, certainly seem to allow such a reading. What if Revelation actually does want its audiences to think that it is somehow all about their own time? What if Revelation is right? How might Revelation be about us today?

One interesting point for our purposes might be the fact that in Revelation's city of God, there is no sea. Once the evil city ("Babylon") is gone, and the vision of the new heavens and earth has come with the divine city of New Jerusalem, "there [is] no more sea." This odd detail has been explained by some as symbolizing the end of the foreign oppressors and forces of chaos symbolized elsewhere by seas and sea monsters.[14] The book of Revelation's insistent negative water and sea imagery has been interpreted as a condemnation of Roman-style colonial militarism; Rome's armies traveled by sea.[15] It has also been interpreted in economic terms, as the end of the Roman empire's unfair trade, which depended upon sea traffic.[16]

Such explanations make a lot of sense. What if, though, we add the possibility that the disappearance of the sea could also be related to *theological* colonialism and foreignness, and to economies of *ideas?* It is a truism of our time and place that there are no oceans for Internet users. Knowledge of God can find its way from Korea to Canada in seconds, and all lands are indeed, in theory at least, now capable of bearing all theological fruits in our contemporary approximation of the timelessly present apocalypse. It seems to me, therefore, that some of the Information Age hype is true, and that the economy of ideas really has been utterly transformed for many of us, allowing us to participate (however imperfectly) in a city of God in which "the knowledge of God" can, in the prophet's words, "cover the earth like water covers the sea." The approach of my North American *City of God* for the present day to other religions would therefore turn out to be very different from Augustine's.

At this point, though, one might reasonably wonder: is it realistic to expect that we can gain knowledge of God from our neighbors, including potentially in this case our fellow global villagers? Is it realistically possible, to be more specific, for people who identify as Christians to see that they have things to learn from non-Christians, as well as things to share? For my part, I wonder why not. One Christian approach that could make it work is the one I have elsewhere called "Conversatianity." A Conversatian Christianity would take Jesus's claim in John's gospel to *be* the truth very seriously, and thus approach intrareligious and interreligious dialogue accordingly. A Conversatian understanding of dialogue within the global village could, in my view, quite easily support the writing of a Christian *City of God for the Pagans.*

A CONVERSATIAN APPROACH TO DIALOGUE

When it comes to truth, "Jesus Christ says something rather remarkable," as John C. Medaille recently pointed out. "He claims to *be* 'the Way, the Truth, and the Life.' This means that the truth is, ultimately, not some object, such as a pure and distinct idea, but a subject, an acting, self-aware person."[17] Now, a personal truth would, like any person, naturally always seem different to different observers, and yet always be the same. This Johannine view of truth could thus explain the shocking universalism of that gospel's opening assertion that the "light" that is Christ the Logos somehow "enlightens *every* human being."[18]

From this point of view, we can also better see and better understand the fact that John's famous *Logos* prologue exhibits a strong Conversatian character. In John's two simple lines, the God of the book of Genesis who creates with a word is related to the Word (Logos) seen by Greek philosophy behind creation, then to the Lady Wisdom (Hokmah) whom Jewish Wisdom literature sees behind creation, and finally to the Cosmic Christ incarnated in Jesus.[19] What I call Conversatianity, then, seems—far from being new—to be an established *implicit* Christian approach to truth.

It is well-known, for example, that perfectly orthodox Christians worship a trinity who is, in words attributed to St. Gregory, "at the same time both unified and differentiated . . . a strange and paradoxical diversity-in-unity and unity-in-diversity."[20] Orthodox Christology further asserts that this paradoxical God became "both fully divine and fully human" in Jesus of Nazareth, making Christian dogma Conversatian at the core. The Christian Bibles are also highly Conversatian texts, and include many assertions and stories that differ sharply.[21] All Christian Bibles, for example, include the four gospel writers' highly contradictory accounts of who came to the resurrected Jesus's tomb and when, how many angels they saw there, and what happened next. Such contradictory accounts—like all other famous scriptural inconsistencies, both real and apparent—could have been edited and harmonized, but apparently the Christians who collected and assembled them were far more comfortable with "scriptural contradictions" than Christians are today. Examples could, of course, be multiplied at great length. Paul's letters tell us that Christians "were saved," and "are being saved," and "will be saved."[22] In the gospels, Jesus teaches that the kingdom of God is both here already unnoticed and "coming soon in a way that will be impossible to ignore," and so on.[23] These early editors shared—or at least respected—the Conversatian approach of Christianity's sacred texts.

Finally, it seems highly significant from a Conversatian point of view that all Christian Bibles include material from texts and systems commonly called non-biblical and non-Christian. The Hebrew Bible cites many scriptures that are lost completely. One reads of the book of the Wars of Yahweh, the book of Jashar, the Acts of Solomon, Visions of Iddo the Seer, and so on.[24] The New Testament, for its part, quotes "pagan" and extracanonical sources quite freely. Acts 17.28, for example, paraphrases Aratus' *Phaenomena* 5. 1 Corinthians 15.33 quotes Menander's *Thais*, Frg. 218. Titus 1.12 quotes Epimenides' *De Oraculis/Peri Chresmon*. Jude 14–15 quotes 1 Enoch 1.9 as an authority, and 2 Peter 2.4–5 also cites Enochic material.

Not only, then, do the Christian Bibles model intrareligious dialogue (i.e., conversation between different Christian systems of thought); they model interreligious dialogue as well (i.e., conversation with non-Christian systems of thought). For many Christians, this is a difficult lead to follow. They are willing to accept the Gospel of John's use of the pagan *Greek* Logos concept, but they do not want to think about the implications of such Christocentric syncretism when it comes to engaging their own pluralistic societies. They are willing to accept that Christian life is, as Edward Moore argues, living in and according to the *Logos* of John's gospel, but they are not willing to engage that Logos in any other extra-Christian guise, even though John's gospel also says that the *Logos* of Christ "enlightens every human being."[25] Many Christians would be unwilling, for example, to think that if John's gospel were written today it might begin with, "In the beginning was the *Dao.*" Such language would make them very uncomfortable, even though it is a perfectly logical way to follow John 1's lead, and even though this is, in fact, exactly the way in which some Chinese Bibles render John 1.1, due to Daoism's emphasis on kenosis and humility, its concept of a preexistent and pervasive creative power, and other attributes. These translations go on to quote Jesus as saying, "I *am* the *Dao.*"[26]

CONVERSATIANITY AND ISLAM

In the aftermath of 9/11, though, most North Americans are more likely to ask if my Conversatian approach could possibly work with Islam rather than Daoism. As far as I can see, the answer is a clear yes, even on the most literal creedal level, and at the points usually considered most deadly to dialogue between Christianity and Islam. The most obvious example is probably the famous Qur'anic denials of Jesus's divinity. These passages in the Qur'an, though, always take the form of warnings against polytheism, against any Messiahs too proud to be earthly creatures or to be called God's apostle, and against mythological ideas of literal (sexual) divine impregnation.[27] A careful Conversatian approach to dialogue with Islam might very well note that orthodox Christians oppose all of these ideas too, thus opening the door for a discussion of a range of ideas about what the Qur'an might mean when it says that Jesus was a "Spirit from God . . . the Messiah . . . His Word cast into Mary."[28] If one is open to the common Muslim view that the Qur'an is capable of bearing many interpretations (one scholar proposed "308,800 potential interpretations" for every single verse!), the door between Christian and Islamic thought may prove easy to open quite wide.[29] Some people may even find that they can become comfortable walking freely back and forth through it, or simply standing with a foot on each side.

Once again, please understand that we do *not* point all of this out in order to suggest that only Christians and/or their friends truly understand Islam. I am only trying to identify examples of potential common ground being wasted by the non-Conversatian Christian majority's present approach to Islam. A truly Conversatian Christianity would not, after all, take the form of a colonial religious tourism that sought to absorb other traditions. It would not seek to identify good ideas as confused Christian ideas. It would not even confine its energy and focus to identifying and building areas of agreement.

As an approach that offered Christian truth to—and sought Christian truth in—the non-Christian "other," a Christian Conversatianity would also welcome constructive disagreements, as well as useful concepts that only non-Christian systems have formulated; concepts that are not readily Christianized and yet seem to Christians to hold truth and beauty. Such an approach would, in my view, allow Christians to share and to learn about the personal truth they love, and to be true to their roots by growing.

In fact, I think it is important to note in concluding this section that although a Conversatian *City of God* would differ from Augustine's in being written *for* instead of *against* "the pagans," I would argue that it would thus be *extending—not opposing*—Augustine's project. After all, even his exclusivist city found room to admit non-Jews such as Job into the "supernal fatherland" of Israel, and even claims the pagan Erythraean Sybil as a citizen in good standing, through a creative bit of textual criticism.[30]

A DIFFERENT VIEW OF VIOLENCE

Another area wherein a post-9/11 city of God would need, in my view, to oppose or extend Augustine's work is in its thinking about violence. It is well-known, for example, that although Augustine considered wars (even just wars) to be a great evil, he did not oppose war per se, preferring instead to Christianize Cicero's idea of the just war.[31] In my opinion, though, 9/11 and its aftermath work against such justifications, however ancient and venerable.

The bare fact that both Bush and bin Laden were undoubtedly, in their own minds, following Augustine's just-war requirements, and the bare fact that many people (including myself) manage to disagree with both of them categorically and simultaneously, seem to me to throw the real-world value of Augustine's system into hopeless doubt. Augustine's own passing notice of the sad reality that only a just state really deserves allegiance, but states as we know them are never just, suffices to hamstring his just-war theory from the start, as it not only raises the question of when a war has *ever* been really just according to the principles he lays out, it also makes one of those principles impossible to satisfy, specifically the necessity of a demonstrably just motive for the war in question, determined by a just and legitimate government.[32]

When I further note that Augustine's *City* equates membership in the divine city with past renunciation of, and future freedom from, war, I cannot help but wonder if a post-9/11 city of God that opposed war itself, instead of simply bemoaning it, might not be said to take Augustine's insights more seriously than he did.[33] I also think it might be possible to correct Augustine by taking him more seriously than he did when thinking about the possible *meaning* of political violence.

A DIFFERENT APPROACH TO THE MEANING OF VIOLENCE

I should probably pause to defend the idea that violence is meaningful. One often hears the phrase "senseless violence," especially in reference to violence perpetuated by an official enemy. This phrase is useful because it effectively excuses both the speaker and the audience from thinking about their own responsibilities when discussing violence, including the basic responsibility of trying to understand violence. Strictly speaking, though, there is of course no such thing as purely senseless violence, in either the personal or the political sphere. When people from Saudi Arabia fly planes into the administrative and symbolic hearts of American big business and American big guns, it means something. When killing machines decorated with little American flags are later rained down in carpet-bombing campaigns over Afghanistan, by fighter planes decorated with little American flags, it means something. When Iraqis execute and record an attack on Americans in Iraq, and the video they send to the television networks includes pictures of torture in American bases in Iraq running along the bottom of the screen, it means something.

These violent acts, with their violent symbolism, are all callous and sick and in my view inexcusable, but they are not senseless. A responsible *City of God* for the present day would stress the intelligibility (and thus question the randomness and inevitability) of violence. It would not limit its treatment of war and violence, as Augustine did, to merely looking down on it all from above somewhere, even while providing excuses for the violence of the powerful. By denying that violence and war are fundamentally unintelligible and inevitable, *and* denying that war and violence are normal and legitimate in the hands of the powerful, it could correct Augustine's instinct to justify human violence while honoring his instinct to find or *make* meaning in the aftermath of human violence.

Augustine's *City of God* proposed, for example, that the destruction by war of Jerusalem and later Rome were in a sense "fortunate falls," because those political disasters created new opportunities for the spread of the knowledge of God.[34] He would probably have seen the Greek colonial wars as similarly providential, as he gives the Greeks credit for further encouraging the spread of Christianity in commissioning and authorizing the Greek Septuagint.[35] He also manages to disapprove of the wars that brought easy communication and interpreters and a common language to the known world, while holding to the hope that such things could be used to build peace.[36]

I would like to see Christians follow Augustine's lead, and extend his insight, by daring to oppose the evils of war and terrorism categorically, and daring to take the responsibility for our own complicity in such evils seriously, even while daring to embrace without reserve any good things that grow in their wake. Ahmad F. Yousif's 2005 article for the journal *Studies in Religion*, for example, acknowledged that the 9/11 attack and its aftermath were a disaster for everyone, including Muslims, but pointed out that Canada had also seen a dramatic increase in awareness and understanding of Islam, and a corresponding "increase in inter-religious dialogue."[37] Is this not clear evidence that it is possible to locate and take control of the meaning of violence for good?

Similarly, North America's developing global city, with its apocalyptic confusion of cross-cultural and cross-national loyalties, can be conflicted and volatile, as many Montrealers will tell you they witnessed at Concordia in 2002. It can also, though, be made to work against conflict. Montrealers could also tell you about seeing the biggest peace march in Canadian history the following year, in 2003, as record numbers of people began to protest the war on Iraq even before it had begun. How did this happen? The same way the well-intentioned but unwelcome and unfortunately degenerated Concordia demonstration happened: People with multiple and cross-national loyalties, armed with cross-national information on violence overseas, and encouraged by cross-national associations formed in opposition to it, decided to insist upon the importance of cross-national awareness, cross-national peace, and cross-national justice.

The global village experience of extended loyalties and multiple loyalties can, therefore, be a force for peace as much as for war, and I see no reason to believe that this fact is less applicable to religious identities and loyalties than to political identities and loyalties. The extent, therefore, to which communities of knowledge in present-day North America are able to participate in a global city, in which knowledge covers the earth "as water covers the sea," and into which the countless nations bring their best offerings, they are able to incarnate the dynamic Conversatian peace of a *City of God.*

CONCLUSION

I know that I will seem, to some, to have strayed a good way from Augustine's *City of God* in imagining my own. I do think, though, that Augustine's *City* contains the right kind of seeds for growing *Cities* like mine, regardless of whether he would have recognized them as legitimate fruits or as unwelcome weeds.

Augustine's City of God and Conversatianity

First of all, the garden of Augustine's *City of God* is not entirely hostile to Conversatian modes of thinking. It is true that he mocks the Greeks for their philosophical discord, but he also feels free to draw quite heavily (as we have seen already with Cicero) upon their work in doing his own, and even seems to respect them: "He speaks with consistent respect for Plato, Varro, Plotinus and Porphyry . . . [I]t is clear that he cannot entirely shake off his respect for the accomplishments, insofar as he understands them, even of those whom he wishes to oppose."[38] A Conversatian *City of God* would build on Augustine's sense of respect for "pagan" wisdom, and try to relate it to his idea of a divine mind that is "infinite" and "capable of comprehending all things," a mind that reveals itself and "enlightens every human being" as a personal truth.[39]

I repeat, though: this idea of human thought and action incarnating an infinite and multifaceted divine wisdom in different ways would not simply assert that we are all really saying the same thing. It would build instead on the kind of religious logic and instinct that led Augustine to believe that the Hebrew prophets and their Greek translators were, insofar as they were equally divinely inspired, equally authoritative.[40] This was, furthermore, true not only of passages that "express the same meaning, but in a different way," but also of "passages which give . . . another meaning" entirely (so long as the two meanings are not "at odds").[41] To me, this idea of real, valid unity in real, valid diversity looks like it could be extended to see different modes and schools of theological thinking as truly different in their messages and yet all somehow related in the infinitely comprehensive mind of God, especially in light of Augustine's idea that theological difference itself may be divinely ordained.[42]

It also seems to me that Augustine's own book illustrates these Conversatian principles. Peter Brown writes: "Above all, *De Civitate Dei* is a book of controversy," which "should never be treated as though it were a static, complete photograph of Augustine's thought."[43] It's also true that Augustine's own translators would, like the Septuagint translators, often decide later to "improve" on his original in ways that seem to make a lot of sense.[44]

Finally, it seems clear to me that when Augustine posits a perfect "concord of the Scriptures regarded as canonical by the Church," and sets it in proud contradistinction to the "discord" of the pagan philosophers, he is basing his case either upon ignorance and illusion, or upon unacknowledged Conversatianity in action, because (as is clearly visible even in the few random examples given above), the dynamic unity Christian Bible as we know it is Conversatian to the core.

Augustine's City of God and Theological Justifications for Political Violence

I have said that I believe a responsible post-9/11 North American *City of God* would work to remove all pretense of divine excuses for human bloodshed. Augustine's *City,* on the other hand, tends to apologize for the state and its violence. He writes, for example, that governments are instituted by God, and that the shaky peace created by governments and their wars is a relative good, even from the Christian point of view, "for, while the two cities are intermingled, we also make use of the peace of Babylon."[45]

As is plainly hinted, though, in this defense of governments and their wars, Augustine admits that Babylon's relatively good peace is created by war's evil means and for the state's evil reasons.[46] He also notes that the murderer Cain founds the first human city, and that neither reason nor revelation point to any human government operating before the fall of the first *City of God.*[47] People are, in Augustine's view, "naturally sociable," but "not naturally political."[48] Human government and its violence come from the *libido dominandi,* he says, and the *libido dominandi* comes from "pride which refuses to accept that all men are by nature equal."[49] Thus, he follows Cicero in suggesting that the state as we know it actually developed from federated banditry, and he quite deliberately "deconstructs the ideology of Rome as the eternal city, whose peace and justice are the peace and justice of the world."[50]

It is not inconceivable from my point of view, then, to take these points in Augustine's *City of God* seriously—perhaps even more seriously than Augustine did—and end up with a *City of God* that accepts, as Augustine did, any good that the wars of the powerful might do, without in any way excusing them as he does. In this way, one might also escape the temptation (familiar to North Americans in the present day) to mix religious authority with governmental authority, or even to justify using the violence of the state to persecute heretics—evils to which Augustine himself unfortunately succumbed.[51]

NOTES

1. CSSR: Canadian Society for the Study of Religion; CTS: Canadian Theological Society; CETA: Canadian Evangelical Theological Association.
2. P. R. L. Brown, "Saint Augustine," in *Trends in Medieval Political Thought*, ed. Beryl Smalley (Oxford: Basil Blackwell, 1965), p. 1.
3. N. H. Baynes, "The Political Ideas of St. Augustine's *De Civitate Dei*," in *Byzantine Studies and Other Essays* (London: Athlone Press, 1955), pp. 288–89.
4. Augustine xi. (I will use *CD* to indicate general *De Civitate Dei* references, and "Augustine" to refer to the Cambridge edition of *The City of God against the Pagans,* trans. and ed. R. W. Dyson [Cambridge: Cambridge University Press, 1998]).
5. Augustine xi.
6. Augustine xii.
7. Augustine xii, xiii.
8. Augustine xi.
9. *CD* 18.40, 41.
10. Isaiah 19:18–21.
11. Matthew 22:39; Mark 12:30–31; Luke 10:27; *Agapêseis kurion ton theon sou en holê tê kardia sou kai en holê tê psuchê sou kai en holê tê dianoia sou.*
12. Augustine xiii, xix, xx–xxi, xxv.
13. See her *The Choice between Two Cities: Whore, Bride and Empire in the Apocalypse* (Harrisburg, PA: Trinity Press, 1999).
14. Rossing, p. 145.
15. Rossing, pp. 145–47; J. Ellul, *Anarchy and Christianity*, trans. G. W. Bromiley (Grand Rapids, MI: Eerdmans, 1988), p. 72.

16. "Even Virgil's Fourth Eclogue envisions an eschatological time when 'the shipper shall quit the sea, nor shall the ship of pine exchange wares; every land shall bear all fruits.' In prophesying an end to the sea, these texts share a longing for an alternate economic vision in which sea trade in luxury goods will be supplanted by an economy that provides the essentials of life 'without payment' (Revelation 21:6; 22:17). In God's New Jerusalem there will be no ships, no maritime commerce or traffic in cargo, for 'the sea is no more'" (Rossing, p. 147; see also pp. 151–53).

17. J. C. Médaille, "Absurd Wisdom: An Apology for Euthyphro," *Theandros* 1, no. 2 (Winter 2003–2004), http://www.theandros.com/euthyphro.html.

18. John 1:9a; *phôtizei panta anthrôpon* - John 1.9b.

19. John 1.1, 1.3; John 1.1's *En arkhê* is an obvious reference to Genesis 1.1's *b'reshith* ("in the beginning"), which suggests a further parallel between the creating "Word" (*ên ho logos, kai . . . panta di autou egeneto*) of John 1 and the God of Genesis 1 who creates by speaking (*wayomer elohim y'hi*) being into being; according to Heraclitus, for example, the *Logos* is "the unity of all things, the measure and the harmony. . . . With reservations, it is Zeus. . . . However, not only is it the universal substance, the source from which all things come but it is the principle that directs the universe." (M. C. Nahm, ed., *Selections from Early Greek Philosophy* (New York: F. S. Crofts and Co, 1934), p. 88; in Proverbs 8.22, Lady Wisdom says God begot (or "possessed" or "created"—*qanani*) her "at the beginning" (or "as the beginning") of his "way" (*reshith darko*), like an architect. Some versions read, "like a little child," but verses such as Proverbs 3.19, Jeremiah 51.15, 10.12, etc., tell us that God created the cosmos "through (W)isdom," supporting a reading of "head worker" or "architect" here. The Wisdom of Solomon calls her the vehicle of all creation (*pantôn tekhnitis*—7.22, 7.21 in Greek), and the image (*eikôn*) of God, who holds creation together (*diêkê de kai khôrei dia pantôn*—7.24). The striking and consistent verbal and theological parallels with Christ as described in passages such as Colossians 1.15f are obvious, and obviously not simply accidental; *kai ho logos sarx egeneto* - John 1.14.

20. *Letters of St. Basil*, number 38.

21. I mean here the various Protestant, Catholic, and Orthodox canons.

22. Romans 8.24; 1 Corinthians 15.2; Romans 5.9.

23. Luke 17.20f; Luke 21.25–32.

24. Numbers 21.14; Joshua 10.12–13, 2 Samuel 1.19–27, and 1 Kings 8.12–13 [in the LXX]; 1 Kings 11.41; 2 Chronicles 9.29.

25. E. Moore, "Some Notes on Orthodox Ethics and Existential Authenticity," *Theandros* 1, no. 3 (Spring 2004), http://www.theandros.com/existential.html.

26. The material in this section is abstracted from my article, "Conversatianity in the Gospel of John," *Theandros* 2, no. 4 (Fall 2004), http://www.theandros.com/convers.html.

27. Qur'an 4.172, 5.72f, 5.75, 19.35f.

28. Qur'an 4.171.

29. B. B. Levy, *Fixing God's Torah: The Accuracy of the Hebrew Bible Text in Jewish Law* (Toronto: Oxford University Press, 2001), p. 180.

30. *CD* 18.23.

31. *CD* 19.5, 7, 8, 12, 28; 22.4, 22; 2.17; 4.15; 15.4; 19.7, 15. See also *ad Bonif.* 189; *ad Marcel* 138, etc.

32. *CD* 2.21; 4.4; 19.21, 24; 19.7 (see also *Contra Faust.* 22.74, etc.); *Contra Faust.* 22.70, 75.

33. *CD* 22.6, 22.23.

34. *CD* 18.46.

35. *CD* 18.42.

36. *CD* 19.7.

37. A. F. Yousif, "The Impact of 9/11 on Muslim Identity in the Canadian National Capital Region: Institutional Response and Future Prospects," *Studies in Religion/Sciences Religieuses* 34, no. 1 (2005): 56.

38. *CD* 18.41; Augustine xxvi.
39. *CD* 12.18.
40. *CD* 18.43.
41. *CD* 18.43.
42. *CD* 18.43.
43. Augustine xiv.
44. Augustine xiv.
45. *CD* 5.21; 19.26 (see also 5.13, 16).
46. Augustine xxiv–xxv.
47. *CD* 15.1, 5; 19.15, etc.
48. Augustine xvii (see also Brown, p. 9).
49. *CD* 19.12 (see also Augustine xvii).
50. Augustine xxiii; *CD* 4.4; Augustine xxix.
51. *CD* 2.19, 26; 5.24, 26.

CHAPTER 12

The Golden Rule and World Peace

Patricia A. Keefe

OVERVIEW OF THE GOLDEN RULE IN HUMAN HISTORY

The golden rule, though phrased in various ways in the major religions of the world, is an aspect of each and expresses a commonality of relationship: "'Do to others as you want others to do to you' and its expression in all of the world's religions is part of our planet's common language, shared by persons with differing but overlapping conceptions of morality. Only a principle so flexible can serve as a moral ladder for all humankind."[1]

There is a well-known poster that contains the golden rule as stated in the major religions of the world. The core meaning has to do with what some call "the ethic of reciprocity." How do these basic ethical formulations relate to a peaceable kingdom on our earth? How does the failure of world religions and their members to abide by the golden rule result in violent conflict and war? Whatever else can be said, the golden rule is not so much an answer to the world's needs as it is an ethical question often not addressed in contexts in which it would be useful for resolving conflict. In this section, the formulations found in Confucian, Jewish, Christian, and Hindu expressions will be explored in some detail.

CONFUCIAN GOLDEN RULE

Confucius (551–479 BCE) is said to have provided the first recorded statement of the golden rule.[2] During a time of political corruption, war, disintegrating society, and declining personal standards, Confucius synthesized and added to traditional Chinese teachings in an effort to reestablish social and political order on a firm foundation. The cornerstone of his edifice was excellence of character, expressed especially in the basic relationships of society, family, political relationships, and friends. Mencius (371–289 BCE) and Chu Hsi (1130–1200 CE) were the major Chinese philosophers who developed the Confucian golden rule. Practice of the golden rule sometimes involves an explicit imaginative role reversal, putting oneself in the other person's situation.

Elements of the Confucian understanding of the golden rule are the following:

1. In comparing self and other, the agent imagines him- or herself in the situation of the recipient. One assumes that others also get hungry and thirsty, desire to succeed, and so on.
2. Though our empathetic understanding of another is not perfect, we do have an intuitive grasp of others.
3. The agent sees the recipient in terms of a relational pattern: father/son, and so on.
4. Comparing is a matter of heart and mind. Separation of these two is un-Chinese. Comparing is a creative, artistic activity. Understanding another is as much an art as a science.
5. In order to elicit the appropriate feeling for a challenging situation, the agent may need to construct an analogy between the immediate situation and one that spontaneously elicits the appropriate feeling. In order to adequately identify with a stranger's situation, the agent may need to take a preliminary step, to bring to mind his or her sympathy for some person closer to the agent.
6. The agent identifies with concrete aspects of the recipient's situation. The agent may need to be able to empathize with the patriotism of the agent if another country is involved.
7. There is a scientific dimension to understanding others. Scientific component of understanding is prominent in Chinese tradition.
8. We can see the recipient in terms of the Way (*tao*) without explicit comparison. One can find the Way in oneself and in the other person. Mencius: "A noble man steeps himself in the Way (*tao*) because he wishes to find it in himself. When he finds it in himself, he will be at ease in it; when he is at ease in it, he can draw deeply upon it; when he can draw deeply upon it, he finds its source wherever he turns."[3]

For Chang Tsai (1020–1077 CE), "Heaven is my father and Earth is my mother. . . . All people are my brothers and sisters."[4]

JEWISH GOLDEN RULE

Rabbi Hillel (active 30 BCE–10 CE) was key in the formulation of the Golden Rule. Upon being asked for a summary of the Torah, he replied: "What is hateful to you, do not do to your neighbor, this is the whole Torah, while the rest is commentary thereon. Go and learn it." The story of Nathan to King David, to illustrate what David had done to take to himself the wife of Uriah, illustrates the golden rule. David acknowledged that the judgment he had made on the rich man, who in Nathan's story had taken the most precious lamb of the poor man for himself, applied by implication to his own action.[5]

Rabbi Arthur Waskow in a recent book, *The Tent of Abraham,* builds on the story of Abraham and his two sons, Isaac and Ishmael. These two brothers were at enmity due to the story of Abraham, Sarah, and the mother of Ishmael, Hagar. At the funeral of Abraham, these two longstanding enemies came together. Waskow notes that the Palestinians and Israelis continue to look past each other as did Isaac and Ishmael until the death of their father. Waskow suggests that only by recognizing that the land over which they are fighting is the land of Abraham for both will they ever stop warring. They are not yet able to stand in the other's shoes, as required by the golden rule. "Both peoples sit unwilling to imagine that there might be a land of Abraham in which his two descendant peoples are entitled to be present, side by side, not dissolved into one but each with its own identity and self . . . each with its own self-determination, each complementary to the other."[6] Waskow is really talking about the golden rule and applying it to this most horrendous of conflicts. Imagination to look differently is what the Confucians understood.

CHRISTIANITY AND THE GOLDEN RULE

The expression of the golden rule in Christianity follows upon the insights of the Jewish religion; Jesus's expression of the golden rule is a strong statement. The flexibility of a rule that remains widely accessible and reasonable while conveying a high standard can be understood as engaging the hearer/reader in a movement through several levels of interpretation.

1. The Golden Rule of Prudence: do to others as you want others to do to you . . . with realistic attention to the consequences of your choices for the long-term welfare of your recipient. This rule must be distinguished from a pseudo-golden rule of self-interest: do to others as you want others to do to you . . . with an eye to avoiding punishment and gaining rewards for yourself.
2. The Golden Rule of Neighborly Love: do to others as you want others to do to you. . . . as an expression of consideration and fairness among neighbors, where the scope of the term "neighbor" extends to all without regard to ethnic or religious differences. Because the neighbor can be the enemy, however, fulfilling a "conventional ethic of fairness" can require extraordinary love, which involves the next level.
3. The Golden Rule of Fatherly Love: Do to others as you want others to do to you . . . imitating the divine paradigm.[7]

When the interior was uncovered the golden rule takes on a deeper interiority: Look into your own heart. Discover what causes pain. Refuse to inflict this pain on anyone else. Are we as focused on the interior as our culture is on exploring the universe? Don't deny the truth of others. Dogmatism can be a kind of idolatry.[8]

GOLDEN RULE IN HINDUISM

"Let no man do to another that which would be repugnant to himself."[9] "Knowing how painful it is to himself, a person should never do to others which he dislikes when done to him by others."[10] "A person should not himself do that act which, if done by another, would call down his censure."[11] "One should never do that to another which one regards as injurious to one's own self."[12] More advanced according to Erik Erikson is: "No one is a believer until he loves for his brother what he loves for himself," which is usually attributed to Islam.[13] In the Upanishads, Erikson finds the most unconditional commitment: "He who sees all beings in his own self and his own self in all beings."[14]

"The Hindu identification of the spiritual self of the agent with the spiritual self of the recipient of the agent's action provides a basis for golden rule thinking."[15]

IS THE GOLDEN RULE BASED SOLELY ON INDIVIDUAL ACTIONS WITH NO IMPACT ON INTERNATIONAL RELATIONS?

The golden rule is first and foremost a principle in the philosophy of living, expressing a personal standard for the conduct of one-to-one relationships.

> If there is righteousness in the heart, there will be harmony in the home. If there is harmony in the home, the nation will be well governed. If the nation is well governed there will be peace in the world.[16]

Political reforms do not necessarily work for a regeneration of righteousness in the hearts of individuals, but "primary leverage occurs at the level of the individual and unless individuals cooperate ideas for reform won't happen."[17] If the limitation of a radical ethics of relationship lies in its inability to cope with systems, its strength is in honoring the way relationships transcend social systems.

Sensitive application of the rule takes into account those indirectly affected by one's actions. If the golden rule is to be a truly universal principle, then there must be threads of consistency linking moral judgments about personal problems with ethical judgments about social, economic, and political affairs.

What the rule does for systems is to prompt questions that imply norms for systems, for example, "Does a national government go beyond intelligent patriotism to assert sovereignty without regard for planetary responsibilities?"

I am primarily interested in the life of the rule, how the rule moves, how its various meanings weave into one another, and how working with it promotes growth. Presenting the golden rule as a principle with emotional, intellectual, and spiritual significance has become, in part, a way to recover a more adequate conception of what it means to be human and a way to move beyond theories of morality that undervalues any one of these dimensions. "[S]o long as the development of religious consciousness functions to deepen, not discard, the concept of the universal family of God, the golden rule with its universal applicability will continue to symbolize the moral expression of religious consciousness."[18]

THE GOLDEN RULE EXEMPLIFIED IN THE PRACTICE OF THE NONVIOLENT PEACEFORCE

An idea that came together at the Hague Appeal for Peace in May 1999, was for the formulation of a nonviolent peace army, or *Shanti Sena,* in Gandhi's terms. After this meeting, research was conducted on the feasibility of third-party nonviolent intervention and structural development was undertaken. In November and December 2002, representatives of forty-five member organizations from around the world, committed to nonviolence, came together in New Delhi, India, to launch the Nonviolent Peaceforce. These representatives chose the international governing council for the Peaceforce and selected, from among proposals from groups in three different conflict areas, the proposal from Sri Lanka.

Thereafter, recruitment of the field team and training took place in collaboration with partner organizations in Sri Lanka. Training involved practice of nonviolent strategies that have been developed through the centuries. These practices include the following:

1. Accompaniment
2. Monitoring
3. International presence
4. Interpositioning

Recruits learn about nonviolence from leaders in movements in every part of the world, including Gandhi, Martin Luther King, Thich Nhat Hanh, and others. Teachings of these and other nonviolent leaders reflect the golden rule. Martin Luther King explained how we can love our enemy, a key aspect of nonviolence: "We must not seek to defeat or humiliate the enemy but to win his friendship and understanding. . . . Every word and deed must contribute to an understanding with the enemy and release those vast reservoirs of goodwill which have been blocked by impenetrable walls of hate. . . . Returning hate for hate multiplies hate, adding deeper darkness to a night already devoid of stars. Darkness cannot drive out darkness; only light can do that . . . Hate multiplies hate, violence multiplies violence, and toughness multiplies toughness in a descending spiral of destruction."[19]

King's words reflect the golden rule in that loving one's enemies requires that one stand in that person's shoes. King recognizes that there is "some good in the worst of us and some evil in the best of us."[20]

Gandhi wrote: "Passive resistance is an all-sided sword: it can be used anyhow; it blesses him who uses it and him against whom it is used. Without drawing a drop of blood it produces far-reaching results. It never rusts and cannot be stolen."[21] Further: "It is the acid test of non-violent conflict that in the end there is no rancour left behind, and in the end the enemies are converted into friends. That was my experience in South Africa with General Smuts. He started with being my bitterest opponent and critic. Today he is my warmest friend."[22]

Gandhi's statements reflect the basic premises of the golden rule. His grasp of nonviolence was based on deep inner awareness that all of us have the same humanity.

Thich Nhat Hahn, a Buddhist monk, writes of mindfulness as the way of nonviolent living: "Nonviolence can be born only from the insight of non-duality, of interbeing. This is the insight that everything is interconnected and nothing can exist by itself alone. Doing violence to others is doing violence to yourself. If you do not have the insight of non-duality, you will still be violent. You will still want to punish, to suppress, and to destroy, but once you have penetrated the reality of non-duality, you will smile at both the flower and garbage in you, you will embrace both. This insight is the ground for your non-violent action."[23] These articulations of nonviolence reflect the deeper meanings of the golden rule. These are understandings of nonviolence that form the basis of training for the Nonviolent Peaceforce field teams.

In 2005, reporter Chris Richards visited Sri Lanka, where Nonviolent Peaceforce field teams were working. His description of one incident:

> What would you do? There is a gang of young men surrounding your car—banging on your doors, your windows and your roof. You do not know how many there are, but when you saw them as you drove by before, there looked to be 20 or 30. Some were drunk. All looked angry—and they were angry with you. This is the time for self-preservation. There's nothing stopping you from driving off to leave it all behind. Except that you're a peace keeper; a peace builder. It's something you believe in to your core. So you wind down the window and talk with them. They say that you have undermined them—stopped a project close to their hearts. They think you are spying on them. They are not prepared to listen . . . except you think that if you stay and engage with them you can transform the situation and defuse their violence. . . . This is the assessment that Peters Nywanda and Atif Hameed make when they get out of their car to talk with the group.[24]

Five days later as Richards drives with Atif past the area, four of the young men who attacked the car earlier wave and smile. Richards concluded: "What is happening in this city could never have been achieved through violence."[25]

In 2006, Atif Hameed of Pakistan and Sreeram Cahulia of India, both veteran field team members in Sri Lanka, joined in an assignment to the Philippines to assess the violent situation in Mindanao. They, whose countries are at loggerheads, show the power of nonviolence, reaching the common humanity of each other and those in the area of conflict.

CONCLUSION

The golden rule has not died. In fact it has developed beyond its original conception and now has a deeper foundation through the work of nonviolent leaders and practitioners. In the Nonviolent Peaceforce, a global organization with now ninety-five member organizations from all over the globe, the wisdom of nonviolence in the world's religions comes to bear on concrete problems and specific conflicts. The golden rule is not just an abstraction. It is as real as the anger of the gang in Sri Lanka and the nonviolent action of the Nonviolent Peaceforce team based on the common humanity of all involved. It is as real as the nonviolent actors in the U.S. Civil Rights Movement who faced angry crowds, water hoses, and death with the strength of nonviolence.

NOTES

1. Jeffrey Wattles, *The Golden Rule* (London: Oxford University Press, 1996), p. 189.

2. Interview of Karen Armstrong by Krista Tippett on National Public Radio, June 17, 2006. Also see Carpenter's piece on Minnesota Public Radio on June 15, 2006.

3. Wattles, pp. 19–22.
4. Wattles, p. 22.
5. Wattles, p. 42.
6. Joan Chittister, Murshid Saadi Shakur Chishti, and Arthur Waskow, *The Tent of Abraham: Stories of Hope and Peace for Jews, Christians, and Muslims* (Boston: Beacon Press, 2006), p. 65.
7. Wattles, p. 67.
8. Karen Armstrong interview.
9. Mahābhārata, book 5, ch. 49, v. 57.
10. Mahābhārata, book 12, ch. 252, v. 251.
11. Mahābhārata, book 12, ch. 279, v. 23.
12. Mahābhārata, book 13, ch. 113;also in *The Mahābhārata of Krishna-Dwaipayana Vyasa*, 3rd ed., trans. Pratap Chandra Roy, (New Delhi: Munshiram Manoharlal, 1972), vol. 11, p. 240.
13. Wattles, p. 112 and fn. 27.
14. Wattles, p. 113.
15. Wattles, p. 112.
16. Wattles. P. 172, adapted from *The Great Learning*, in *A Source Book in Chinese Philosophy*, trans. and comp. Wing-Tsit Chan (Princeton, NJ: Princeton University Press, 1963), p. 88.
17. Wattles, p. 172
18. Analysis in this section is from Wattles, pp. 171–74.
19. Martin Luther King Jr., *Strength to Love* (Philadelphia: Fortress Press, 1977), pp. 51–53.
20. King, p. 51.
21. Mahatma Gandhi, *All Men Are Brothers, Life and Thoughts of Mahatma Gandhi as Told in His Own Words*, comp. Krishna Kripalani (Ahmedabad: Navajivan Publishing House, 1960), p. 128.
22. Gandhi, p. 128.
23. Thich Nhat Hanh, *Anger, Wisdom for Cooling the Flames* (New York: Riverhead Trade, 2002), pp. 65–70.
24. Chris Richards, "The Challenge to Violence," *New Internationalist* 381 (2005): 9–12.
25. Richards, pp. 9–12.

CHAPTER 13

World Religions and World Peace: Toward a New Partnership

Brian D. Lepard

In this chapter I will explore how world religions can become a force for peace in the world rather than a cause of division and war. I will first review the history of religion-based violence and conflict. I will then examine the contribution that world religions can make, based on their peace-inducing teachings, to the mitigation and resolution of conflict. I will suggest that world religions and world peace need to form a new partnership, in which peacemaking efforts can benefit from certain unique perspectives on peace gleaned from the scriptures of the major world religions.

RELIGION AND CONFLICT IN THE WORLD TODAY

First of all, there is no need to recount the tragic and disgraceful history of wars and conflicts instigated, pursued, and escalated under the banner of religion and religious ideologies—a history that regrettably persists in the twenty-first century. We need look no further than the Middle East, not to mention many other regions of the world, to perceive the destructive effects of religious prejudices and hatreds. Moreover, even where entreaties by religious leaders and adherents to fight rival religions or secular ideologies do not result in outright war, they create in too many regions today a tense and electrified atmosphere of what we might call pre-conflict, in which at any moment a misguided act of terrorism or an isolated attack on an individual could spark a new religion-inspired conflagration.

In centuries past, religion was such a volatile instigator of war that religious wars led to the first calls for the creation of a secular international law based on respect for sovereignty and the freedom of countries, if not individuals, to follow the religion of their choice. This was, for example, the outcome of the Thirty

Years' War, which resulted in the Peace of Westphalia of 1648, regarded by many scholars as the inauguration of the modern-day state system and of contemporary international law. As a result of this pathetic history, many secular observers believe that peace, and respect for international law, can only be achieved by keeping the world religions at bay.

HOW CAN WORLD RELIGIONS BECOME A FORCE FOR WORLD PEACE?

In this chapter I suggest by contrast that the world religions can and must become wholehearted supporters of world peace, and in fact that a durable and profound world peace cannot be achieved without respect for and adherence to fundamental moral teachings shared by all religions. Religion-inspired conflict is based on religious prejudice and fanaticism, which defy the essential teachings of the world religions themselves as articulated in their most revered scriptures. If we look at these teachings, we see many commonalities that offer moral hope in a divided and traumatized world. I review some of these commonalities in my recent book, *Hope for a Global Ethic: Shared Principles in Religious Scriptures.*[1] In particular, we find in the world's great scriptures a unique and multilayered conception of peace that can make a positive contribution to resolving all conflicts peacefully, whether or not they are religious in origin.

COMMON MORAL PRINCIPLES IN WORLD SCRIPTURES RELATING TO PEACE

What are some of these common principles that can serve as the foundation for a new conception of peace?

The Spiritual Nature of Human Beings

A first is the common religious teaching that all human beings have a spiritual nature and have the capacity to acquire spiritual qualities. For example, according to the Hebrew scriptures, we are all created in the image of God. Buddhist scriptures counsel us, "Even as a mother watches over and protects her child, her only child, so with a boundless mind should one cherish all living beings, radiating friendliness over the entire world, above, below, and all around without limit."[2] Jesus teaches us, "be perfect, therefore, even as your heavenly Father is perfect."[3] According to the Qur'an, the reason God has created us is so that we can cultivate good relations with one another, especially those different from us: "O mankind, We have created you male and female, and appointed you races and tribes, that you may know one another. Surely the noblest among you in the sight of God is the most godfearing of you."[4] And Bahá'u'lláh counsels humanity, "O friends! Be not careless of the virtues with which ye have been endowed, neither be neglectful of your high destiny."[5]

By virtue of this spiritual nature not only do we have an obligation to respect others as spiritual beings, but we ourselves have the capacity to rise above animalistic urges, including the desire for blood or revenge, and treat others with compassion, kindness, and justice. Unlike materialistic theories that view humans as just another form of animal, inebriated with the desire for power and with lust and greed—a view that sees war as inevitable and unavoidable—this spiritual conception of humanity's purpose sees war as a product of humanity's failure to rise to the spiritual heights of which it is fully capable, which, indeed, is the divine will for humanity.

This teaching thus makes it a moral imperative that we pursue peace and the eradication of unjust wars. It can give us the resolve to keep trying because of a recognition of humanity's divine potentialities and a shared belief that we are not mere animals, consigned to a life of competition and combat either for limited resources or for power, glory, or other materialistic values.

The Unity of the Human Family

A second unique spiritual teaching of the world's religions is that all human beings are, first and foremost, members of one human family, a family that morally ought to strive day and night to become ever more united, both materially and spiritually. Thus, for example, the Bhagavadgītā of Hinduism asserts that the "whole world" is "united" and affirms that if we achieve true enlightenment we will be one with all beings.[6] The Hebrew scriptures ask, "Have we not all one Father? Did not one God create us?"[7] Buddhist scriptures affirm that we should love all other beings in the entire world, free from ill will or hatred.[8] The Analects of Confucius teaches that we are all brothers and sisters.[9] Through the story of the Good Samaritan, Jesus asserts that we are all spiritual neighbors who should love one another. The Qur'an announces that all humanity was created of a "single soul."[10] The Bahá'í writings declare, too, that "all peoples and nations are of one family, the children of one Father, and should be to one another as brothers and sisters!"[11]

In short, according to the scriptures, we are neither mere individualistic automatons intended to pursue our self-interests nor simple appendages of our communities, whether religious, local, or national. Rather, we are fundamentally members of a single world-embracing family. At the same time, the scriptures elevate to a moral value the diversity of thoughts, opinions, beliefs, and aspirations that characterize the human family. They see this diversity as an evidence of the divine good pleasure and a value we ought to cherish rather than lament or oppose in the interest of creating an artificial homogeneity of thought and belief. For example, the Qur'an declares that the variety of our "tongues and hues" is a sign of God.[12]

This teaching of the unity of the human family has a number of implications for peacemaking. For example, it counsels us to make peace with others because they are fellow family members. No one is an enemy. Furthermore, the goal is not mere toleration of others we view as fundamentally different from ourselves; it is to achieve a profound level of mutual understanding. Belief in the unity of the human family, coupled with recognition of humanity's spiritual character, implies, too, that we ought to be simultaneously optimistic and pragmatic about peace-building efforts. We ought to reject the pessimism that can infect purely secular approaches. The teaching of the unity of the human family furthermore can fortify our resolve to keep trying to settle seemingly intractable conflicts rather than to give up.

PEACE AS A MORAL IMPERATIVE

Third, all the world's revered scriptures uphold peace as a moral imperative. It is not some vague social good, to be aimed at where possible. Rather, the promotion of peace, at both the interpersonal and international levels, is the raison d'être of our social lives on this earthly plane of existence. For example, the Bhagavadgītā instructs us to practice nonviolence and harmlessness (*ahimsa*). The Hebrew scriptures teach us to "seek amity and pursue it."[13] Buddhist scriptures counsel us to purify ourselves from anger and to promote peace. Confucian writings condemn cruelty, arrogance, and vengeance while praising social peace. In the New Testament Jesus announces, "Blessed are the peacemakers, for they will be called children of God."[14] Thus, we are all called upon to be engaged as peacemakers. The Qur'an declares that it is "a Book Manifest whereby God guides whosoever follows His good pleasure in the ways of peace."[15] And the Bahá'í writings teach, "When a thought of war comes, oppose it by a stronger thought of peace. A thought of hatred must be destroyed by a more powerful thought of love."[16]

A DYNAMIC CONCEPTION OF PEACE

Fourth, however, the religious scriptures articulate a dynamic conception of peace rather than a static notion of peace as the mere absence of overt conflict. This includes seeing peace as intimately intertwined with justice, with the elimination of extremes of wealth and poverty, and with the practice of open-minded consultation. This dynamic vision of peace is sorely needed today, because we are often tempted to see war and peace in black-and-white terms—like a light switch that simply is turned on or off. We are tempted to define peace simply as the absence of war and to be willing to trade off virtually any other values to achieve it.

I will elaborate on each of these points in more detail.

Peace and Justice

With respect to justice, all the scriptures affirm that peace and justice go hand in hand, and that true peace must encompass a just ordering of society, including the punishment of wrongdoers. For example, the Bhagavadgītā extols both "harmlessness" and "uprightness." The Hebrew scriptures affirm that the "work of righteousness shall be peace, And the effect of righteousness, calm and confidence forever."[17] Buddhist scriptures recognize that sometimes the use of force may be necessary to achieve justice and prevent unjust wars. Confucian writings also endorse "uprightness" along with peace, and indicate that we should respond to wrongdoing with justice rather than kindness.[18] The New Testament also repeatedly emphasizes the imperative of justice alongside peace, as does the

Qur'an. And the Bahá'í writings assert that peace must be "based on righteousness and justice."[19]

Regrettably, today, as in times past, such as the events leading up to World War II, we witness attempts to appease gross human rights violators in the name of achieving peace. But the scriptures indicate that long-lasting peace includes justice and respect for human rights, which are an integral element of peace—that, indeed, peace without justice and human rights is an illusionary peace, morally as well as practically.

Peace and the Elimination of Poverty

Further, recent events make clear that attempts to impose or create peace without economic justice in particular are doomed to end in disaster. A failure to address the injustice of millions living in abject poverty while others benefit from enormous riches inevitably leads to chronic frustration and anger that can easily bubble to the surface and result in war or terrorism.

Religious scriptures categorically reject the materialism that is insinuating itself into global culture, led by the West, which is only destined to create more dissatisfaction. They call upon us not only to pursue spiritual values rather than material goods in our own lives, but to take effective action to help the less fortunate. For example, Hindu scriptures extol the virtues of generosity and detachment from material things. The Hebrew scriptures, the Buddhist scriptures, and Confucian writings all require that we give to the needy as a strong moral obligation. In the New Testament, Jesus advises us to "give to everyone who begs from you, and do not refuse anyone who wants to borrow from you."[20] The Qur'an teaches us to provide sustenance to the "needy, the orphan, the captive" because of love for God and not expectation of appreciation or any personal benefit."[21] And Bahá'u'lláh advises us to "be a treasure to the poor, an admonisher to the rich, an answerer to the cry of the needy."[22]

Of course, this compelling principle in the scriptures calling upon us to assist the needy does not imply that the mere existence of poverty excuses conflict or terrorism. But there is no doubt that it creates justified grievances that must be remedied in order for a lasting peace to be built. The right to economic justice and development is another facet, then, of peace with justice.

Peace and Open-Minded Consultation

According to the world's religious scriptures, open-minded consultation is also an essential element of peace. Open-minded consultation is a process by which we solve problems through freely expressing our own views with an attitude of courtesy and respect while inviting and seeking to learn from the views of others, ultimately with the goal of reaching a unified consensus. All the scriptures endorse open-minded consultation instead of conflict. For example, the Hebrew scriptures teach that magistrates should "not be partial in judgment," but instead "hear out low and high alike."[23] Buddhist scriptures recount the parable of the blind men and the elephant, teaching that we can only apprehend truth in all its fullness through open-minded consultation as opposed to engaging in useless argumentation.

Confucian writings indicate that everyone else can be a teacher for us, and that we must seek out the opinions of others with a humble attitude. The New Testament likewise praises consultation and a process of mutual learning and encouragement.[24] The Qur'an also exhorts us to practice open-minded consultation, affirming, "Take counsel with them in the affair; and when thou art resolved, put thy trust in God."[25] The Bahá'í writings affirm, "Take ye counsel together in all matters, inasmuch as consultation is the lamp of guidance which leadeth the way, and is the bestower of understanding."[26]

Again, too often today we strive for the illusion of a peace based on a fragile truce, a peace that is false because the parties involved are not able or willing to talk with one another. This kind of peace through mutual bare toleration inevitably breeds renewed tensions, and ultimately new conflicts. If individuals, nations, or peoples experiencing tension with one another can begin to engage in open-minded dialogue, inspired by recognition of their common humanity, they can better avoid conflict. And in the aftermath of conflict they can pursue through consultation a long-lasting peace. Moreover, we have learned that consultation must involve all elements of society, including historically marginalized groups and individuals such as women. A peace among leaders alone that does not nurture the full participation of ordinary citizens is likely to be transient and ephemeral.

THE LIMITED USE OF FORCE

Finally, as intimated by the title of this section, the world's great scriptures also teach us that sometimes the use of force may be justified, and even necessary, to promote justice and peace. This view of the use of force is consistent with the scriptures' recognition that peace and justice are two sides of the same coin; true peace cannot exist without justice, and justice may require the use of some kind of force. In this connection, the concept of just war appears in all the scriptures.

Obviously, when abused, just-war theory has served as ideological fuel for the kinds of atrocious interreligious conflicts I described at the outset of this chapter. But the scriptures themselves indicate the primacy of peaceful methods of dispute resolution and impose strict limitations on the use of force, limitations that render it more in the nature of a police operation than what we traditionally have called war. Indeed, these limitations correspond closely with emerging standards of just war under international law, including those that appear in the Charter of the United Nations. It is critical to emphasize, too, that the scriptures, as a general rule, emphatically declare that religious prejudice is morally inexcusable and can never justify war between members of different religions.

Let me give here just a few examples of these scriptural warrants for the limited, and pure-minded, use of force to achieve peace, justice, and the protection of others. The Hebrew scriptures authorize certain limited wars, but also provide some of the world's first protections for innocent combatants, and indicate that war must be used as a last resort. Buddhist scriptures likewise authorize wars to promote justice after all peaceful attempts at resolution have failed.

According to Buddhist scriptures, the Buddha affirmed, "All warfare in which man tries to slay his brother is lamentable, but [the Buddha] does not teach that those who go to war in a righteous cause after having exhausted all means to preserve the peace are blameworthy. He must be blamed who is the cause of war."[27]

Confucian texts authorize wars to liberate people oppressed by tyrants, and arguably only such wars. As we are aware, Christian doctrine has evolved a concept of just war grounded in biblical teachings involving love and justice. The Qur'an prohibits aggressive war but allows wars in self-defense and wars to protect the innocent from oppression. Finally, the Bahá'í writings, while outlawing "holy war" based on religion, imply that in some cases war may be necessary as a last resort to inhibit an aggressor or protect human rights victims, and that the world needs to establish a system of collective security for these purposes.[28]

As noted earlier, in our praiseworthy quest for peace today we often are tempted to insist on peace at any price, and regard the use of force as inherently morally reprehensible or forbidden. The scriptures can serve as a correction to these myopic well-intentioned views. The scriptures teach us that, regrettably, in a world in which tyrants and human rights violations are ubiquitous, the use of force may be the only way to forestall conflict, stop it once it has occurred, or rescue imperiled human rights victims. This is an important teaching of the scriptures. But the scriptures also emphasize that the use of force, which importantly can take forms far short of what we think of as war, must be carefully regulated and calibrated. Some scriptures imply that ideally, where possible, legitimate uses of force should be supervised by global institutions that operate under a principle of open-minded consultation. These checks and balances help ensure that the use of force is morally justified and appropriately limited. These shared ethical principles in the scriptures point to the imperative of adhering to, but also where necessary reforming, similar rules and limitations that have found their way into contemporary international law. These include rules in the U.N. Charter, which allows military action only in self-defense or where it has been authorized by the U.N. Security Council.[29]

CONCLUSION

To conclude, despite the sordid record of religious instigation of war, any successful effort to achieve durable peace in the world must take into account and draw inspiration from the shared teachings concerning peace and the just use of force in the scriptures of the world religions. We thus need a new partnership between world religions and world peace. If members of religious communities around the globe can work together to perceive and act on these common principles, the world may yet avoid the resurgence of hatred and violence that seems to be on the immediate horizon.

NOTES

1. Brian D. Lepard, *Hope for a Global Ethic: Shared Principles in Religious Scriptures* (Wilmette, IL: Bahá'í Publishing, 2005).
2. Edward Conze, trans., *Buddhist Scriptures* (London: Penguin Books, 1959), p. 186.

3. Matthew 5:48. All quotations from the New Testament are from *The Holy Bible Containing the Old and New Testaments: New Revised Standard Version* (New York: Oxford University Press, 1977).

4. 49:13. All quotations from the Qur'an are from A. J. Arberry, trans., *The Koran Interpreted* (New York: Simon and Schuster, 1955).

5. Bahá'u'lláh, *Gleanings from the Writings of Bahá'u'lláh,* 2d rev. ed., trans. Shoghi Effendi (Wilmette, IL: Bahá'í Publishing Trust, 1976), p. 196.

6. See, for example, 5:7, 11:7. All quotations from the Bhagavadgītā are from Franklin Edgerton, trans., *The Bhagavad Gītā* (Cambridge: Harvard University Press, 1972).

7. Malachi 2:10. All quotations from the Hebrew scriptures are from *Tanakh: A New Translation of the Holy Scriptures according to the Traditional Hebrew Text* (Philadelphia: The Jewish Publication Society, 1985).

8. See Conze, p. 186.

9. See Analects 12:5, as translated in E. Bruce Brooks and A. Taeko Brooks, trans., *The Original Analects: Sayings of Confucius and His Successors* (New York: Columbia University Press, 1998).

10. 4:1.

11. 'Abdu'l-Bahá, *Paris Talks: Addresses Given by 'Abdu'l-Bahá in Paris in 1911–1912,* 12th ed. (London: Bahá'í Publishing Trust, 1995), no. 42.11.

12. See 30:21.

13. Psalms 34:15.

14. Matthew 5:9.

15. 5:18.

16. 'Abdu'l-Bahá, no. 6.7.

17. Isaiah 32:17.

18. See, for example, Analects 14:34.

19. 'Abdu'l-Bahá, *The Compilation of Compilations Prepared by the Universal House of Justice, 1963–1990* (Maryborough, Victoria: Bahá'í Publications Australia, 1991), vol. 2, p. 165.

20. Matthew 5:42.

21. 76:8–9.

22. Bahá'u'lláh, *Epistle to the Son of the Wolf,* rev. ed., trans. Shoghi Effendi (Wilmette, IL: Bahá'í Publishing Trust, 1979), p. 93.

23. Deuteronomy 1:17.

24. See, for example, 1 Corinthians 14:26, 14:29–31.

25. 3:153.

26. Bahá'u'lláh, *Tablets of Bahá'u'lláh Revealed after the Kitáb-i-Aqdas,* trans. Habib Taherzadeh (Haifa: Bahá'í World Centre, 1978), p. 168.

27. Paul Carus, comp., *The Gospel of Buddha* (Chicago: Open Court, 1915), p. 148.

28. See, for example, 'Abdu'l-Bahá, *The Secret of Divine Civilization,* 2d ed., trans. Marzieh Gail (Wilmette, IL: Bahá'í Publishing Trust, 1970), pp. 70–71; Bahá'u'lláh, *Tablets of Bahá'u'lláh,* p. 165.

29. See, for example, U.N. Charter articles 2(4), 39–51.

About the Editor and Contributors

ARVIND SHARMA is Birks Professor of Comparative Religion in the Faculty of Religious Studies at McGill University in Montreal, Canada, and has published extensively in the fields of Indian religions and comparative religion. He was the president of the steering committee for the global congress on World's Religions after September 11, which met in Montreal from September 11 to 15, 2006, and is currently engaged in promoting the adoption of A Universal Declaration of Human Rights by the World's Religions.

RAMAZAN BICER graduated from Erciyes University in Islamic and religious studies. Following this, he received an M.A. at Marmara University in Istanbul. He was awarded a Ph.D. in 1999 for a religious studies thesis on Islamic Theology. Bicer has written or translated some fifty articles and books on a variety of topics. He has several articles in Turkish, Arabic, French and English. His research interests include religious studies, theology, philosophy of religion, philosophy of ethics, New Age religious movement, and Turkish-Islamic culture. Bicer is currently an Associate Professor as head of the department of Islamic theology on Ilahiyat Faculty, Sakarya University.

PAMELA CHRABIEH holds a Ph.D. in sciences of religions from the University of Montreal. She is finalizing postdoctoral research at the Canada Research Chair in Islam, Pluralism and Globalization (University of Montreal) and at the Institute of Islamic-Christian Studies (St-Josef University of Beirut). She has published several scientific articles in Canada and Lebanon on interreligious dialogue, the politics-religions-society relations in the Near Eastern area, as well as the role of Lebanese civil society and diaspora in constructing peace. She has also published *Icônes du Liban, au carrefour du dialogue des cultures* (2003) and *À la rencontre de l'Islam, itinéraire d'une spiritualité composite et engagée* (2006).

JEAN DONOVAN is an assistant professor of theology at Duquesne University, teaching systematic theology, sacraments, and liturgy. She graduated from the University of Notre Dame with a B.A. in Philosophy in the first class of women. Following missionary work with the Holy Cross Fathers in Nairobi, Kenya, she pursued an M.A. in theology and an M.Div. at Catholic Theological Union, and a Ph.D. at Fordham University. She has worked as both professor and full-time minister since then. Her work in ministry has included campus ministry, parish ministry, hospital ministry, crisis counseling with women survivors of domestic violence, and hospice chaplaincy.

STEPHEN HEALEY holds degrees in Religion and Society from Eastern Nazarene College (B.A.), Andover Newton Theological School (M.A.), and Boston College (Ph.D.). He was the director of the Program in World Religions at the University of Bridgeport in 1998, where he is also an associate professor. His research and publications have focused on religion and human rights, globalization in religion, and public theology. His primary teaching and research methods are the comparative analysis of religions and enquiry into the public dimensions of religious belief and practice.

PATRICIA A. KEEFE is Outreach Coordinator for the Nonviolent Peaceforce. She has been on the Nonviolent Peaceforce staff since 2000 helping to establish this global organization and raising funds to develop it. Patricia has an M.A. in Theology and a J.D. She was a legal services attorney for eight years in Minnesota. She worked in the Legal Office of Amnesty International's Secretariat in London for a year. As Director for Justice and Human Development for the Archdiocese of Oklahoma City, Patricia helped found the Oklahoma Coalition to Abolish the Death Penalty and received awards from the Oklahoma Chapter of the American Civil Liberties Union and the Oklahoma Human Rights Commission.

HEERAK CHRISTIAN KIM is visiting professor of biblical studies at Asia Evangelical College and Seminary in India. Professor Kim has held many prestigious academic fellowships, such as the Lady Davis Fellowship at the Hebrew University of Jerusalem in Israel during the 1996–97 academic year. Professor Kim has coined a literary device, called "key signifier," which identifies words and phrases which trigger collective memory and compel the audience to action. Besides working in literary criticism, Professor Kim has published widely on Jewish studies and biblical studies, such as *Hebrew, Jewish, and Early Christian Studies.* Professor Kim is very active in the Korean community and has worked as the official court Korean Interpreter for Palisades Park (NJ) Municipal Court.

BRIAN D. LEPARD is professor of law at the University of Nebraska and a specialist in international law. A graduate of Princeton University and the Yale Law School, he is the author of a number of books and articles relating to international law, human rights, peacemaking, world religions, and global ethics. His most recent book is *Hope for a Global Ethic: Shared Principles in Religious Scriptures,* published in 2005. He also wrote *Rethinking Humanitarian Intervention: A Fresh Legal Approach Based on Fundamental Ethical Principles in International Law and World Religions,* which was published in 2002. He is a member of the International Board of Consultants of the Global Ethics and Religion Forum. Prior to entering law school, he served for three years at the United Nations Office of the Bahá'í International Community, where he worked on human rights issues.

WILLIAM R. O'NEILL, S.J., is a professor of social ethics at the Jesuit School of Theology at Berkeley and a visiting professor of ethics at the Jesuit School of Theology in Nairobi. His writings address questions of human rights, ethics and hermeneutical theory, social reconciliation, and refugee policy. He received a Newcombe Fellowship, a Lilly Theological Research Grant, and held the Jesuit Chair, Georgetown University (2003–2004). He has served on the Editorial Board of the *Journal of the Society of Christian Ethics* and serves on the Board of the Society of Christian Ethics and of the journal *Theological Studies.*

AARON RICKER is presently at McGill University in Montreal writing an M.A. thesis on the politico-rhetorical context of Mark 10:42 and its Synoptic parallels, focusing particularly on teasing out the marks and the implications of the rhetoric's oddly Roman and imperial character. Aaron is interested in the underexploited dialogical and anarcho-pacific potential of Christian traditions and their critical study.

MARCIA SICHOL investigates the need for new perspectives in just war theory for the twenty-first century, addressing the significance of taking a woman's perspective in discovering the incarnational principle underlying the just war tradition. Marcia has a doctorate in philosophy from Georgetown University and is the treasurer and director of communications for the Sisters of the Holy Child.

LLOYD STEFFEN is Professor of Religion Studies and University Chaplain at Lehigh University in Bethlehem, Pennsylvania. An NGO representative to the United Nations, Steffen is the author of six books in philosophy of religion and ethics, including the award-winning *Executing Justice: The Moral Meaning of the Death Penalty,* and, most recently, *Holy War, Just War: Exploring the Meaning of Religious Violence,* published in 2007.

KATHERINE K. YOUNG, James McGill Professor, teaches in the Faculty of Religious Studies and is a member of the Centre for Medicine, Ethics, and Law at McGill University. She publishes in three fields: Hinduism, ethics, and gender and religion. She has coauthored *Hindu Ethics* (1989) and has coedited *Religion and Law in the Global Village* (2000). She is currently writing a book on the peaceable ideal of manhood in the cultures of Indian Brahmans, orthodox Jews, Mennonites, and Swedes. On the topic of gender, she has collaborated with Arvind Sharma on twelve books on women in world religions and has co-authored with Paul Nathanson *Spreading Misandry: The Teaching of Contempt for Men in Popular Culture* (2001) and *Legalizing Misandry: from Public Shame to Systemic Discrimination against Men* (2006).

Index